DEVON AND CORNWALL

New Series, Vol. 25

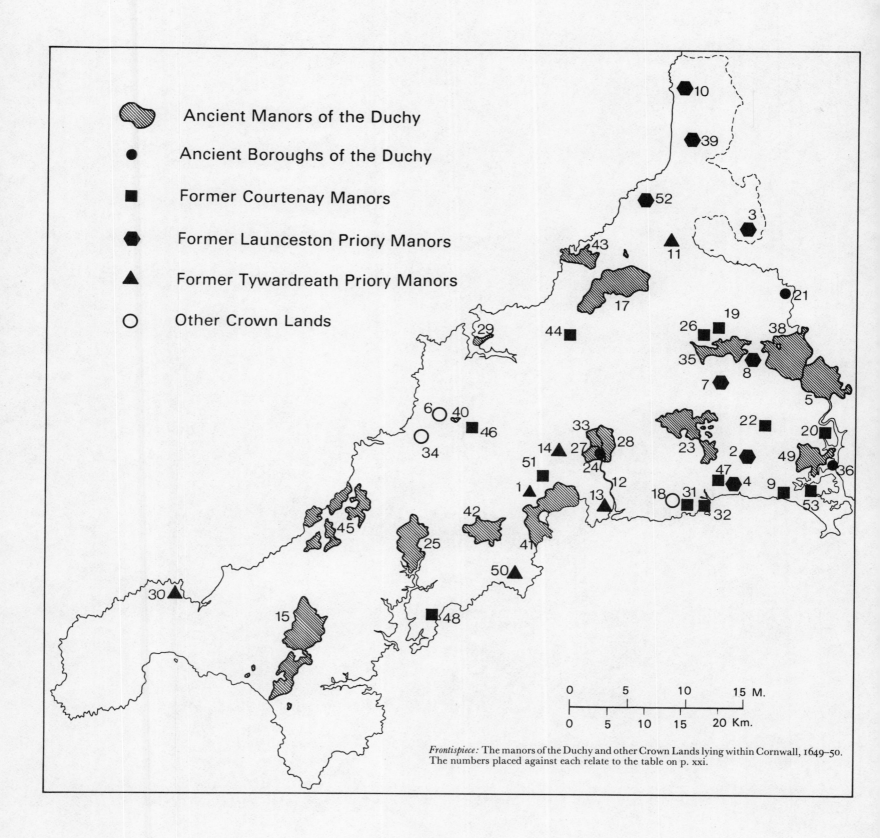

Ancient Manors of the Duchy

Ancient Boroughs of the Duchy

Former Courtenay Manors

Former Launceston Priory Manors

Former Tywardreath Priory Manors

Other Crown Lands

0   5   10   15 M.

0   5   10   15   20 Km.

Frontispiece: The manors of the Duchy and other Crown Lands lying within Cornwall, 1649–50. The numbers placed against each relate to the table on p. xxi.

EVON & CORNWALL RECORD SOCIETY

New Series, Vol. 25

THE
PARLIAMENTARY SURVEY
OF THE
DUCHY OF CORNWALL

PART I
(Austell Prior—Saltash)

Edited with an Introduction by

NORMAN J. G. POUNDS

Printed for the Society by
THE DEVONSHIRE PRESS LTD.
TORQUAY
ENGLAND

1982

ISBN O 901853 25 2

FOREWORD BY HIS ROYAL HIGHNESS THE PRINCE OF WALES, DUKE OF CORNWALL, K.G., K.T., G.C.B., A.D.C.

It is not without a sense of irony that I write this foreword. The mid-seventeenth century represents the nadir of Duchy history and as a result of these surveys its lands and rights were sold off. Happily, it arose phoenix-like from the ashes in 1660. The information contained in the surveys will be of interest to all those who wish to know more of the social, economic and agricultural history of England during this century of transformation.

Surveying is now intrinsic to the management of landed estates. It is above all a practical art and for this reason the work surveyors have done is of interest to subsequent generations. The Duchy has commissioned several major surveys of its estates since the mid-seventeenth century. William Simpson produced detailed terriers and maps in the 1780's. Henry Spry surveyed Duchy holdings in Cornwall in 1813. In the 1970's there were comprehensive surveys of the Duchy's main agricultural interests. Both Spry and Simpson used the Parliamentary surveys as a basis for their own work, while in turn, the recent reporters examined Simpson and Spry. Thus, faint echoes of the surveys carried out more than three hundred years ago still exist and can be found in the modern Duchy.

It is remarkable that the archive of a great agricultural estate such as the Duchy of Cornwall has never been very fully published. The material it contains provides not only a unique series of documents relating to Duchy history, but, by its nature, an important national archive stretching back to the thirteenth century. I am indebted to Professor Pounds for his important contribution to our national and local history.

CONTENTS

INTRODUCTION

All governments in the seventeenth century found it difficult even in times of peace to make ends meet. The Commonwealth was no exception. Indeed it was particularly hard pressed for money, and any expenditure above the ordinary led it to look for additional sources of income.[1] The cost of the war in Scotland had forced King Charles to call Parliament, and his reluctance to comply with its demands had led to the Great Civil War. The war itself was expensive for both sides, and Parliament decreed[2] that those who had brought it about should be made to contribute to its cost. When it was over the cases were pursued vigorously against the so-called 'delinquents', and heavy fines were imposed.[3] But the obligations of the government continued to increase. In the late 1640s the pay of the Army was in arrears, and there was dangerous discontent amongst the soldiery. The war itself had not yet been terminated; resistance to Parliament was continuing in the Isles of Scilly; Ireland had still to be reconquered, and the execution of the King in January 1649 was followed by the proclamation in Scotland of his son as King Charles II.

Parliament resorted to many devices to raise money. The episcopate of the Anglican Church had been abolished by ordinance of Parliament – the 'act' never received the royal assent – and in November 1946[4] Parliament ordered the estates and other possessions of the bishops to be surveyed and offered for sale.[5] Two and a half years later the estates of the Deans and Chapters, whose offices had been suppressed at the same time, were also surveyed and put on the market.[6] The amounts raised were totally inadequate to meet the needs of Parliament, and the government resorted to the sale of the landed possessions of the King and royal family. The sale of Crown lands appears to have been first mooted in February 1649,[7] when a committee of the House was appointed to prepare and introduce an act for the survey and sale of the royal manors and parks.[8] The bill was laid before Parliament on May 9. It was debated, and some amendments were made. On July 9 the House was told that its passage was a matter of great urgency, because the government was in desperate need of the money that the sale of the crown lands would provide. In the end it was passed on July 16 1649.[9] The new law enacted that, since 'the late King, the Queen, and their eldest

---

[1] S. R. Gardiner, *History of the Commonwealth and Protectorate 1649–1660*, London, 1894, vol. 1, 95–7.
[2] *Acts and Ordinances of the Interregnum*, ed. C. H. Firth and R. S. Rait, Record Commission, 1911, vol. 2, 168–9. The essential documents were first published by Henry Scobell, *A Collection of Acts and Ordinances of General Use, made in the Parliament*, London, 1658.
[3] *Calendar of the Proceedings of the Committee for Compounding 1643–1660*, Record Commission, 1889–92, vol. 1, vii–x.
[4] *Acts and Ordinances*, 1, 879–81.
[5] *ibid.*, 879–83.
[6] *ibid.*, 2, 81–104.
[7] The new style of dating is used both in this Introduction and in the text.
[8] S. J. Madge, *The Domesday of Crown Lands*, London, 1938, 65–76.
[9] *Acts and Ordinances*, 2, 168–91.

son have been the chief authors of the late wars and troubles', they should be made to bear the heavy cost that resulted. Their honours, castles and other houses, their manors, parks and all rights from which they derived any financial advantage were to be confiscated, surveyed and sold.

Parliament's previous experience, first with the episcopal lands and then with the lands of the Deans and Chapters, led on this occasion to a very precise and workmanlike piece of legislation.[10] The estates themselves were vested in Trustees, who were to arrange for their survey and sale. No land might be sold without preliminary survey and evaluation. The Trustees appointed William Webb, the Surveyor General, to supervise the survey of the Crown lands. Under him was a number of assistant surveyors, of whom there were in all over a hundred, many of them working in a single county, or at most in two. Most of the manors of the Duchy were surveyed by the same five assistant surveyors, who added their names at the ends of all the surveys made in 1649–50. They were George Crompton, George Gentleman, George Goodman, Edward Hore and Gabriel Taylor. Of these Gabriel Taylor appears to have been the most experienced. His name appears in surveys conducted in no less than fourteen counties.[11] The others were employed only in Devon and Cornwall. Crompton was Receiver General of the Duchy, but only Hore was a local man.[12]

The surveyors proceeded by the time-honoured method of impanelling a jury in each manor, putting it on oath, and then demanding detailed information about the extent and occupation of each tenement or parcel of land. Answers were not always unambiguous, and, indeed, one would be surprised if some of the information required were readily available.

Most of the surveys of Crown and Duchy lands in Devon and Cornwall were made between November 1649 and November 1650. A few had, however, to be delayed. The war was continuing in the Isles of Scilly, and here the survey was not completed until September 1652. The surveyors were John Fiske, Samuel Cottman and John Hadocke, all of whom had been employed widely in other parts of England. The survey of the fishing rights in the River Fowey was delayed until late in 1656. Their possession by the Crown was not known to the surveyors when they were surveying Lostwithiel and Fowey, and knowledge of it reached the Trustees only through information supplied by Anthony Rowse. The same happened in the Honour and Manor of Bradninch, part of which was not surveyed until 1658.[13]

The surveyors began their work in the Tamar Valley with the manor of Landulph. From here they moved westwards to the group of manors which centered in Rillaton. Each survey contains the date of its transmittal to London, and by this means the surveyors' itinerary can be traced in broad outline. They made a practice, however, of holding the completed surveys until three or four were ready for transmittal, so that their precise route cannot be reconstructed. The survey of the manors in the Tamar valley was followed by that of the manors near the south coast and in the Fowey valley. These were completed by late February, 1650. The work appears then to

10 S. J. Madge, *op. cit.*, 79–91.
11 See S. J. Madge, *op. cit.*, Appendix 3 for tables of the names of officials engaged in the survey.
12 Mary Coate, *Cornwall in the Great Civil War 1642–1660*, Oxford University Press, 1933, p. 268.
13 Number 55 of the text.

have been interrupted for about a month, for the next survey, that of the small manor of Trelugan, is dated March 30. A campaign in mid-Cornwall followed in April, and this in turn by the completion of the West Cornwall manors in May. The journey back to Devon was by way of Fentrigan in North Cornwall and the Borough of Saltash on the shore of Plymouth Harbour. In June and July the surveyors visited the North Cornwall manors from Rialton in Colan parish to Eastway in Morwenstow, together with the North Devon manor of Bradford. In August they were at Lydford in Devon; in September at Carnanton in Mawgan in Pyder, which had curiously been omitted from the earlier expeditions, and Launceston; and in November they visited Trematon Castle and the remaining manors in Devon.

The whole task had occupied a little more than a year, though it seems to have been interrupted for short periods. Figure 1 is an attempt to reconstruct the route of the surveyors. It is clear that they travelled far greater distances than was necessary. It is even possible that they may have had difficulty in locating some of the smaller manors, and perhaps Carnanton, for which no detailed information is supplied, was not visited at all. The dates of submittal suggest that the survey of the manor of Porthea was taken at the part of the manor that lay in St Anthony in Meneage rather than at St Ives. There is no evidence in the text to show that the surveyors were in any way assisted by the local officials of the Duchy. Indeed, the evidence for the non-payment of rent suggests that the latter had not been particularly active in recent years.

Once completed, fair copies were made of each survey, and at least two copies were sent to Worcester House in the Strand, which became the administrative headquarters for the survey of the Crown lands. On reaching London they were endorsed with the date of receipt and the time – usually *eodem die* – when they were passed to the Surveyor General. William Webb read them at once, making marginal notes, which are included in this edition, on actions to be taken. Within two or three days they were passed to the Trustees who proceeded at once with the formalities for the sale of the lands surveyed. The assistant surveyors had left many questions unanswered. These arose mostly from rival claims to lands and privileges and from the loss of documents from which such claims might be substantiated. In order to expedite the process Parliament set up a Committee for the Removal of Obstructions to the sale of Crown lands,[14] which is occasionally referred to in the endorsements to the surveys recounting the decisions reached. One is constantly amazed in reading the surveys at the meticulous care shown by William Webb who himself read and commented on all the surveys for England and Wales, with the exception only of those for the county of Rutland.

Parliament had prescribed an oath to be taken by all surveyors of Crown lands. They undertook to use 'their best endeavour and skill to discover the estate . . . and every part thereof . . . and to finde out the true values and improvements thereof . . . [and to] make true surveys according to [their] best skill and cunning, and the same from time to time to deliver, or cause to be delivered in writing close sealed up, unto the Register . . . and also a true

---

[14] *Acts and Ordinances*, 2, 338–42 and S. J. Madge, *op. cit.*, 94.

copy or duplicate thereof close sealed up, unto the said Trustees . . .'.[15] The surveyors furthermore undertook not to accept 'any gift or reward . . . except such allowances as the said Trustees . . . shall think fit to make . . .'.

The surveyors were given precise instructions both for the presentation of their results of their enquiries and also for their evaluation of the Crown lands preparatory to sale. Amongst the documents in the possession of the Duchy of Cornwall is one entitled 'Surveyors' Instructions for Method of Making Surveys'.[16] They were to begin by listing the quit rents of the free tenants, following with leasehold and customary rents and all obligations and services in kind. They were instructed to use any accounts that might be available of later date than 1641 in order to compute the value of these perquisites. Demesne lands, together with any manor house and woodland, were to be recorded. In the case of land that had been let or leased, the reserved rent was to be noted in the left margin of the page, and the 'improved', or estimated market value, in the right. In the case of land let by lease, all conditions and exceptions were to be listed, and if a lease was for 'lives', the names and ages of the 'lives' were to be noted. In the case of copyhold or conventionary tenements, the dates of the copies and details of rents, fines, heriots and other obligations were to be recorded, as well as the duration of the tenenacy and the 'lives' by which it was held.

All woodland over and above that needed 'for the maintenance of necessary bootes' was to be recorded and valued. Charges and 'reprises' against manors and other sources of income were to be listed. The bounds of manors were to be given, 'if cleerely and notoriously knowne but if dubiously given you, it were better bee silent therein'. The customs of the manor were also to be recorded in so far as they were relevant to the purpose of the survey. A rental or list of tenants, with their monetary obligations, and an abstract of the rents and improved values were to end the survey of each manor. Both the survey and the duplicate were to 'bee fairely ingrossed without bloting or scraping', and to be 'made agreeable in the folio and contents in each follio'.

The surveyors were also required to give an evaluation of the current worth of all properties that were not subject to a fixed rent. This was expressed as an 'improved value above the present rent'. The discrepancies between the current rent and that which the surveyors thought that the property would bear were sometimes very large. This undervaluation of lands, due in the main to the inflationary trend of the previous century, had long been troubling the administrators of Crown estates, though there is no real evidence that the Duchy had tried to raise its revenue in line with the enhanced value of its property.

The Trustees proceeded to the sale of the Crown lands as soon as William Webb had approved and endorsed the relevant surveys. Sales were entrusted to Henry Colbron, the 'Register', who presided over the Contractors for the Sale of Crown Lands. Land was not to be sold for less than thirteen years' purchase, and for leaseholds on lives a scale of payment was devised, based on the expected lifespan of the 'lives' in question. For thirty

---

[15] *Acts and Ordinances*, 2, 172–3.
[16] Duchy of Cornwall, Baynes Papers. There is a copy in the British Library, Add. 44937. The text is printed in S. J. Madge, *op. cit.*, 334–9. See also *Royal Commission on Historical Manuscripts Report VII*, part 1, 685–8.

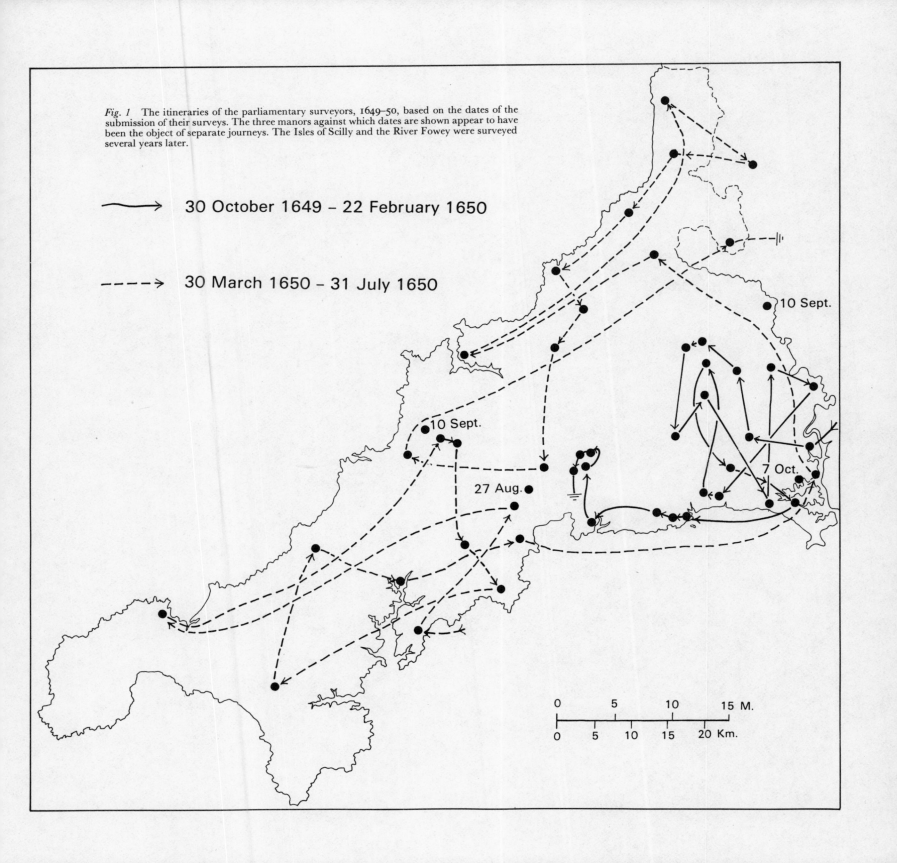

Fig. 1 The itineraries of the parliamentary surveyors, 1649–50, based on the dates of the submission of their surveys. The three manors against which dates are shown appear to have been the object of separate journeys. The Isles of Scilly and the River Fowey were surveyed several years later.

30 October 1649 – 22 February 1650

30 March 1650 – 31 July 1650

10 Sept.

10 Sept.

27 Aug.

7 Oct.

0   5   10   15 M.

0   5   10   15   20 Km.

days after the announcement of the sale the present tenant had a right of refusal. Only after the expiry of this period could land be offered for public sale.[17]

The Duchy lands were quickly sold. The purchasers were in part local gentry of the Parliamentary persuasion, eager to round out their estates; in part local bourgeois, and in part soldiers in Cromwell's army with money to spend.[18] But all that they acquired were the rights previously exercised by the Crown or Duchy. The rare attempts by the new owners to change manorial customs were quickly defeated. Local traditions had a way of asserting themselves and, as Mary Coate observed, 'life on the Duchy manors after 1650 continued much as before'.[19]

After the Restoration Parliament declared all sales to be null and void, and Crown and Duchy resumed possession of their lands. But, as Madge noted,[20] 'forbearance on the one hand and "concealments" on the other resulted in a greatly modified resumption of the King's honors, lands . . .' In fact, many of the fee farm or freehold rents were lost for good, and the Crown lands actually recovered were 'but a shadow of their ancient bulk'. The resulting loss of income to the Crown was an important factor influencing Parliament when it settled a regular income on the King. The unscrambling of the Parliamentary settlement of the Crown lands still remains obscure in many respects,[21] but in Devon and Cornwall the ancient owners seem in general to have resumed possession of their lands, and in so far as the Duchy is concerned, most of those surveyed remain today the property of the Duke of Cornwall. The only significant loss since 1650 has been the sale in the 1790s of certain lands in connection with the land tax redemption act.

THE CROWN ESTATE Medieval monarchs were expected to 'live of their own', and for this purpose they held an extensive though fluctuating estate.[22] The Crown lands were at intervals increased by escheats and confiscations and diminished by grants to favourites and members of the royal family. Amongst the largest and most important of such grants was that made in 1337 to the newly created Duke of Cornwall. The lands in question had not long been in royal hands. They had been accumulated during the thirteenth century by Richard and Edmund, successively Earls of Cornwall.[23] They reverted to the Crown on the death of Earl Edmund in 1300, and were granted in turn to Piers Gaveston, Queen Isabella and John

---

[17] S. J. Madge, *op. cit.*, . . . and Mary Coate, *Cornwall in the Great Civil War*, 270–1.
[18] *ibid.*, 271–4.
[19] *ibid.*, 274.
[20] S. J. Madge, *op. cit.*, 263; also *Guide to the Contents of the Public Record Office*, H.M.S.O., 1963, vol. 1, 89.
[21] See M. P. Ashley, *Financial and Commercial Policy under the Cromwellian Protectorate*, London, 1934; G. B. Tatham, 'The Sale of Episcopal Lands during the Civil Wars and Commonwealth', *English Historical Review*, vol. 23 (1908), 91–108; H. Egerton Chesney, 'The Transference of Lands in England, 1640–1660', *Transactions of the Royal Historical Society*, 4th series, vol. 15, 181–210; H. J. Habakkuk, 'Public Finance and the Sale of Confiscated Property during the Interregnum', *Economic History Review*, vol. 15 (1962), 70–88. The classic study of a local area on the basis of the Parliamentary Surveys is Reginald Lennard, *Rural Northamptonshire under the Commonwealth*, Oxford Studies in Social and Legal History, vol. 5, Oxford, 1916.
[22] B. P. Wolffe, *The Royal Demesne in English History*, London, 1971, 52–3.
[23] Mary Coate, 'The Duchy of Cornwall: its History and Administration', *Transactions of the Royal Historical Society*, 4th series, vol. 10 (1927), 135–69.

of Eltham, younger son of Edward II, who died in 1336.[24] John of Eltham
was the last Earl of Cornwall. He died while still a minor, and the lands of
the earldom again escheated to the Crown. A year later they were granted
by Edward III to his eldest son, Edward of Woodstock, more popularly
known as the Black Prince.[25]

This grant, however, differed fundamentally from those that had pre-
ceded it. Edward of Woodstock was created *Duke* of Cornwall, and the lands
of the former earls were made an inalienable endowment of the Duchy.
Both title and lands, furthermore, were attached to the firstborn son of the
monarch either from birth or from the accession of his father to the throne.
This grant was confirmed in an act of Parliament, so that no future
monarch was able, at least in theory, to vary it at will. Exemptions were,
however, made. The future Henry VIII was granted the title and lands
after the premature death in 1502 of his elder brother Arthur, Prince of
Wales. Similarly Charles I was made Duke of Cornwall when Prince
Henry, elder son of James I, died during his father's lifetime, the terms of
the original charter being altered to *filius primogenitus existens*.

When the reigning monarch had no son the estates of the Duchy reverted
temporarily to the Crown, the King acting 'as if he were Duke', and the
Duchy income augmenting the royal revenue. This was indeed the case for
nearly two-thirds of the time hat elapsed between the creation of the Duchy
and the execution of the Parliamentary Survey in 1649–50.

Nor were the estates of the Duchy always treated as inviolate. On several
occasions Duchy lands were alienated, but most were eventually recovered.
The most serious offender was Elizabeth I, who sold a number of manors
which her successor, James I, managed to get back. In point of law the
original charter constituting the Duchy was conceived as having been
granted by Parliament: *communi assensu et consilio praelatorum, comitum,
baronorum et aliorum . . . in praesenti Parliamento*. Parliament could therefore
amend the charter, and it was by act of Parliament that the Duchy was
deprived in 1540 of the Honors of Wallingford and St Valery, and was
compensated with lands previously held by the Marquis of Exeter and the
Priories of Launceston and Tywardreath. For this there was a precedent in
the early fifteenth century. In 1421 Henry V gave the Duchy manor of
Isleworth to Sion Abbey, which he had recently founded, and repaid the
Duchy with lands in Somerset, Lincolnshire and elsewhere that had
escheated to the Crown.

THE DUCHY LANDS   In the seventeenth century the lands of the Duchy
of Cornwall were made up of three distinct groups of manors, rights
and privileges. Foremost amongst these were the *maneria antiqua*, the
group of seventeen manors, all of them in Cornwall, with which the
Duchy had originally been endowed. They had suffered losses, but all
had been recovered, and their extent in the mid-seventeenth century

---

[24] On the extent of the lands at this time see *Ministers' Accounts of the Earldom of Cornwall,
1296–1297*, ed. L. Margaret Midgley, Camden Society, 3rd series, vol. 66, and the inquisition
post mortem of Earl Edmund, *Calendar of Inquisitions Post Mortem*, Edward I, vol. I no. 604,
pp. 456–87, and of Edward the Black Prince, *ibid.*, vol. XV (1–7 Richard II), nos. 166–178,
pp. 67–77.
[25] *The Complete Peerage*, vol. 3, 433–5.

was much as it had been three centuries earlier. The seventeen manors were:

Calstock (5)
Helston in Kerrier (15)
Helston in Trigg (17)
Liskeard (23)
Moresk (25)
Penkneth (27
Penlyne (28)
Penmayne (29)
Restormel (33)

Rillaton (35)
Stoke Climsland (38)
Talskidy (40)
Tewington (41)
Tibesta (42)
Tintagel (43)
Trematon, with the borough of
Saltash (36, 48)
Tywarnhayle (52)

To this list must be added the rights which the Duchy exercised over the borough of Lostwithiel (24), originally part of the manors of Restormel and Penkneth, over the castle and borough of Launceston (21), the fishing of the River Fowey (12), and the toll tin of the western manors of Helston in Kerrier and Tywarnhayle.

The second group was made up of the *forinseca maneria*.[26] They had been part of the Duchy from its inception, but lay outside the county of Cornwall. They included:

the borough and manor of Lydford (57) and the Chase of Dartmoor
the manor and borough of Bradninch (55)
the fee farm of the City of Exeter[27]
Sutton Pool (62) and the river of Dartmouth (56)

as well as scattered lands in southern and eastern England. The manor of South Teign, generally considered to belong to this group, was attached to the Duchy in 1342.[28]

The last category of Duchy manors was made up of the *annexata maneria*. Most were added to the Duchy estates by either Henry V or Henry VIII in compensation, as has already been noted, for certain honors and manors that had been separated from it. They were a widely scattered group. Those which lay in south-west England were annexed to the Duchy by an act of Parliament of 1540 and derived from three separate sources:

1. The lands of Henry Courtenay, Marquis of Exeter, who had been attainted and executed in 1538,[29] consisting of:

Crafthole borough (9)
Landreyne (19)
Landulph (20)
Leigh Durant (22)
North Hill (28)
Portloe (31)
Portpigham borough (32)

Tinten (44)
Tregamere (45)
Trelowia (46)
Trelugan (47)
Treverbyn Courtney (50)
West Antony (53)

together with the fee farm of the Isles of Scilly (37)

[26] Mary Coate, 'The Duchy of Cornwall . . .', *passim*.
[27] Charles Croslegh, *Bradninch, being a short Historical Sketch of the Honor, the Manor, the Borough and Liberties and the Parish*, London 1911, 45. Rougemont Castle was reckoned to be the *caput* of the Honor of Bradninch.
[28] This is a lost place-name. It has been identified with Teigncombe in Chagford parish: J. E. B. Gover, A. Mawer and F. M. Stenton, *The Place-Names of Devon*, English Place-Name Society, vol. IX (1932), 425–6.
[29] *The Complete Peerage*, vol. 4, 330–1.

2.   The lands of the dissolved Priory of St Stephen, Launceston, consisting
of the manors of:[30]

Bonyalva (2)	Climsland Prior (8)
Boyton (3)	Eastway (10)
Bradford, Devon (54)	Stratton Sanctuary (39)
Bucklawren (4)	Treworgie (51)
Carnedon Prior (7)	

3.   The lands of the dissolved Priory of St Andrew, Tywardreath, consisting of:[31]

Austelprior (1)	Gready (14)
Fentrigan (11)	Porthea Prior (30)
Fowey borough (13)	Trevennen (49)

All the lands and perquisites surveyed in 1649–50 in Devon and Corn-
wall were part of the Duchy, with the exception of the manors of Rialton
and Reterth (34), Killigarth (18) and Carnanton (6) in Cornwall, and in
Devon the manors of Shebbear (59) and West Ashford (63, 64). Rialton and
Reterth had formed part of the possessions of the Priory of St Petroc at
Bodmin. After the Reformation they were jointly leased to John Mondy,
whose family still held them at the time of the Survey.[32] The rights of the
Crown in the manor were, however, settled by Charles I on his Queen,
Henrietta Maria, as part of her jointure.

Killigarth had been the property of Sir James Badge, but was confiscated
by the Exchequer because of his debts to the Crown. Carnanton had formed
part of the estates of the Nevilles, earls of Warwick, and was by the Neville
heiress Anne conveyed to Henry VII. It was thereafter held of the Crown on
lease.[33] The Devon manor of Shebbear had also been a Neville property[34]
and probably came to the Crown at the same time. The Crown acquired the
manor of West Ashford in Heanton Punchardon parish through the attainder of Henry Gray, Duke of Suffolk in 1554.[35] The Honors of Okehampton
and Plympton, the foremost feudal honors in Devon, had passed to the
Courtenays and escheated to the Crown along with the rest of the Courtenay lands in 1538.[36] The surveys of these royal but non-ducal manors are
printed below in order to complete the record for the two south-western
counties.

TENURES AND CUSTOMS

The varied origins of the lands which made up the Duchy of Cornwall in
1649–50 is reflected in the variety of their tenures and customs. In all
manors, with the exception of Talskidy, there were free tenants who owed
only a quit rent or, in a few instances, a petty service. Some owed only suit of
court. One was obligated to meet his lord at Polson Bridge whenever the
latter visited Cornwall, a far from onerous duty since he scarcely ever came.

---

[30] G. Oliver, *Monasticon Dioecesis Exoniensis,* Exeter, 1846, 23.
[31] *ibid.,* 47.
[32] Sir John Maclean, *The Parochial and Family History of the Deanery of Trigg Minor,* London, 1873,
vol. I. 137.
[33] D. and S. Lysons, *Magna Britannia,* vol. 3 *Cornwall,* London, 1814, 220.
[34] D. and S. Lysons, *Magna Britannia,* vol. 6, *Devon,* London, [1822], part 2, pp. 437–8.
[35] *The Complete Peerage,* vol. XII, part 1, 462.
[36] *Victoria County History, Devon,* vol. I, p. 551; I. J. Sanders, *English Baronies,* Oxford, 1960,
pp. 69–70; 137–8.

A few held their lands of Launceston, Trematon or Bradninch by knight service. The resulting obligations by this time were not even nominal, and it is clear that the Duchy had by and large lost track of the military duties of its free tenants.[37] Free tenants held their lands 'freely to themselves, their heirs and assigns' for ever. These tenancies had been in existence in many cases for centuries, and the real value of their rents had been diminished by inflation, so that by the mid-seventeenth century their value to the Crown was quite small. In fact, the total rents that the Duchy was receiving from this source in 1649–50 was less than a quarter of the whole Duchy income from Devon and Cornwall.

The Dukes of Cornwall had never been resident lords on any of their manors in the South West. There was thus no need for a demesne, and in those few instances where a vestigial demesne had survived, it was leased to a tenant farmer. The unfree lands of the manors of the Duchy were held by conventionary tenants. Their status was strictly speaking unfree, but the evidence for their 'unfreedom' was rapidly disappearing. On the *antiqua maneria* the conditions of conventionary tenure were unique. The tenants were required to renew their tenancies at an Assessions Court held in each manor every seven years. This mode of tenure was devised early in the fourteenth century, when land was scarce and the pressure of population acute.[38] The seven-yearly assessions allowed the Duke's steward to increase rents by the simple process of permitting any peasant to bid for the tenement. The sitting tenant was usually able to renew his tenancy though not infrequently at the price of an enhanced rent. In the later-fourteenth and later centuries land-hunger had abated. The Assession Rolls show unoccupied tenements, and the steward was more concerned to hold the tenants he had than to exact higher rents. The old obligation on each conventionary tenant to bid again for his land lapsed, and a degree of security of tenure developed. Indeed, Richard Carew wrote in 1602 that 'a kind of inheritable estate acrued' to the conventionary tenants of the Duchy.[39] John Norden, the Duchy Surveyor, demurred, and reckoned that these tenants held only *ad voluntatem domini*[40] an opinion strongly supported by a warrant addressed to the Duchy steward in 1639, informing him that the tenants pretend 'to have some estate of inheritance by custom, whereas they have none'.[41]

Such subtleties, however, were not revealed to the surveyors who, ten years later, surveyed the assessionable manors. In manor after manor the jury of tenants deposed that every seventh year a court was held 'at which the tenants of the said manor are to claime theire estates and to enter the same, not because theire estates doe then determine but that the Lord may know his present tennants, and the way of payinge his rents may be

---

[37] See the comment of the surveyors in their survey of Trematon: 'we cannott finde whoe are the present tenants in fee of the foresaid lands', nor, it might be added, could they have located some of the lands that owed knight service if they had tried.
[38] British Library, Add Ms. 30209, 'Brief Collection concerning the Mannors of the Dutchy of Cornwal'. Also J. Hatcher, *Rural Economy and Society in the Duchy of Cornwall*, Cambridge University Press, 1970, 80–101.
[39] Richard Carew, *The Survey of Cornwall*, edn. of 1811,]11–3.
[40] John Norden, *Speculi Britanniae Pars: A Topographical and Historical Description of Cornwall*, London, 1728, 21.
[41] Duchy of Cornwall Office, Enrolment Book 1639–42, quoted in M. Coate, "Duchy of Cornwall . . ."

preserved (which were otherwise uncerteine), there hapening divers altera-
cions and changes every yeare, the customary tennants haveing power to
surrender away any parte of his tenement at his pleasure'.[42]

This frequent and regular renewal of tenancies was, however, made the
occasion for financial impositions on the tenants. The tenant paid a fine,
called 'Old Knowledge Money', to renew his tenancy. Payment was spread
over the next six years, thus causing some awkward sums in the surveyors'
tabulations of manorial incomes. A change of tenant elicited another payment, known for obvious reasons as 'New Knowledge Money', which was
commonly double the rent.

The conventionary tenant on the *antiqua maneria* was clearly approximat-
ing the status of a freeholder, and the surveyors were constantly puzzled by
the lingering evidence of servile status. Ultimately, but not until 1828–9,
the claim of the conventionary tenant to be a freeholder was tested in the
case of Rowe v. Benton.[43] Although the Duchy established its case that
conventionary tenures on the assessionable manors were essentially unfree,
the judgment was so out of line with the times that an Act of Parliament of
1844[44] in effect converted assessionable tenancies into freehold.

The *annexata maneria* had an entirely different tenurial structure.[45] Assessionable tenancies were unknown in them. Instead, apart from freehold
lands, tenancies were held either by lease granted by King or Duke, or by
copy of the court roll. As a general rule the leases which the Duke granted
by indenture or the King by letters patent, were for substantial holdings.
Their term was commonly for 31 years; occasionally for 99 years or three
lives. In many instances the lessee is recorded to have sublet the lands
almost immediately, and it is apparent that they were held as an invest-
ment, especially as the rent to the Duchy was often very much below the
level of the 'improved' rent.

Tenements held by copy of the court roll were invariably small, rarely
more than a family holding of about 30 acres, and often only a small fraction
of this. They were usually held by two or three lives in succession. When the
last 'life' was in possession, the tenement was usually granted in reversion
to another tenant, often a relative of the tenant in occupation. Invariably
copyhold tenants paid, in addition to their rent, a fine when they received
their tenements and a heriot on the death of each 'life'. Fines varied greatly,
and were anything from five to fifteen times the annual rent. The sale value
of a copyhold tenement clearly depended on the number and ages of the
'lives' by which it continued to be held, and, as was noted above, a scale was
devised by Parliament to guide the contractors in their sale of copyholds.

Between the groups of *annexata maneria* there were also differences in
tenurial arrangements. Those which derived from the estates of the Marquis of Exeter were almost wholly devided into small copyhold tenements.
Those which had formerly belonged to the Priories of Launceston and
Tywardreath were leased in relatively large units for terms of years. These
contrasts must have derived from late medieval tenurial conditions, before
these manors were annexed to the Duchy.

[42] No. 5 (Calstock).
[43] George Concanen, *A Report of the Trial at Bar Rowe v. Brenton*, London, 1830.
[44] 7 and 8 Victoria, cap. 65.
[45] Mary Coate, 'Duchy of Cornwall . . .', p. 145.

Many tenements, especially assessionable and copyhold, had come to be minutely subdivided. This was especially so in the manor of Liskeard, where the same tenant is represented as holding fractions of several tenements. While the number of tenements is determinable for each manor, that of the tenants is uncertain owing to the repetition of their names. Table 1 is an attempt to enumerate the tenements of each category in each of the manors surveyed, the numbers at the left indicating the numerical sequence in the text.

TABLE I

	Freehold	Leasehold	Assessionable	Copyhold
Maneria antiqua				
5 Calstock	14	1	142	
15 Helston in Kerrier	27		106	
17 Helston in Trigg	28		96	
23 Liskeard	31	1	109	
25 Moresk	29		61	
27 Penkneth	7		6	
28 Penlyne	6		15	
29 Penmayne	9		33	
33 Restormel	1	1	13	
35 Rillaton	6		34	
38 Stoke Climsland	17	1	66	
40 Talskidy			10	
41 Tewington	35		62	
42 Tibesta	23		54	
43 Tintagel	18		45	
48 Trematon	38		68	
52 Tywarnhayle	16		51	
	305	4	971	
Courtenay Lands				
9 Crafthole	14			4
19 Landreyne	4			8
20 Landulph	3			20
22 Leigh Durant	3			16
26 North Hill	8			2
31 Portloe	6			11
32 Portpigham	57			
44 Tinten	15	1		37
45 Tregamere	6			5
46 Trelowia	4	2		7
47 Trelugan	9			5
50 Treverbyn Courtney	14	3		13
53 West Antony	13			17
	156	6		145

	Freehold	Leasehold	Assessionable	Copyhold
Lands of St Andrew, Tywardreath				
1 Austelprior	10	4		
11 Fentrigan	10	3		
13 Fowey borough	36			
14 Greadow	32	4		
30 Porthea Prior	28	2		
49 Trevennen	11	2		
	127	15		
Lands of St Stephen, Launceston:				
2 Bonyalva	5	4		
3 Boyton	13	9		
54 Bradford, Devon	3	5		
4 Bucklawren	1	10		
7 Carnedon Prior	62	22		1
8 Climsland Prior	6	10		
10 Eastway	6	4		
39 Stratton Sanctuary	6	7		
51 Treworgie	21	4		
	120	70		1
Total	708	95	971	146

The legislation which terminated the status of the assessionable tenancies on the *antiqua maneria* was accompanied by the preparation of maps of each of them.[46] These were prepared on a large scale and in a style which closely resembled that of the contemporary tithe maps. Each manorial map was accompanied by a schedule listing the separate properties, their area and occupancy. On the maps themselves the different forms of tenure: freehold, conventionary and common land were distinguished. A map of the manor of Stoke Climsland, derived from this source, was prepared by R. L. Clowes.[47]

The monetary value of each manor is given in the abstract which concludes each survey, together with the 'improved' or current value. Table 2 presents the current income from each category of tenure in the Duchy and Crown manors of the South West. It omits, however, the value of 'timber trees' and woodland and also some other small and irregular sources of income. It also excludes the appraised value of properties that were 'in hand' at the time of the survey. The totals given do not in all cases agree with the abstracts printed at the ends of most chapters. The latter are as

[46] There are sets of these maps in the Duchy of Cornwall Office, the Public Record Office and the Cornwall County Record Office.
[47] Unpublished London MA thesis, a copy of which is in the Duchy Office. Maps of some Duchy manors, apparently derived in part from those compiled about 1940, were used in M. W. Beresford, 'Dispersed and Group Settlement in Medieval Cornwall', *The Agricultural History Review*, vol. 12 (1964), 13–27.

TABLE 2

	Freehold rents and perquisites of court	Rents of leasehold lands	Rents, fines etc. of conven. tenants	Copyhold rents	Other income	Total
	£ s d	£ s d	£ s d	£ s d	£ s d	£ s d
1. Austelprior	1 14 11	4 0 8				5 15 7
2. Bonyalva	1 9 11	6 6 8				7 16 7
3. Boyton	1 14 1	17 1 6				18 15 7
4. Bucklawren	3 19 2½	25 12 1½				29 11 4
5. Calstock	11 4 9½	148 18 0	42 10 5½		3 13 4	206 6 7
6. Carnanton		52 8 4				52 8 4
7. Carnedon Prior	9 7 11¾	11 12 6		3 4		21 3 9¾
8. Climsland	8 3	6 17 7			2 10 0	9 15 10
9. Crafthole	1 3 10½			12 4½		1 16 3
10. Eastway	16 2	6 11 0				7 7 2
11. Fentrigan	2 0 10	1 13 10				3 13 10
12. Fowey River						—
13. Fowey Borough	1 13 4	1 8				1 15 0
14. Greadow	9 1 4	2 15 2				11 16 6
15. Helston/Kerrier	11 7 7		55 14 7			67 2 2
16. Helston Toll Tin		6 8				6 8
17. Helston/Trigg	14 2 6½	10 13 4	57 17 5¾			83 3 9¾
18. Killigarth	1 12 3	8 8 8			19 2	10 15 1
19. Landreyne	1 0 8			2 12 8		3 13 4
20. Landulph	1 5 7			13 14 5		16 0 0
21. Launceston	9 4 0½	2 3 4			15 0 0	26 7 4½
22. Leighdurant	1 3 3			9 3 7		10 6 10
23. Liskeard	16 8 5	25 13 0	53 5 5½			95 9 10½
24. Lostwithiel	9 10 11½	2 0 0				11 10 11½
25. Moresk	9 14 3½		24 18 8¼			34 12 11¾
26. North Hill	12 9			16 0		1 8 9
27. Penkneth	1 2 2½		3 17 8			4 19 10½
28. Penlyne	2 9 7		4 7 10			6 17 5
29. Penmayne	2 8 2		7 13 4			10 1 6
30. Porthea	7 16 7	1 12 4				9 8 11
31. Portloe	4 7 8½			15 12 8		20 0 4½
32. Portpigham	3 4 8½					3 4 8½
33. Restormel	7 2	28 7 0	5 12 6½		6 8	34 13 4½
34. Rialton/Reterth		60 0 0				60 0 0
35. Rillaton	4 3 4		11 13 5		8 13 0	24 9 9
36. Saltash	3 0 0				1 0 0	4 0 0
37. Isles of Scilly	40 0 0					40 0 0
38. Stoke Climsland	30 4 0	10 18 4	26 5 3		5 6 2	72 13 9
39. Stratton	1 10 4	6 8 6				7 18 10
40. Talskidy			4 10 6¾			4 10 6¾
41. Tewington	15 3 3¾		28 4 5			43 7 8¾
42. Tibesta	7 12 7		31 17 2½		1 0	39 10 9½
43. Tintagel	2 13 10½	2 2 10	34 12 5¼			39 9 1¾
44. Tinten	5 5 0	2 17 0		27 10 11½		35 12 11½
45. Tregamere	1 6 1			2 16 8		4 2 9
46. Trelowia	6 9	2 13 8		4 6 8		7 7 1
47. Trelugan	1 2 6	1 4 10		4 5 0		6 12 4
48. Trematon	15 0 0	1 16 9	43 2 2¼			59 18 11¼
49. Trevennen	6 12 9	3 2 0				9 14 9
50. Treverbyn Courtney	2 16 2½	1 10 1		5 16 11	4 0 0	14 3 2½
51. Treworgie	5 1 7	3 19 0				9 0 7
52. Tywarnhayle	10 11 4		15 4 7¾			25 15 11¾
53. West Antony	5 2 3			13 16 7¾		18 18 10¾
Devon						
54 Bradford	1 2 2	6 8 1½				7 10 3½
55. Bradninch	14 16 1	1 15 0		48 12 9½	1 10 0	66 13 10½
56. Dartmouth River		14 13 4				14 13 4
57. Lydford	4 10 0*					4 10 0
58. Honors of Okehampton and Plympton	39 2 10	6 16 8				45 19 6
59. Shebbear		5 0 0				5 0 0
60. Southteigne	11 17 0					11 17 0
61. Sidmouth Mills		4 13 4				4 13 4
62. Sutton Pool		13 6 8				13 6 8
63/4. West Ashford		11 18 3				11 18 3
	366 9 1½	524 7 9	451 18 2	150 0 8¼	42 19 4	1535 15 0¾

* Amended to £11 3 4 in 1658.

given in the manuscript, but in some instances they incorporate arithmetical errors which, it is hoped, have been eliminated from the table.[48]

THE MANUSCRIPT   Fair copies of the survey were prepared in the field and were despatched, usually in groups of two or three, to Westminster. They were uniform in style. All were written on sheets of paper of about 305 mm by 375 mm. Those for each manor were sewn at the head and placed within a cover of the same paper. A title and number were added to each of the latter, and such endorsements as were made were placed on the back of the last sheet. The two sets of surveys are *almost* identical. There are minor discrepancies in pagination, and a very few copying errors have been found, though it is impossible to say which copy represents the data presented by the jury.

Two incomplete sets of the surveys of the Duchy manors are available, but only one of the surveys of other Crown lands in the South West. Both sets were endorsed by William Webb. The set in the records of the Duchy of Cornwall lacks the survey of the Isles of Scilly; that in the Public Record Office is short of the surveys of Bucklawren and Treverbyn Courtney, but has two copies of that of the Water of Fowey. The last named was surveyed at a later date than most of the rest of the manors, and clearly more than two copies were submitted.

The condition of the surveys is in general good. Those in the Public Record Office are in a few instances faded and stained with damp, and for a complete reading must be supplemented by the copies in the Duchy Office.[49] The Duchy Office also contains a number of eighteenth century copies of the surveys. In one instance these had to be used to complete data which had been torn from both the originals.

Wherever relevant the surveys give the area of tenements either by estimation or 'admeasurement'. One does not of course know how careful or expert the surveyors were in estimating the size of tenements, but too many are given in the traditional units of 30 acres to inspire much confidence. On the other hand many pieces of land were measured. It may be that this was done only when the jury failed to agree on the size of a tenement or piece of land. On a number of manors – most of them *antiqua maneria* – the old measure, the Cornish acre, was used. This was a variable unit which is generally assumed to have been on average about 60 acres.[50] It was divided into four farlingates or furlongs.

EDITING   The great length of the manuscript and the repetitive nature of much of the text have combined to prevent it from being printed in its entirety. The practice has been adopted of printing in full the first entry of each type – preamble, free tenants, etc. – in order to show its style, and of

---

[48] The totals have been taken from the abstracts at the end of each survey. These do not always agree with the figures given in the text of the surveys, but discrepancies are very small.

[49] All Parliamentary Surveys in the Public Record Office were listed by county in the *Seventh Report of the Deputy Keeper of the Public Records*, 1846, Appendix 2, pp. 224–238, and the *Eighth Report*, 1847, Appendix 2, pp. 52–80. On page 81 is a list of the surveys deposited in the Duchy Office.

[50] E. Smirke, 'Notice on the Old Land-Measure called a Cornish Acre', *Archaeologia Cambrensis*, vol. 9 (1863), Appendix 2; also printed in *The Forty-second Annual Report of the Royal Institution of Cornwall*, Part 2 (1861), 29–40.

calendaring the remainder. Where a portion of the text is quoted in the calendar it is enclosed by quotation marks.

A number of abbreviations has been used in order to shorten the text; these are listed on page xxiv. In the manuscript most dates are given by regnal years. These have been translated into calendar years, using the new style with the year beginning on January 1. The surveyors were evidently as confused by the use of regnal years as some modern readers are likely to be, and a number of mistakes was made, including the attribution of a lease to a non-existent date. These are noted in the text.

The text printed is that found in the Duchy of Cornwall office, supplemented where necessary by that in the Public Record Office. Discrepancies between the two are noted. A note at the beginning of each survey gives the class marks in both series, as well as the location of the manor or property surveyed, and the circumstances under which it passed into the possession of either the Duchy or the Crown.

There are in the text some 1500 place-names. Many of these are field-names, and no attempt has been made either to locate them or to identify their present forms. The rest are settlement names. Most have been identified, using large-scale Ordnance Maps, maps in the Duchy Office, Symons' *Gazetteer*[51] and the lists compiled by Charles Henderson, now in the possession of the Royal Institution of Cornwall at Truro. Nevertheless a considerable number of names remains unidentified. Some of these will be known to persons with a deeper local knowledge than that possessed by the editor. Further research will doubtless reveal the identity of others. In all cases this edition gives place-names exactly as written in the text, even where a name is spelled in more than one way. The modern form of the place-name, where it is known, is given in square brackets. If the form in the text is the same as that in use today this is indicated by *id*.

The surveyors occasionally omitted significant detail, such as Christian names and part of a date. Such an omission is shown in this edition by [. . .]. In the larger manors a tabulation, usually alphabetical is given of free and conventionary tenants, together with their rents, fines and other obligations. Since this merely repeats what is given elsewhere in the text, it has been omitted. The tabulations, however, occasionally provide a useful guide to the interpretation of otherwise illegible figures in the text. Nevertheless, there are discrepancies between the body of the text and these tabulations. It is assumed that figures given in the text are correct, and that these discrepancies result merely from copying errors in preparing the tabulations.

Rents, heriots and fines are given in the manuscript in the left-hand margin, as required by the 'instructions to Surveyors', and improved values in the right. These have been re-arranged in this edition in order to save space.

The second volume of this survey will contain the manors from the Isles of Scilly to West Antony in Cornwall, all the Duchy's possessions in Devon and an Index to the whole work.

[51] R. Symons, *A Geographical Dictionary or Gazetteer of the County of Cornwall*, Penzance, 1884.

ACKNOWLEDGEMENTS

The editor, with the Council of the Devon and Cornwall Record Society, wishes to express his deep gratitude to H.R.H. Prince Charles, Duke of Cornwall and his Council both for their kindness in allowing the records of the Duchy to be consulted and transcribed and also for their generous help towards the cost of this publication.

The editor also wishes to thank Mr J. W. Y. Higgs, Secretary to the Duchy, Sir Anthony Gray KCVO, his predecessor in that office, Dr Graham Haslam, Records Clerk to the Duchy, and Miss Henrietta Sweeting of the Duchy Office for their kindness and help.

Others whose help he acknowledges are Mr Leslie Douch, Curator to the Royal Institution of Cornwall, Professor Leo Solt of Indiana University, Mr Peter Hull, Archivist to the County of Cornwall and his assistant, Mrs Christine North, Mr P. A. S. Pool, and lastly Professor Joyce Youings of the University of Exeter, editor of the Record Society, without whose help and encouragement and command of the minutiae of editing this manuscript could not have been made available.

Cambridge   N. J. G. Pounds
December 1981

ABBREVIATIONS

ac.	acre
ac. C.	Cornish acre
als	alias
bro.	brother
clk	cleric, clerk
d.	daughter, death
dec.	deceased
esq.	esquire
f.	father
farl.	farlingate ($\frac{1}{4}$ of a Cornish acre)
gent.	gentleman
indent.	indenture
kt	knight
L. I.	lease indented
L. P.	letters patent
Md.	memorandum
mess.	messuage
s.	son
sis.	sister
sp.	spinster
w.	wife
wid.	widow

THE PARLIAMENTARY SURVEY OF THE DUCHY OF CORNWALL

1 MANOR OF AUSTELL PRIOR

DCO Surveys/3; PRO E 317 (c)/3. The manor lay within St Austell parish and included the churchtown. It was bounded by the manors of Tewington (no. 41) on the south and by Treverbyn Courtney (no. 50) on the north. Formerly the property of Tywardreath Priory; added to the Duchy in 1540.

'A survey of the mannor of Austelprior with the rights, members and appertynances thereof, lying and being in the county of Cornewall, partes of the annexed Dutchie and parcell of the possessions of Charles Stuart late Duke of Cornewall but now settled on trustees for the use of the Comon Wealth, held as of the mannor of East Greenewich in free and comon soccage by fealtie onely, taken by Edward Hore, George Crompton, George Gentleman, Gabriel Taylor and George Goodman and by them retorned the first day of April anno domini 1650.

FREE TENNANTS OF THE SAID MANNOR

The heires of Clearke and Cole hold freely to them and theire heires for ever in soccage certeine land in Bonamaris for which Oliver Saule esq. paieth to the lord p.a. . . . 2s.
Clowberry holdeth . . . land in Boonamaris . . . 4s; [. . .] . . . land heretofore Burgis in Bonamaris . . . 4s 6d; Oliver Saule esq. . . . land in Austell heretofore Rosagans . . . 5½d; The said Oliver . . . land there heretofore Delamanies . . . 2s; The said Oliver . . . land there heretofore Bonallackes . . . 1s; The said Oliver Saule . . . one tenement there . . . 6s; Clowberry . . . land there . . . 5s 6d; William Carlyon of Menagwins [id.][1] . . . land there . . . 6s 5d; Oliver Saule . . . land there . . . 1s ½d.

Some total of the said rents p.a. 32s 11d.

LEASE HOLDERS OF THE SAID MANNOR

Nicholas Saule esq. by letters pattants[2] bearing date at Westminster [17 February 1627] hath made and graunted to him, his executors and assignes all those Five Tenementes and Mill and one acre and a halfe of land English with their appurtenances, scituate, lying and being in Austell with all and singuler the profitts, comodities, emoluments and hereditaments whatsoever thereunto belonging or in any wise apperteyninge. Habend' for and dureing the end and terme of thirty and one yeares next followinge the feast of Michael the Archangell before the date of the said letters pattents. Redd' inde yearely for one of the said tenements and mill the rent of forty sixe shillings and eight pence and for the other tenement and acre and halfe of

---

[1] The ancient seat of the Scobell family.
[2] Grants of leases were by indenture if made by the Prince of Wales as Duke of Cornwall, but by letters patent if by the King when the properties of the Duchy were vested in the Crown.

land nine shillings at the two most usuall feasts of the yeare by equall porcons, all which foresaid premisses are worth at an improved value besides the present rent p.a.   £6.

There is excepted out of the said graunt all greate trees, timber trees, woodes, underwoodes, mines, and quarries in uppon or belonginge to the premisses.

It is provided that if the said rents shall not be paid in parte or in whole by the space of forty dayes next after it shall grow due that then the said graunt shold be voide.

The said Nicholas [is] bound to keepe all the premisses in good and sufficient repaire and soe to deliver it up at the end of the terme, alsoe to doe suite and service to the Lords Cortes when they shalbe there holden, and to plant the number of three trees of oake, ash, or elme yearely on the premisses.

There is allowed to the said Nicholas all sortes of bootes as necessary to be expended on the premisses and not elsewhere.

Oliver Saule esq., sonne and heire of the said Nicholas, hath now the possession of the premisses.'

Joseph May, 8 May 1628, tenement in Austell sometime in the tenure of Luke Vivian and late Richard Lestons; 5½ acres; term of 99 years from 21 March 1628 [sic] on lives of Ralphe, George, and Theophilus, sons of Joseph. Rent 10s. Herriot 10s. Improved value £4. Exceptions, provisions and conditions as above. Lives: Ralphe aged 34; Josephe 32; Theophilus 'supposed to be alive being gone in the East Indies and lately heard from (if soe) he is alsoe aged 30 yeares'.

Joseph Stephens, 28 May 1628, tenement in St Austell with 3 acres English; term 99 years on lives of wife Joan and their sons John and Lionell. Rent 5s. Heriot 10s. Improved value £4. Exceptions etc. as above. Lives: John, now in possession, 40 yeares, Lionell 30.

John Came, 3 November 1626, tenement in Austle and 3½ acres English; term 99 years on lives of John, Agnes Hore (daughter of Stephen Hore of Roch) and Elizabeth Hore (daughter of John Howe [sic], son of Stephen Hore of Roche. Rent 10s. Heriot 20s. Improved value £3 15s. Exceptions, etc. as above. Lives: Agnes Howe, now Agnes Came widow, 45 years, Elizabeth Hore 26.

'BOUNDES

This mannor of Austelprior lyeth within the Churche Towne of St Austell and is bounded on all sides with the mannors of Tewington [No. 41] and Treverbin Courtney [Treverbyn, No. 50].

There is belonginge to the tennants of this mannor a pasture comon conteying twelve acres wherein the said tennants claime right of comon.

CUSTOMES

There ought to be kept every yeare foure courtes, viz. two Law Courtes and two Courtes Barron to which all the tennantes are to doe theire suite.

There is one of the customary tennants of the said mannor every yeare chosen (as it shall come to his turne) to execute the office of Reeve, whoe is to collect the Lord's rents and to be accountable for the same.

The free tenements of the said mannor pay on every death or alienacon a Relieffe according to the custome of the mannor. The leaseholders [? and] customary tennants pay a Herriott according as is expressed in theire severall leases, which the Reeve is alsoe to collect, and likewise all such fines, amerciaments, estrayes and other perquisites which doe yearely accrue within the said mannor and will amount to communibus annis [in an average year] 2s.

AN ABSTRACT OF THE PRESENT RENTS AND FUTURE IMPROVEMENTS OF THE SAIDE MANNOR

Rents of Assize and Perquisites of Courtes p.a.   34s 11d
Rents of the Leaseholders for lives and yeares p.a.   80s 8d
    Some totall of the present rentes p.a.   £5 15s 7d
Improved value of the landes and tenements in lease after the death of the lives and expiracon of the yeares is (besides the present rent) p.a.
        £17 15s.

    This is an exact survey of the said mannor taken and [blank] by us, [signed] Ed. Hore, G. Garman, G. Crompton, G. Gentleman, Gabr. Taylor.
Ex[amined] Wi. Webb, Surv[eyor] Gen[era]ll.'

2   MANOR OF BONYALVA

DCO S/3; PRO E 317 (C)/4. The manor lies in the western part of St German's parish; formerly belonged to Launceston Priory, and was attached to the Duchy in 1540.

'A survey of the mannor of Bonialva . . . retorned the [blank] day of February . . . 1649.

FREEHOLDERS WITHIN THE SAID MANNOR

John Moyle esq. holdeth freely to him and his heires for ever
certeyne lands in East Bonialva for which he payeth p.a.   5s 5d
George Ketchwitch esq. . . . land in Treswinger   10s
Charles Vaughan esq. . . . land in Trethewe [Trethew in Morval]   1s 5d
Philip Mayowe esq . . . land in Poulca [? Polcatt in St Germans]   7s
Richard Briyn gent. and Robert Couch . . . land in East Bonialva   3s 7d
          [Total]   27s 5d

LEASEHOLDERS WITHIN THE SAID MANNOR

West Bonialva
William Ketchwich by Letters Pattents beareing date at Westminster [24 May 1626] hath made and graunted to him . . . All those Two Tenements with the Appurtenances in Westbonialva late in the Tenure of Thomas Gache or his Assignes, Alsoe All that Tenement called Janes Tenement, And All that one other Tenement and Mills . . . late in the Tenure of Walter Gache and John Elliott . . . All which conteyne by estimacion one hundred and Thirty Acres of land . . . Habend' for and dureing the terme of Ninety nine yeares if Jane Ketchwich wife of the said William, George Ketchwich and William Ketchwich theire sonnes or one of them shold soe long live. Redd' inde annuatim for the Tenements called Gatches the some of Twenty three shillings [and] foure pence; for Janes Tenement Twenty one shillings [and] eight pence, And for the other Tenement and Mills Twenty six shillings [and] eight pence at the most usual feasts (vizt) Michaeltide and

Lady Day by equall porcions . . . All which are worth upon Improvement besides the present rent p.a.   £60'
Exceptions, provisions and conditions; six trees to be planted p.a.
Md.: 'There is allowed to them sufficient of all sortes of bootes needefull to be onely expended on the premisses and not elsewhere. Alsoe to take sufficient Timber by the appointment of the Steward and not otherwise.
There are now groweing on the premises certeine Timber Trees and Saplins worth now to be sould   £13
The lives are all in beinge and Aged: Jane about 56 yeares; George about 38; William, 35.'

Thomasin Gache, sp., 25 May 1626, messuage, orchard, garden with an acre of meadow and 3 acres of land, late Thomas Gache, and 1½ acres of wood. Term: 99 years, on lives of Thomasin Gache (40), Francis Ketchwich (30), s. of John K. gent., dec., and Thomasin Pawley (26), d. of Edward Pawley.   Rent 6s.   Imp. val. £4 5s.
Exceptions, provisions and conditions, as above. Lessee 'not to cutt the Woodes and Under Woodes graunted them but once in Tenn yeares dureing the whole Terme. And after every such cutting are to enclose and encoppice the same And to keepe it from hurt or spoyle by beasts. And alsoe to leave on every acre sufficient Staddells according to the Statute. And lastly . . . to plant Two Trees yearely.'

Thomas Axford gent., 26 May 1628, Knights Tenement and 48 acres. Term: 99 years, on lives of Honor Axford (50), w. of Thomas A, and Nicholas and Thomas (both dec.) their sons.   Rent 25s.   Imp. val. £24.
Exceptions, provisions and conditions, as above; to plant 3 trees p.a. Trees now growing worth £15.

Thomas Chubbe of Morval, 25 March 1627, messuage late Stephen Hodge, and 48 acres. Term: 99 years, on lives of Elizabeth Chubbe (50), w. of Thomas C (dec.), and John (37), their s. Rent 24s. Imp. val. £24.
Exceptions, etc., as above; to plant 6 trees yearly. Trees now growing worth £5.

'BOUNDS

The said Mannor is thus Bounded: On the East with a Lake called Pollebba Lake[1] which ariseth out of the lands of John Moyle esq. called Mill Towne [probably Wilton] and thence runneth into a River called Seaton River which runneth towards Hessenford, and from thence by the lands of the foresaid John Moyle called Mill towne on the North to a little Brooke which runneth between the Lands of the said John Moyle and Sir John Trelawney and Mr Eliotts lands called Cuttenbeake [Cuddenbeak in St Germans] Mannor. And on the West by the said River called Seaton River untill it comes to Pollebba Lake aforesaid where it begun.

CUSTOMS

There is kept foure Courtes yearely in the said Mannor (Vizt) Two Law Courtes and Two b[aro]n Courtes to which all the Tennants of the said Mannor are bound to performe theire suites.

---

[1] Almost certainly the unnamed stream to the south-east of Bonyalva farmstead. The term 'lake' was commonly used for a small stream.

Att one of the said Courtes there is usually chosen one of the Tennants by Lease to execute the office of Reeve which he is to doe upon Oathe, whose office is to Collect the Lords rent and to be accountable for the same to the Lord. Alsoe all such Fines, perquisites of Courte which will amount to, Communibus Annis 2s 6d

AN ABSTRACT OF THE PRESENT RENTS AND FUTURE IMPROVEMENTS OF THIS MANNOR

Present rents and perquisites of court		29s 11d
Present rents of leasehold lands		£6 6s 8d
Total	£7 16s	7d
Improved rents after the leases have expired	£112 5s	
Trees and saplins valued at	£30	

This is an exact survey . . .'

3 MANOR OF BOYTON AND BRADRICH BARTON

DCO S/3; PRO E 317 (C)/5. Lies mainly in Boyton parish with an extension across the Devon boundary into St Giles on the Heath. Formerly belonged to Launceston Priory; was attached to the Duchy in 1540.

'A Survey of the Mannor of Boyton and the Barton of Bradrich . . . Retorned 31 July 1650.

THE BARTON OF BRADRICH WITH THE BARTON HOUSE

The said Barton house Consisteth of a faire lardge Hall at the West end whereof is a Kitchen and at the East end a Larder with other Convenient Roomes thereto Adjoyninge there belowe staires. Over the said lower Roomes or above staires there is a faire dininge Roome at the East end of which are two lodging Chambers with a Clossett and at the West end Three lodgeing Chambers with a Clossett, all in very good repaire. Without doores there are Two Barnes with other outhouses to them adjoyning.

The Scite of the said House Consisteth of one Paved Courte on the South West side and another on the North East side of the saide house with one garden and a bowling Alley with [blank] Orchards and one Meadow below the house. All which Scite conteyneth in the Whole fifteene Acres of land.

THE DEMEASNES LETT IN LEASE WITH THE FORESAID HOUSE

All those thirtie eight parcells of Meadow, Pasture, Arrable and Wood ground, conteyning in the whole by mensuracion Six hundred fiftie and foure Acres, besides the Scite of the house aforesaid, And which with the said house and Scite are valued to be worth upon Improvement £203.

The forementioned premises are in the present Tenure and Occupacion of Thomas Gewen esq. whoe holds the same by Letters Pattents from the late King for the Terme of Ninety nine yeares if Three lives live so long, Under the yearely rent of Tenn Pounds. Which said Letters Pattents the said Gewen refused to show unto us by which meanes Wee cannott Certifie what the Excepcions and Provisoes are, Nor what Condicions or Covenants the said Gewen is bound to performe.

We are informed that there is but one of the Three lives in being, Viz Christopher Gewen, his sonne, whoe is aged about 30 yeares.

The Timber Trees and Sapplins growing on the foresaid lands (if Excepted) are valued to be worth in ready money now to be sould £60.

The Woodes and Under Woodes groweing on parte of the foresaid premisses being 141 Acres (if Excepted) are also worth in ready money . . . £564.

Md. [added later] that the said Gewen came before us and made Claime to the said Barton and alsoe for the Mannor of Boyton upon pretence of haveing an estate of Inheritance therein, but produced noe Deede nor writeing to make good the said Claime.

[Marginal, in a different hand] The Clayme is made good by the order Entered on the Backside of the foregoing sheete.

[Added at the bottom of the membrane] I find by the Copie of the originall Grant proved upon oath before the Commissioners for rem[oval] of obst[ructions] dated [6 June 1628], That the premisses are granted under two distinct rents amounting in the whole to £10 yeerlie, viz. for the Lands £6 13s 4d and for the Woode and Underwoode (with an Exception of the Great Trees and Tymber Trees) £3 6s 8d.

FREE TENNANTS OF THE SAID MANNOR

John Lea holdeth to him and his heires for ever in Knights service one Messuage or Tenement called Southbeare [South Beer in Boyton], with Two Gardens, Three orchards, 10 Acres of Meadow, 20 Acres of Pasture, 2 Acres of Woode, 100 Acres of Furse ground and 20 Acres of moore for which he paieth p.a. 5s 8d.

These tennants followinge are (and have beene) accounted to hold freely of the said Mannor but by what Tenure wee cannott finde.'

John Arscott gent. and Thomas Shepland in right of his w., land in Southbeare, 3s 1d; Gartride Rolles wid., ten. called Nordon, 1s 6d; Richard Spoore esq., ten. in Dunnes [Dunns in Boyton], 5s; Marke Cottle esq., lands in Boyton, 6d; Henry Randall gent., lands in Newton [*id.* in Boyton], 1s 8d; Samuell Gilbert gent., lands in Newton, 1s 8d; Robert Martin gent., lands in Newton, 7½d; Richard Curry gent., lands in Newton, 7½d; William Risden esq., lands in Hole, als Holehamm [Hele in St Giles on the Heath, Devon], 1s; The Lady Prideaux, a Headweir in Northcott [*id.* in St Giles], 1s; John Glanvill, by the d. of George G his f. and John Williams alias Bartlett, lands in Southbeare, 3s 1d; Robert Lovis, lands in Blagdon [in North Tamerton] suit of court only.

Total   25s 5d.

LEASEHOLDERS OF THE SAID MANOR

Henry Randall gent., by L.P. of 2 May 1627, ten. in Boyton of 31 ac. Term: 99 years, on lives of Margaret (32), Grace (30) and Wilmott Randall (28). Rent 13s 9d. Imp. val. £15 16s. Exceptions, etc., as above; to plant 4 trees p.a. Premises assigned 4 January 1646 to George Anderton of North Petherwyn and Thomasin Lea of Boyton.

John Olver, by L.P. of 30 November 1632: mess. and corn mill in Haunch [*id.* in Boyton]; a pasture called South Park of 3¼ac.; meadow of 3½ ac.;

arable called Crosse Park of 3 ac.; two meadows called the Little Meadow of 3½ ac.; pasture called Higher Lease of 3 ac.; arable called Middle Lease of 3¼ ac.; arable called Lower Lease of 8 ac.; two woods called Upper and Lower Woodground of 7½ ac.; meadow called Millmeade of 2 ac.; pasture called Hamm of 3 ac. Term: 99 years, on lives of Alice, w. of John Oliver, and John (26) and Stephen (24) their sons. Rent 18s 10d. Heriot 20s. Imp. val. £30 15s. Exceptions, etc., as above. Trees on premises valued at £3.

John Pentire, by L.P. of 26 June 1628, moiety of ten. called Haunch, of 18 ac. Term: 99 years, on lives of John P. (63), Mary (64) his w., and John (24) their s. Rent 5s 8½d. Imp. val. £11 10s 6d. Exceptions, etc., as above.

Henry Berdowne, by L.P. as above, the other moiety of Haunch of 31 ac. Term: 99 years, on lives of Henry B. (48), Rebecca B. (40) his sister, and John Olver alias Broadway (dec.). Rent 5s 8½d. Imp. val. £14 10s 6d. Exceptions, etc., as above.

Thomas Gewen esq., by L.P. of 16 June 1628, ten. [i] in Boyton lately held by Prudence Veale, of 42 ac.; another ten. [ii] in Boyton, lately held by Peter Bawden, of 32 ac. Term: 99 years, on lives of Christopher Gewen (30), Thomas G. (dec.) and Mary G. (dec.). Rent 14s 5d [in margin, 24s 10d] and 10s. Imp. val. £32 11s 4d.
Thomas Gewen assigned his right in [i] to Prudence Veale, 12 Oct. 1629, at the same rent, 'the Improvement whereof being deducted out of the foresaid Improved value is p.a. £18 1s 6d.'
T. G. assigned [ii] to Richard Langford gent., 5 April 1630. R. L. assigned his right in one close called Crosse Park and an adjoining meadow to John Pentire, 6 April 1630 at a rent of 1s 8d, 'being part of the reserved rent . . . the Improved value of which Close being taken out of the Improved value of the whole is p.a. 46s 6d.'
Richard Langford assigned a close called Worth Park of 11 ac. to Henry Randall, 16 July 1628 at a rent of 2s 6d, part of the reserved rent. Imp. val. £5 2s 6d.
R. L. assigned the residue, consisting of 15 ac., to John Lange [no date given]. Rent 6s 5d, the remainder of the reserved rent. Imp. val. £7 1s 1d.

Henry Parsons, by L.P. of 30 Nov. 1627, ten. called Dorsett [Dorset] of 72 ac. Term: 99 years, on lives of H. P. (50), Edith (44) his w., and Grace (24) their d. Rent 20s. Heriot 20s. Imp. val. £33. Trees worth £15.

Thomas Parsons, by L.P. [no date], a cottage. Term: 99 years, on lives of Christopher (34), Mary (24) and Blaunch (28), children of T.P. Rent 1s 8d. Imp. val. 25s. Exceptions etc., as above.

Walter Duncanson, gent., by L.P. of 13 Sept. 1626, ten. in Tamerton [in North Tamerton parish], lately held by Leonard Tome, of 64 ac. Term: 31 years, beginning 25 March before date of L.P. Rent 24s. Imp. val. £27 16s. By d. of W. D. the ten. came to James Anderson of London, merchant, and William Anderson of London, jeweller, executors of W. D., who assigned it to Richard Langford, 19 June 1630, who on 10 March 1633 assigned it to Leonard Tome. Leonard Tomes [sic], s. of L. T. is the present tenant.

Another ten. in Tamerton of 70¼ ac. is occupied by Widow Stanbury, relict of William S. Rent 24s. Imp. val. £29.

Widow Stanbury claims possession in virtue of 'a bargaine betwixt one Nicholas Paine of Stratton and her foresaid husband'. Nicholas Paine claims the tenement by an assignment made to him by Richard Langford, who had it assigned to him by the executors of Walter Duncanson, 'but neither the said Widow Stanbury nor the said Paine produced any Deede or Assignment to make good theire foresaid Claimes'.
[Marginal note] 'The grant to be produced.'

'THE BOUNDS OF THE SAID MANNOR

This Mannor is bounded on the East with the River of Tamer, on the South with the parish of Werrington, on the West with a Brooke or Water called Tala and on the North with the Barton of Bradridge.
Md. that the Two last mentioned Tenements lying in the Towne and parish of Tamerton with the Barton of Bradrich are not included within the foresaid bounds neither cann wee bound them particularly.

CUSTOMES OF THE SAID MANNOR

There hath been usually kept within the said Mannor two Courtes Leete and Two Courtes Barron to which all the Tennants as well free holders as Leaseholders are bound to doe suite and service.
There is chosen every yeare by the homage a fitt person of the Leaseholders to execute the office of Reeve which he is to doe upon Oathe and is to Collect the Lords Rents and to be accountable for the same Alsoe the said Reeve is to Collect all fines, Amerciaments, Relieffes, Herriotts, Wayfes, Estraies, felons goodes, with other Casualties accrueing to the Lord within the said Mannor, which said Casualties will amount unto, Communibus Annis, 8s 8d.'

AN ABSTRACT OF THE PRESENT RENTS, FUTURE IMPROVEMENTS AND OTHER PROFITS

Rents of Assize and perquisites of court	£1	14s	1d
Rents of leaseholders	£7	1s	6d
Rent of Bradrich Barton	£10		
Total rents	£18	15s	7d
Improved value of leasehold tenements	£196	4s	4d
Improved value of Bradrich Barton	£203		
Total improved value	£399	4s	4d
Trees and saplings on leasehold lands are worth	£18		
Trees, etc. on Bradrich Barton are worth	£224		

'This is an Exact survey . . .'

4 MANOR OF BUCKLAWREN

DCO S/3. This survey is not listed in the *Seventh Report of the Deputy Keeper of the Public Records*, and the copy held by the Duchy of Cornwall appears to be the only one extant. The manor lay in the parish of St Martin by Looe. It belonged to Launceston Priory and was acquired by the Duchy in 1540.

'A Survey of the Mannor of Bucklawren Bucke . . . Retorned 25 Jan. 1649/50.

FREE-HOLDERS OF THE SAID MANNOR

Robert Spoore gent. holdeth freely to him and his heires for ever severall houses in East Lowe within the said Mannor for which he doth suite to the Lords courtes And payeth p.a.   1s.'

Philip Hix gent. several houses in East Looe, suit of court and   4d.
Edmond Dyar gent. and Thomasin Pope divers houses there, suit and   2d.

LEASEHOLDERS OF THE SAID MANOR

John Wilshman, by L.P. dated 11 March 1626: 'all those two Messuages or Tenements and one hundred and eleven Acres of land thereunto belonginge with foure Acres of woode parte of the premisses, And the Tithes from tyme to tyme comeing and encreassing on the said Two Tenements, with all and singular profitts . . . for the terme of Ninety Nine yeares if the said John Welshman (58), Grace (50) his wife, and William (30) theire sonne or one of them shold soe long live.'
Rent of ten., wood and tithes, £4 7s 4d. Heriot 20s. Imp. val. £69.
Exceptions, etc.; 'not to cutt the woodes graunted to them but when they shalbe of the groweth of tenn yeares and then onely in time convenient, and upon every cutting are to leave sufficient storrers and staddels on every acre and after every cutting are to enclose and preserve the same woode from spoyle or hurt by beasts. And are to plant . . . six trees . . . yeerely'. Now growing, trees worth 40s.

Edward Russell gent., by L.P. of 24 May 1626, mess. and 33 ac. Term: 99 years, on lives of Edward R. (49) and John (30) and Rebecca R. (dec.), s. and d. of John Russell of Liskeard. Rent 28s 6d. Heriot 40s. Imp. val. £27. Exceptions, etc.; to plant 3 trees yearly.

Denzill Hore, by L.P. of 30 May 1628 mess. and 46 ac. with all woods, underwoods and tithes, in the village of Bucklawren. Term: 99 years, on lives of John (30), Margarett (32) and Joan (dec.), children of D. H. Rent 45s. Heriot £3 6s 8d. Imp. val. £23. Exceptions, etc.; to plant 6 trees yearly. Now growing, trees worth 20s.

John Hoskins, by L.P. of 25 May 1626 mess. and 53 ac. with tithes, woods and underwoods. Term: 99 years, on lives of Thomas H. (dec.), Henry H. (dec.) and Reginald H. (30). Rent 44s 4d. Heriot 26s 8d. Imp. val. £28. Exceptions, etc.; to plant 6 trees yearly, clause regarding cutting, as above. Trees now growing worth 40s.

John Ivie, by L.P. of 25 May 1626, mess. in Overtreveria [Higher Treveria in St Martins] and 31 ac. Term: 99 years, on lives of J. I. (40), Grace Heskett (dec.) d. of John Heskett of St Germans, John Knight (dec.) s. of John K. of Treveria. Rent 28s 6d. Heriot 28s 6d. Imp. val. £17 5s. Exceptions, etc.; to plant 4 trees yearly.

John Knight, by L.P. of 11 March 1626, 2 mess. and 77 ac. with all woods and underwoods in Nether Treveria [Lower Treveria in St Martins]. Term: 99 years, on lives of J. K. (dec.), William (25) and Elizabeth (dec.) s. and d. of J. K. Rent 48s 5½d. Heriot £4. Imp. val. £32 18s 6d. Exceptions, etc.; to plant 6 trees yearly; clause regarding cutting, as above.
Lease of one of the tenements assigned by J. K. to Richard Langston gent. by deed of 25 March 1642 at 'proportionable' rent and heriot. Now growing, trees worth 30s.

John Hoskin, by indent. of 2 June 1621, mess. and 40 ac. in Nether Treveria. Term: 90 years (sic), on lives of Zenobia (56) late w. of J. H., Wilmott (dec.) and John (dec.) d. and s. of J. H. Rent £6 10s. Heriot £3. Imp. val. £12 2s 6d. Exceptions, etc.; to plant 4 trees yearly.
Zenobia, now w. of [blank] Dingle, now in possession.

Daniell Burte, by L.P. of 11 March 1626, all the messuages and 47 ac. in Overbodigga [Bodigga in St Martins]. Term: 99 years, on lives of D. B. (45), Joan Penny d. of Thomas P. of Blisland, and Walter Burte, bro. of Daniell, one of whom [name not given] is alive and aged 40. Rent 32s 6d. Heriot 32s 6d. Imp. val. £24 10s. Exceptions, etc.; to plant 4 trees yearly.

William Birte of Bodigga, by L.P. of 10 July 1626, mess. and 47 ac. in Bodigga. Term: 99 years, on lives of W. B. (50), Katherine (50) his w. and John (dec.) their s. Rent 32s 6d. Heriot 20s. Imp. val. £24 10s. Exceptions, etc.; to plant 3 trees yearly.

John Chubbe, by L.P. of 11 March 1626, ten. called Pollescourte [Polliscourt in St Martins], with 9 closes lately divided into 12 closes of land and pasture, with a hopyard, in all 25 ac. and 3 corn mills on the premises, with suit of mill. Term: 99 years, on lives of J. C. (dec.), Henry (40) and Philip (dec.) his sons. Rent 35s. Heriot £3. Imp. val. £23 15s. Exceptions, etc.; to plant 6 trees yearly.

[Rental of Manor omitted]

'THE SAID MANNOR IS THUS BOUNDED (VIZT;

From the salt water of Millin Draught [Millendreath Beach in St Martins] unto the Corner of the Hedge belonginge to a garden now in the Tennure of one Thomasin Broade; thence by a Hedge unto a Highwaye; by the Highway unto a peece of land called Noe Mans Land on the West. From the said land by a hedge over against Mr Mayowes land unto a hedge that bounds Mr Langdales land and thence by the water unto Mr Thomas Langdales land, and by the said land unto one Mr Wills land and the said land unto Mr Thomas Tonkins land, and by the same land to a bridge in the Highway called Church bridge on the North. From thence it is bounded by the Mannor of Treloy [Trelowia in St Martins] unto a certeine wood called Bockenver Woode [Bokenver Wood in St Martins] now in the possession of Mr Langdon, and thence the water Bounds it to the corner of a Hedge in Mr

Bullers land, and thence by a hedge unto a highway against Richard Langstones land and by that hedge southward into a Corner in the highway called Penveeth (Penvith) gate. Thence by the said hedge unto a spring called South Towne Spring, And thence by a hedge unto Dinnboule Corner, and soe forward to an Orchard in the Marquesse of Winchesters land; thence to the highway, and from thence the hedge bounds it unto the South Sea on the East, and soe by the Sea unto Millin Draught where it began.

Md. the Tennants . . . do enforme upon Oathe that some of the Community of the Manor of Pendrine [Pendrim in East Looe, to the West of Bucklawren] have encroached upon a certeine peece of land (conteyninge by estimacon Two Acres) which adjoynes to the lands of Henry Chubb and lies betwixt the water leate accounted to the Auntient bounds of this Mannor and the Mill leate taken out of the former leate and which the Tennants of the said Mannor of Pendrin doe Account the bounds of the Mannor of Bucklawren aforesaid whoe as they say have enoiyed it tyme out of minde and are now in possession of it. But we finde that there was a Commission directed from the Councell table for the Dukedom of Cornewall beareing date the 9th of April 1638 unto John Moyle esq, Walter Langdon and Christopher Ough gent. for the vieweing and examining the said boundes. And they by certificate under theire hands retorned the boundes of the said Mannor of Bucklawren in that parte of the Mannor to be bounded by the Water leate, not the Mill leate; And that the Tennants of the Mannor of Pendrine have nothing to do beyond the said water Leate. And furthermore we haveing viewed the said bound doe conceave and are in our iudgments fully satisfied that the Auncient Waterleate is the bounds of the Mannor of Bucklawren aforesaid and not the Mill leate, And the rather because the Mill leate hath beene taken out of the said Water leate and there is noe rent ot acknowledgement paid for the same to the Mannor of Pendryn; alsoe because that the tennants of the Mannor of Bucklawren whose lands adjoyne to the same leate doe cutt home to the said leate and betwixt the leates and both above and below the place where the said Mill leate is taken out. Moreover if the Mill leate were the bounds of the said Mannor then shold the Princes Mill be in the Mannor of Pendrym and not in the Mannor of Bucklawren. And Lastly for that the saide John Chubb hath a hoppyard betweene the Two leates which is parte of this Mannor and alsoe as soone as the said Water is past the Mill it falls againe into the Auncient leate which is then the bounds of the Mannor as it was above the place where the Mill leate was taken out. All which wee leave to the farther Consideracion, the said lands which is thus encroached on by the said Tennants being worth p.a. 40s.

THE CUSTOMES OF THE SAID MANNOR

There is usually kept in the said Mannor Two law Courtes and Two By Courtes yearely, at one of which Law Courtes there is usually chosen a Reeve whose office is to sumon the Courtes which are to be kept at the Reeves house. Alsoe to collect the Lords Rents which he is to be Accountable for.

Alsoe he is to gather the fines, Herriotts, Wayfes, Strayes, felons goods and other perquisites of Courte, which said Casualties doe amount to, Communibus Annis, £3 7s 8½d.

The Tennants of this Mannor as well free as Tennants by Lease are bound
to doe suite and service to the said Courtes, the free Tennants paying on
every death or alienation for a Relieffe double the Rent which they pay.
Alsoe if any estate fall in hand the present Tennant is used to hold the same
paying halfe the value of the said Tenement, And to take lease for the same
in case he be not able to pay the Fine and nowe is to take except the Tennant
doe refuse to give Tenn yeares purchase for a New State therein.
Md. the Tennants of the Demeanes called Bucklawren are free from tithe
but pay in way of acknowledgement to the Minister forty shillings yearely.'

AN ABSTRACT OF THE PRESENT RENTS, FUTURE IMPROVEMENTS
AND OTHER PROFITS OF THE SAID MANNOR

Rents of assize and perquisites of Court	£3 19s 2½d [sic.]
Rents of leasehold land	£25 12s 1½d[1]
Total	£29 1s 4d [sic.]
Improved rents after the expiry of the leases	£282 1s 0d.
[Trees growing to the value of £6 10s.][1]	

'This is an Exact Survey . . .'

5   MANOR OF CALSTOCK

DCO S/3; PRO E 317 (C)/6. An ancient manor of the Duchy. Its boundaries corre-
sponded closely with those of Calstock parish.

'A Survey of the Mannor of Calstocke . . . retorned [25 Jan. 1649/50].

DEMEASNES IN LEASE

There hath beene lately built by John Connocke jn. esq. a faire dwellinge
house with a barne, stable and other outhouses upon parte of the premisses
called Harewoode [Harewood in Calstock] which among other things was
let to him by Letters Patents as followeth:
The said house consisteth of one faire hall, one buttery, one kitchin and one
pantrie below staires and of foure roomes above staires, and to the backside
of the said house adioynes a wash house and brewhouse. There belongs to
the said house a little garden and orchard. The scite of which houses,
barnes, stable garden and courtes conteynes by estimacon one acre and is
worth at an improved value p.a.   £6'
Four closes adjoining the house, 12 ac., imp. val. £6;   Wood called
Hirewood or Harewood, 140 ac., imp. val. £33 6s;   Wood called North
Helewood, 16 ac., imp. val. £3 12s;   Wood called South Helewood, 12 ac.,
imp. val. £2 14s;   Wood called Hawkemoor [Hawkmoor] Wood, 13 ac.,
imp. val. £1 19s;   2 woods called Torniscombe and Castle Wood, 68
ac., imp. val. £8 10s.
House and premises granted by L.P. of 19 June 1628 to John Connocke jn.
esq. Term: 99 years on lives of J.C. (dec.), Alice (40) his w., and Nicholas C.

[1] Torn from the DCO copy; supplied from an eighteenth century copy (DCO S/75). This copy
also gives the value of rents of assize and perquisites as £3 9s 2½d, thus making the addition
correct.

(dec.) s. of John C. sn. of Treworgie esq. Heriot £3. Rent £8 10s. Imp. val. £62 1s.

Exceptions, etc.; tenant 'not to cutt the woodes and underwoodes . . . but once in tenn yeares and after every such cuttinge . . . to enclose and encopice the said woode and to preserve and keepe the said woodes from biteinge, treadeing and spoyleing by beasts, and alsoe are to leave in every acre sufficient staddells according to the statute.'

Edmond Fowell esq. is in occupation by virtue of his marriage with Alice, relict of John Connocke.

A wood called Raniescliffe alias Caponsham of 22 ac. is held by Thomas Major of London, to whom it was granted by L.P. of 8 June 1642 for 31 years. Rent 8s. Imp. val. £3 6s.

Exceptions, etc., as above.

Lease assigned 20 Jan. 1644 to Richard Langford of Liskeard.

[Endorsement on membrane 3] 'By the Commissioners for removing obstructions in the sale of the honors . . . of the late King, Queene and Prince', Peirce Edgcombe claims the 'fishinge and weare of Calstocke' for his life and the lives of Richard and Winifrede Edgecombe, his s. and d. Trustees appointed by the Commissioners on 5 May 1653 reported 'that it appears by a copye produced taken out of the Journall Booke of the late Commissioners for the Prince's revenues under the hand of Thomas Major and . . . attested upon oath by George Neylie [. . . July 1653] that the said court did the [10 Nov. 1640] contract with the petitioner for a graunt to be made to him of the said fishing and of a certeine old weare called Pinocke Weare within the Manor of Landolph [Landulph] . . . for the lives (aforesaid) under the yearly rent of [£10] to the Dutchy and [26s 8d] to the Exchequer for the said fishing and [4s p.a.] for the said weare for which he was to pay a fyne of (£200).

That it appears by certificate under the hand of John Downes auditor, dated [8 June 1653] that the said summe of [£200] was paid unto Robert Napper Receiver General of the Dutchy of Cornwall for the year 1642 and by him accompted for unto the Committee of Revenue . . . it appeares by a certificate from Haberdashers Hall under the hand of John Leech . . . that Peirce Edgcombe . . . hath compounded for a franke tenement wherein he was seized dureing three lives of and in a certeine fishing and weare standing and being in the River of Tamar in the parish of Calstocke which he held by demise from the Prince as part of the Dutchy of Cornwall at a yearly rent and was worth before the troubles over and above the rent reserved £40. . . .

All that weare or fishing of Calstocke . . . and all that water of Tamar . . . and all those fishings and severall fishings in the foresaid weare and water . . . from the gulfe or weare of the late Abbotts of Tavistocke called Collysworthy Hatch alias Collworth in the upper parte unto the Rocke of Toplington alias Tocklington on the lower parte of the said water, formerly in lease unto John Connocke esq.' Term: 99 years on three lives, all of which are deceased. The fishery is now in hand and is worth £140.   Rent 26s 8d.

'Md. Pearse Edgecombe esq. claimeth an interest in the saide weare of Calstocke and water of Tamar by vertue of an order of composition from the Councell boarde of the late Duke for the Dukedom of Cornewall beareing date [1 Dec. 1644] under the hande of the Lord Lumley, Sir David Coning-ham, Sir Charles Herbert, Richard Lane and others it was ordered that upon the paying of [£200] fine and alsoe upon the surrender of Jane Hunkin, one of the lives in being, that a good lease shold be made of the premisses unto the said Pearse Edgecombe for the terme of [99] yeares if he, the said Pearse [40], Richard [10] his sonne and Winifrede [11] his daughter or one of them shold soe long live under the severall yearely rents aforesaid and that as soone as the same shuld be done by lease, and in the meane tyme shold have power to dispose of and lett the same to his best advantage . . .' Jane Hunkin died 7 March 1644/5. P. E. has possession of the weir.

'There are groweing on Kingswoode alias Comonwoode [Kingswood] within the said mannor . . . 1500 old trees . . . worth' £150

FREE TENANTS OF THE MANOR

Lady Mary Greenvile holds 'one peece of land called Golyhatche', rent 1s;   Pierce Edgecombe esq. 2½ ac. C. in Cuthell [Cotehele in St Dominick], being 1/8 of a knight's fee, owing suit of court;   William Brendon gent. mess. and 30 ac. in Cuthell, rent 3s;   Anthony Osborne, mess. and ½ ac. C. in Lechley [Latchley] by knight service, rent 3s;   Samuell Dowrish, mess. and ½ ac. C. in Denisham [Dimson] by knight service, rent 3s;   John Axworthie, mess. and 3 farl. in Sandholcke, rent 5s 1d;   John Dodge, mess. and ½ ac. C. in Mederhill [Metherell], rent 3s 2d;   John Martin, close called Slade Park in Mederhill, rent 9d;   Pierce Edgecombe esq., mess. and 1 farl. in South Newton, hatches work 1d, rent 1s 8d;   *id.*, mess. and 1 farl. at Morden Mill, hatches work, 1d, rent 1s 8d;   *id.*, mess. and 1 farl. at Westenhole, hatches work 2d, rent 1s 8d;   John Buttersby gent. 4 ac. C. in Westherber [West Harrowbarrow] by knight service, 'for which he payeth for tenn mens worke at the Hatches' 10d, rent nil;   *id.*, 'divers tenements [in Westenhele] by a rent called berbage rent . . . and for the worke of [150] men at the Hatches', 12s 6d, rent 20s 4½d;   *id.*, lands in Eastherber, rent 'one pound of Coming seede or sixe pence';   *id.*, 'for a streame of water called Hedweare for the mill of Westherber', rent 4d.

CONVENTIONARY TENANTS

	Fine	Rent	Berbage rent[1]	Hatches rent[2]
In Todesworthy [*id.*]				
William Newett, mess. and 30 ac. in ½ ac. C.	22s	5s 8d	—	2d
William Harrie 1/8 of a moiety of a ten.;				
Thomas Combe, the same; Thomasin				
Harrie, John Bealberrie and Richard				
Northy the rest [¾]	10s	4s	9d	2d

[1] Hals claims (*Lake's Parochial History of the County of Cornwall*, 1867–73, Vol. 1, p. 173) that berbage was a rent paid for fishing rights in the River Tamar, and derived from *barbague*, a barbed fishing spear. J. Hatcher's opinion ['Non-Manorialism in Medieval Cornwall', *Agric. Hist. Rev.*, Vol. 18 (1970), pp. 13–4] that it originated as a tax on sheep, but became a fixed levy on land, is far more likely.

[2] A payment in lieu of work on the fish hatches in the Tamar; see P.L. Hull, *The Caption of Seisin of the Duchy of Cornwall* (1337), Dev. and Cornw. Rec. Soc., Vol. 17 (1971), p. xliii.

	Fine	Rent	Berbage rent	Hatches rent
Reall Bond, John Baker, Thomas Combe and Anthony Rundell, mess. and 18 ac. in ½ ac. C.	20s	3s 6d	9d	—
Timothy Turner, ¼ and 1/8 of ten. and 16 ac.; Thomas Combe 1/16, and Mary Adams the rest	9s	3s 6d	9d	2d
Nicholas Strippe ½ and ¼ of ten. and 13 ac. in ½ ac. C.; Barbara Sannue ¼	6s 8d	3s 6d	9d	2d
In Hill [? Trehill]				
Roger Bealberrie, mess. and 18 ac. in ½ ac. C. in Hill	12s	3s 9d	—	2d
Joan Carne, mess. and 18 ac. in ½ ac. C. in Hill	13s 4d	3s 5d	—	2d
id., moiety of ten. and 18 ac. in ½ ac. C. in Hill; Christopher Reade, ¼ and ⅓ of the other moiety; Annis Bealberrie ¼ of the said moiety, except the ⅓	6s 6d	1s 8½d	4½d	2d
Roger Bealberrie mess. and 18 ac. in ½ ac. C. in Hill	11s	3s 5d	—	2d
Assigns of Andrew Edgecombe, ½ mess. and ½ ac. C. in Hill	6s 6d	1s 8d	4½d	1d
In Trewin				
Thomas Tozer, mess. and 21 ac. in ½ ac. C.	13s 4d	3s 5d	9d	2d
In Albeston [Albaston]				
Elizabeth Coysgarden, mess. and 18 ac. in ½ ac. C.	8s	3s 4d	—	—
id., mess. and 19 ac. in ½ ac. C.	8s	3s 4d	—	2d
Tristram Axworthy, mess. and 19 ac. in ½ ac. C.	12s	3s 5d	9d	2d
John Chapman, moiety of cott. with curtelage in Albeston; John Jeffery, ¼; Degorie Simons, ¼	nil	10d	—	—
John Grosse, moiety of mess. and 19 ac. in ½ ac. C.; Thomas Grosse the other moiety	8s	3s 4d	—	2d
In Newton [*id.*]				
Marke Martin, Marke Hunn and Robert Topsome, mess. and 20 ac. in ½ ac. C.	13s	4s 5d	—	2d
Marke Martin, Nicholas Spiller and Pierce Edgecombe esq., mess. and 24 ac. in ½ ac. C.	30s	5s 6d	—	3d
In Childesworthy [Chilsworthy]				
Samuel and Richard Dowrish, mess. and 9 ac. and 2 ac. of 'land wast'	9s	2s 1d	5d	2d
Thomas Bond, by surrender, ¼ except 1/20 of ten. and 9 ac. in 1 farl.; Elenor Hill, the 1/20; Nicholas Harry, the rest, viz 'a house and garden'	9s	2s 1d	4½d	2d

	Fine	Rent	Berbage rent	Hatches rent
Anthony Dowrish, Thomas Young, Stephen Torr and William Colborne, mess. and 19 ac. and a 'pearche' in ½ ac. C.	9s	3s 5d	9d	2d
Anthony Dowrish, mess. and 9 ac. in 1 farl.	9s	1s 9d	4½d	2d
id., cott and 1 ac.	1s 6d	6d	—	—
Samuell Dowrish, mess. and 14 ac. in ½ ac. C.	6s 8d	2s	—	2d
Thomas Young and Richard Baulhatchet, mess. and 19 ac. in ½ ac. C.	16s 8d	3s 4d	—	2d
Richard Dowrish, close in Lechley Highway in Childsworthy	nil	9d	—	—
'All the tenants . . . hold the passage of the River of Tamer'	12s	4s 6d	—	—
James Stephen, John Stephen, Henry Moore and Thomas Young, mess., 20 ac. and ½ ac. of Meadow in ½ ac. C. in Hatches [*id.*]	20s	4s	—	—
Annis Stephen and Henry Moore, 1 ac. waste in Hatches	4d	1d	—	—
Mess. and 24 ac. in North Woode devided into divers parts by surrender; held by John Hunn,⅓; Edward Wills and Grace Wills, 1/16; Samuell Hunn, the rest	13s 4d	2s 6d	—	2d
John Hunn, Jane Young wid., Tristram Axworthy, Jane Blowey, Margarett Bridge, Richard Ragland, John Warren, Richard Jetson and John Blowey, mess. and 18 ac. in ½ ac. C. in Sandocke	6s 8d	3s 4d	—	2d
Nicholas Rowe, 16 ac. waste in Hawkes Moore [Hawkmoor]	6s 8d	2s 6d	—	—
In Lachley [*id.*] Mess. and 14 ac. in ½ ac. C. 'devided into severall partes by surrender', held by Hillary Courter, ¼ and 1/16; Tristam Axworthie, ¼; John Adams, 1/16; Edward Phillipps, 1/9; Thomas Combe, 1/30; Sibill Edwards, Flower Edwards and Richard Edwards, the rest	13s 4d	2s 2d	—	2d
The same: 'like partes of one other tenement there' and 30 ac. in ½ ac. C. and 'one Marish called Comerish Marsh'	13s 4d	2s 8d	—	2d
Roger Tooker, Parnell Tooker and Walter Slade, mess. and 30 ac. in ½ ac. C. and 'one Marish called Corderish Marsh'	13s 4d	4s 3d	—	—

	Fine	Rent	Berbage rent	Hatches rent
Mess. and 14 ac. in ½ ac. C. 'devided into divers parts', held by Katherine Dodge, 1/30 and 1/6; Thomas Bond, 1/8; John Wills, 1/8 and 1/36 [sic.], and John Adams, the rest	14s	2s 2d	—	2d
The same hold like parts of another ten.	14s	2s	—	2d
Mess. and 30 ac. in ½ ac. C. divided by surrender, held by Henry Hallamow, 1/8; Francis Staddon, ¼; John Stenteford, 1/8; John Young, ¼; William Looes, 1/8	31s	4s 10d	10d	2d
John Stenteford, Thomas Jefford, Richard Jefford, mess. and 16 ac.	11s 6d	2s 7d	4½d	1d
John Adams, mess. and 31 ac. in ½ ac. C.	48s	5s	—	—
Thomas Combe, Sibill Edwardes, John Adams and Marke Stenteford, mess. and 14 ac.	13s 4d	2s 2d	4½d	1d
Thomas Combe, Sibill Edwardes, mess. and 14 ac. in 1 farl.	1s	10d	—	—
John Stenteford, Thomas Jefford and Richard Jefford, mess. and 16 ac.	11s 6d	2s 7d	4½d	1d
John Axworthie, pasture called Parcke Caporisham alias Caponsham of 10 ac. 3 rods 24 perches at Parocke Park	2s 6d	1s	—	—
Nicholas Adams, Samuell Hunn and John Reade, 2 mess. and 40 ac. and 20 perches in Northendardon alias Wimple [*id.*]	6s 6d	6s 1d	9d	—
Anne Bealberry, Marke Hunn and Annis Cudlip, ten. and 27 ac. in ½ ac. C. in Newton	28s 4d	6s 3d	—	4d
William Stenteford and Thomas Baylie, mess. and 30 ac. in ½ ac. C. in Honycombe [Honicombe]	18s	3s 10d	—	2d
John Martin, John Knight, John Dodge, Roger Dodge, James Bligh, Roger Cornock and Robert Edwards, mess. and 36 ac. in 3 farl. in Heging	35s	6s 8d	9d	—
George Martin, William Bond, Anthony Adam and Walter Jane, mess. and 22 ac. in Herbere [Harrowbarrow]	25s	4s 6d	—	—
John Spiller, John Bennett, Annis Woodland, Richard Dodge and William Bond, 2 mess. and 12 ac. in Herbere	30s 6d	4s	—	2d
John Knight, Robert Kelly, James Kelly, Nicholas Elliott, Robert Stephens, 2 mess. and 22 ac. in ½ ac. C. in Harbere	28s	4s 6d	9d	2d
Richard Edgecombe esq., Joane Facy, Jane Fox, Annis Record and Anne Slade, mess. in Northendridon, Southendredon,				

	Fine	Rent	Berbage rent	Hatches rent
Spinkeford and King Garden, 40 ac. and 4 ac. of waste in Wimple and 1 rod of meadow	nil	7s 1d	1s	2d
Richard Edgecombe esq., Jane Fox and Joan Facy, 20 ac. of waste in King Garden	8s	1s 4d	—	2d
Thomas Combe, John Dodge, Andrew Sands, Annis Nute, Samuell Hunn, mess. and 9 ac. in Beassell Crosse	4s	1s 9d	4½d	2d
'Thomas Combe and the rest', another mess. and 20 ac. in ½ ac. C. in Beassle Crosse	11s	1s 9d	4½d	2d
In Kingsgarden				
Richard Edgecombe esq., Jane Fox, Sampson Hawkin and Joan Farne, 20 ac. of waste	8s	1s 9d	—	2d
Joan Galsworthy, 3 parts of a ten. and 24 ac.; Peter John, ¼ of the same	25s	4s 6d	9d	2d
John Bealberry, Sampson Bowdon, Thomas Combe, Peter John, Peter Northen, John Jane, Robert Edward and Elizabeth Coysagarden, mess. and 14 ac.	30s	4s 0d	—	2d
Thomas Hendson, John Honnycombe and Peter John, 12 ac. of waste 'nigh Dunscombe Hill'	9s	1s 0d	—	—
Richard Dodge, James Bligh, William Bond, Peter John, mess. and 16 ac.	20s	5s 4d	—	1d
Robert Bond, George Bond and James Kelley, mess. and 19 ac.	nil	4s 10d	—	1d
John Knight, mess. and 12 ac.	13s 4d	2s 0d	—	1d
Thomas Bond, James Kelley, Walter Jane, Robert Edward, Nicholas Elliott, James Bligh and Samuell Hunn, mess. and 11 ac.	7s 2d	2s 2d	4½d	2d
In Mederhill [Metherell]				
John Marten, mess. and 21 ac. in ½ ac. C.	28s	5s 0d	—	2d
William Bond, Marke Hunn, John Marke, Annis Grose, John Bealberie and Thomas Stephen, mess. and 19 ac. in 1 farl.	25s	4s 7d	9d	2d
Marke Hawkin and Bartholomew Hawkin, mess. and 21 ac.	29s	5s 0d	9d	2d
John Bealberrie, Anthony Bealberrie, mess. and 22 ac.	33s 4d	4s 7d	1s	2d
John Dodge, Roger Dodge, Thomas Bond, Thomas Sernell, mess. and 19 ac.	25s 4d	4s 8d	9d	

	Fine	Rent	Berbage rent	Hatches rent
John Dodge, Roger Dodge, Thomas Stephen and Annis Wadlin, mess. and 19 ac.	26s 8d	4s 8d	—	2d
John Bond, 'One whole tenement' and 19 ac. except 1/8 part held by John Bligh	30s	4s 8d	—	2d
Ferdinando Bligh, moiety of ten. and 19 ac. in Mederhill; John Bligh, ¼, and John Bennett, ¼	25s	4s 8d	—	2d
Marke Hawkin, John Hill, John Bligh, John Martin, John Dodge, Roger Dodge, William Slade, Thomas Stephen and William Stenteford, mess. and 13 ac.	33s 4d	5s 1d	—	2d
John Marten, Richard Edgecombe, John Hornebrooke, Griffith Bond and William Bond, mess. and 9 ac.	12s	3s 4d	4½d	2d
Thomas Bond, mess. and 9 ac.	13s 4d	2s 2d	4½d	2d
Mathew Bond and Joan Bond, ¾ of moiety of ten. and 19 ac.; Thomas Bond, a moiety except 1/12 and a close; John Bligh, ¼ of the said 1/12; John Dodge, the rest	26s 8d	4s 7d	9d	2d
John Hill and Mary Hill, a ten.	33s 4d	5s 0d	9d	2d
Thomas Bond, ¼ mess; John Bligh, 1/10; Rabisha Bealey, 1/20; John Hornebrooke and Marke Bealey, the rest	25s 0d	3s 4d	—	2d
Marke Bealey, cott. and garden	4d	4d	—	—
Thomas Bond, mess. and 14 ac.	20s 0d	3s 4d	—	2d
John Marten, Thomas Bond, Richard Edgecombe and William Bond, mess. and 19 ac.	31s 0d	4s 7d	1s 0d	2d
Pierce Edgecombe, a corn mill	nil	26s 8d	—	—

IN CALSTOCK CHURCHTOWN[3]

	Fine	Rent
Thomas Combe, close called Midle Parke and 16 ac.	23s 4d	11s 1d
Alice Fowell, close called Haryodiate of 8 ac.	16s 1d	5s 4d
Christopher Reade, meadow called Calstocke Meade	3s 9d	1s 3d
id., another parcel there of 3 rods	8s 0d	2s 8d
Christopher Reade, John Marten and Richard Marten, Robert Doble and Joan Hornedon, 26 ac. 'nigh Cemiter called the Floodeland'	58s 6d	19s 2d
Christopher Reade, piece of land 'in the marsh of Calstocke' of 4 ac.	7s 6d	2s 10d
id., 1 ac. of meadow	3s 9d	1s 3d
Nicholas Adam, a garden	10s 0d	3s 4d

[3] The cluster of cottages and tenements that lay near Calstock parish church.

	Fine	Rent
Thomas Combe and Nicholas Hunn, 5 ac. 'nigh Sandway'[4]	10s 0d	3s 4d
Robert Doble and Thomas Facy, close called Bromer Close of 8 ac.	14s 0d	4s 8d
Christopher Reade, mess. and close called Chocke Parke	16s 0d	5s 2½d
Robert Doble and Thomas Facy, a piece of wood	2s 0d	8d
Christopher Reade and Thomas Facy, piece of meadow with a garden	8s 0d	2s 9d
Robert Doble and Thomas Facy, 6½ ac. and 20 rods	3s 4d	4s 5d
Christopher Reade and Thomas Facy, close called Gill Park	4s 6d	2s 9d
Assignees of Elizabeth Sterkey, piece of meadow	3s 0d	1s 0d
Alice Fowell, 'meadow or marshground called Herriott Meadow under the wood called Herriott Wood alias Harewood'	nil	25s 8d
Pierce Edgecombe esq., 2 'mills built on a water called Clamorigam, viz a corne mill and a bloweing mill'[5]	nil	1s 4d
Edward Maning, a cott.	1s 0d	4d
Tenants of Lechley and Childesworthy, 'pasture of a certaine wast ground called Greenehill'	nil	11d
Katherine Gees and Christopher Reade, piece of marsh	7s 6d	2s 6d
Pierce Edgecombe, piece of meadow	5s 0d	1s 8d
Anthony Barlett and Nicholas Adams, 'one pigeon house with the fishing of Tamar'	nil	4s 0d
James Webb and William Osborne, a cockrode	nil	3d
John Leane, 22 ac. 'on the east side of Sandway'	44s 0d	14s 8d
Anthony Barlett, John Jane and Kathern Gee, piece of ground called garden	10s 0d	3s 4d
Anthony Barlett, ½ ac. of meadow	2s 6d	1s 8d
Katherin Gee and John Jane, 19 ac. and a rod	38s 10d	12s 10d
Anthony Barlett, close called Killy Parke	24s 3d	8s 1d
Christopher Reade, piece of meadow	5s 0d	1s 8d
id., ¼ of a garden	1s 0d	2½d
id., close of 8 ac. near Harewood	16s 0d	5s 4d
id., 4 ac. in Hill	8s 0d	2s 8d
id., 'divers parcels . . . on the west side of Sandway'	17s 0d	5s 7d
Alice Fowell and Christopher Reade, piece of land called Southehele	3s 0d	1s 0d
John Adams and the tenants of Childesworthy, pasture of 'ground called Joneshey nigh Dunisham'	nil	4d
Tenants of Childesworthy, pasture of 'peece of wast land in Childesworthy'	nil	1s 0d
Richard Raglande, pasture of 'ground called Wickslade alias Plusha Parke' of 6 ac.	nil	1s 1d

[4] A customary right of way for conveying sea-sand from the coast or from a navigable river to the fields; see N. J. G. Pounds, 'Sandingways to the Sea', *Dev. and Cornw. Notes and Queries*, Vol. 22 (1946), pp. 289–91.
[5] A smelting house for tin in which the bellows were worked by waterpower.

	Fine	Rent
Oliver Hunn, Thomas Jago, Annis Stephen, with the tenants of Sandy Parke, pasture of Tothatches	nil	8d
Thomas Tozer and tenants of Albeston: pasture of Albeston	nil	10d
Margarett Stephens and Margarett Jago, cott. in Winkeslade	6s 0d	2s 0d
Grace Jane, a cott. in Okenhay [Oakenhays]	nil	8d
Thomas Combe, piece of land 'nigh Hensdone [? Hingston] called Heighemanskend	nil	2s 0d
William Newett, 'parcel . . . nigh St Anns Well'	nil	8d
Griffith Bond and the tenants of Westmetherell, piece of land called Glamarigan		3s 4d
John Knight, Robert John, Joan Crosworthy and Peter John, pasture of Papowell and Holes	nil	1s 1d
Marke Hunn, piece of land in Lache Millway	nil	2d
Samuell Dowrish and tenants of Childesworthy, pasture of Woodles in wood called Trerett	nil	8d
Thomas Bond and tenants of Mederhill, piece of land called Domishcombe [Dunescombe] alias Blished	nil	10d
Thomas Combe, ten. near St Anns Chappell [S. side of Hingston Down]	—	1s 0d
Nicholas Adam and Thomas Facy, cott. with curtelage	—	2d
Tenants of the said manor, 'one way called Sowndway alias Sandkey' [i.e. Sandingway]		7s 0d
Samuell Hunn, John Warne, Edmond Newcombe, Grace Jane, John Helland, Margarett Jago and Andrew Sonds, pasture of Drakeland (Drakelands) of 60 ac.	nil	5s 0d
Christopher Reade, Thomas Facy and Robert Doble, piece of meadow in Herriott	8s 0d	2s 8d
Nicholas Doble, 1 ac. C. called North Parke	6s 8d	1s 2½d
Nicholas Rowe, piece of land called Gollyhatche, of 3 rods	2s 0d	4d
Roger Kernishe, 2 mills viz. 'a stamping mill[6] and a bloweing mill by Gollyhatche'	8s 0d	2s 0d
Robert Bond, 2 mills in Herbere	2s 0d	2s 0d
Pierce Edgecombe, the Royaltie of Birding	6d	1s 0d
id., 'the fishing of the River of Tamer from a weare called Colworthey in the lower parte unto a water called Sherwill Combe in the upper parte	—	4s 0d
Thomas Combe and the tenants of Todesworthy, piece of land called Boneslande	—	1s 8d.

'All the tennants are to pay within foure yeares next after every Assession a certeine some of money called old recognition money which in the whole is seven pounds six shillings eight pence, and doth amount unto' on average 20s 11¼d and 1/7 of 5 farthings.

THE BOUNDARIES OF THE MANNOR

This mannor lyeth wholely in the parish of Calstocke and is bounded on the east with the River of Tamer, on the north with the manor of Stoke

---

[6] A mill for crushing tin-bearing rock preparatory to separating the ore from the waste.

Clymsland, on the west with Carlington [Callington parish], and on the south with the parish of St Dominicke'.

CUSTOMS OF THE MANOR

Two law courts are held yearly at which free and conventionary tenants must perform suit, and also a three-weekly court which only customary tenants are bound to attend.

The reeve is chosen at one of the courts. His duties include the collection of perquisites which are worth on average £8 16s.

Free tenants pay a relief and customary tenants a heriot.

An Assessions court should be held every seven years, and should record changes in tenancies. New recognition money, payable by new tenants, is worth on average £4 4s.

Widows have the right to continue to hold their late husbands' tenements.

'There are severall tyn workes within the lands of the customary tennants which ought to be kept under bounds, and when there is any tyn wrought in the same there hath beene and is of custome paide to the Lord of the said Mannor a fifteenth parte of the tyn that is wrought out of the said workes which comes to' on average £2 3s 4d.

AN ABSTRACT OF THE PRESENT RENTS AND FUTURE IMPROVEMENTS AND OTHER PROFITS

Rents of assize and perquisites	£11 4s 9½d
Quit rents and old knowledge money paid by conventionary tenants	£26 8s 2¼d
Barbage rent	£1 0s 2d
Hatches rent	9s 10d
Fines paid in the six years after each Assessions, av.	£11 18s 3¼d
New recognition money, average	£4 4s 0d
Toll of tin mines valued at	£2 3s 4d
Rent of demesne lands and of the weir at Calstock	£148 18s 0d
Total	£206 6s 7d
Improved rents of the manor	£57 8s 0d
Trees standing on Kings Comon valued at	£150 0s 0d

'This is an exact survey . . .'

6 MANOR OF CARNANTON
(In St Mawgan in Pydar parish)

PRO E 317 (C)/7. This was a crown manor (see Introduction). It lay in the parish of Little Colan.

'A Survey of the Mannor of Carnanton . . . Retorned [10 Sept. 1650].

All those Rents of Assize and Quitt rents due and payable by the Free and Conventionary Tennants, And alsoe all those royalties, viz. wreckes of the sea, fellons goodes, fellons de se, Wayfes, estraies, Fines, amerciaments with all other Regalities, Herriotts, fines, alienacons and other Perquisites

of Courte . . . graunted to Edward Savage esq.' by L.P. of the late King . . .
[1633–4.] Term 21 years. Rent £52 8s 4d. Imp. val. of rents and perquisites
£60 0s 8d.
Md. Humphrey Noye[1] claims rents and royalties by virtue of an assignment
made to Edward Waye gent. and his heirs by Edward Savage, and also the
reversion of the lease for a term of 600 years. 'But the said Humphrey Noye
produced neither the said Letters Pattents nor any assignment of them
whereby to make good his said Claime.'

CUSTOMS OF THE SAID MANOR

1   No one can be a tenant 'but by descent from his Parents, surrender
made in open courte, or by the demise of the Lord or farmer, or by warrant
from either of them published in open courte.'
2   Customary tenants hold according to the custom of the manor. On the
death of a tenant, his wife is 'to enjoy the same Customary land whereof he
died seized, dureing her Widowhood onely and she to come into the Courte
paying sixe pence for her knowledge and to be sworne and admitted tennant
dureing her widowhood . . . and after the death or marriage of the said
widow the homage to present the next heire at the Comon Law.
3   That if the heires be female and more than one, then the oldest daughter
or other female and her heires to be onely admitted Tennants.
4   That if the said heires at the comon law doe not come into the Courte
and claime the said lands and tenements and doe as is aforesaid, not being a
woman married or within age or being imperfect minde and not out of the
Realme or in the Princes service or in prison dureing the tyme of seven
yeares, that then it shall be lawfull for the Lord or Farmer or theire deputies
to seize the said tenement or lands and the same to demisse according to the
custome.
4   If any tennant doe some murther manslaughter or doe kill himselfe . . .
then the tenements . . . to Escheate to the Lord.
If any tennant doe graunt his Tenement or any parcell thereof . . . in fee
simple, fee tayle generall or speciall for life, lives or yeares except it be from
seven yeares to seven yeares onely or by surrender as aforesaid, shalbe
forfeited to the Lord . . .
That on every surrender and death . . . the lord . . . is to have theire best
beast for ever tenement.
That every escheate and forfeiture shalbe found first by the whole Homage
or twelve of them at the least.
That if any tennant goe from his tenement and leave it without sufficient
distresse for rent and reparacions by the space of one whole year that then it
shalbe lawfull for the lord or farmers to enter into the same and to demise it
according to the Custome.
That all ordinary fees of the customary tennants to be paid to the steward;
for all manner of actions is one penny; for presentments of Bloudshed or
other like, foure pence; for entering judgment, Twelve pence; for venire
facias, twelve pence; and for reparacions, one penny.
That all resi[d]ents within the mannor And all other strangers, being
arrested for any action, shall pay the Steward foure pence.

[1] Humphrey Noye was the second son of William Noye, d. 1634, Attorney-General to
Charles I. In fact, his elder brother, Edward, inherited Carnanton.

That if any tennant or other stranger doe finde any kinde of wreacke within the mannor . . . thereof the Lord or Farmer is to have the one halfe and the other halfe to the inders.

5   That noe suite or action shalbe commenced or presented betweene any the tennants of the said Mannor, either freeholders or customary, or betweene any residents or inhabitants within the same in any Courte out of that mannor for any cause or matter determinable within the same. That noe kinde of processe for any cause or matter shalbe executed within the said Mannor without the licence of the bayliffe of the said Mannor first had and obteyned.

That tennants of this Mannor claime by vertue of letters pattents graunted from the late King James beareing date at Westminster [2 July 1623], as alsoe by theire auntient custome, to be freed from paying any tolle, pannage, passage, murage or comeing within the statute for erecting Cottages.

Md. that the said Mannor lyeth for the most parte in the parish of Little St Colan, but cannot be bounded for that it is dispersed into divers partes.

This is an exact survey . . .'

7   MANOR OF CARNEDON PRIOR

DCO S/3; PRO E 317 (C)/9. This manor, later known as Caradon, lay mainly in the parishes of Linkinhorne and North Hill. It formerly belonged to Launceston Priory, and was attached to the Duchy in 1540.

'A Survey of the Mannor of Carnedon Prior . . . retorned [21 Dec. 1649].

The tennants of this Mannor are of two sortes, viz: freeholders [and] farmers by lease and letters pattents, onely one cottage in Midlewood which is holden by copy of courte rolle.

The freeholders hold in free soccage whoe owe suite to the lords courte twice every yeare, and there is due from the moste parte of them upon every death or alienation a relieffe certeine as it is set downe at theire severall holdings. The farmers by lease or letters patents owe suite to the lords courte when they are there unto called and are bound to performe divers Condicions which is mentioned in their severall graunts as followeth.

FREEHOLDERS WITHIN THE MANNOR AFORESAID . . .

William Hooper gent. holdeth to him and his heires for ever in free soccage one halfe acre of Land Cornish in Linkinhorne for which he payeth to the Lord a quitt rent [p.a. 3s] and upon every death or alienacion for a relieffe 6s 3d.'

	Rent	Relief
Edward Roberts cottage and 1 ac. in Linkinhorne	1s 8d	—
Thomas Andrew, $\frac{1}{3}$ ac. C. in Odicroft (nr Rilla Mill)	1s 2½d and $\frac{1}{3}$ of ½d	4s 2d
John Lampen, $\frac{1}{3}$ ac. C. in Odicroft	ditto	4s 2d

	Rent	Relief
William Hooper gent. and heirs of Edward Kempe, $\frac{1}{3}$ ac. C. in Odicroft	ditto	4s 2d
John Budge, 1 ac. C. in Sutton [in Linkinhorne] and Knoll Parke [Knowle in Linkinhorne]	6s 0d	12s 6d
John Escott, 1 farl. C. in Sutton [*id.*]	1s 6d	3s 1½d
Richard Budge, 1 farl. C. in Sutton	1s 6d	3s 1½d
John Escott, ½ ac. C. in Upton [in Linkinhorne] alias Steartes [Sterts, nr Upton], Cowparke and Dunsley [in Linkinhorne]	3s 0d	6s 3d
John Dingle, ½ ac. C. in Upton alias Hall	1s 9d	6s 3d
Heirs of Sampson Manaton esq., ½ ac. C. in Knoll	2s 0d	6s 3d
John Dingle, ½ ac. C. in Orchard	1s 8d	6s 3d
John Kneebone, ½ ac. C. in Netherton [nr Rilla Mill]	3s 0d	6s 3d
Heirs of John Dingle late of Christorr [Christa in Linkinhorne], ½ ac. C. in Orchard alias Christorr	1s 8d	6s 3d
Henry Spoore, ½ farl. C. in Kingbeare [in North Hill]	1s 5d	1s 6¾d
John Reade, ½ farl. C. in Kingbeare	1s 5d	1s 6¾d
Henry Spoore, ½ of 1/12 of Twelvemennsmoore [Twelve Men's Moor in North Hill][1]	2d	2s
id., 3 parts of 1/12 of same	3d	3s
John Reade, ½ of 1/12 of same	2d	2s
Heirs of Nicholas Crinnis, 1/12 of same	4d	4s
id., 1/12 of same	4d	4s
John Pethen, 1/12 of same	4d	4s
Heirs of John Vincent, 1/12 of same	4d	4s
id., 2 parts of 1/12 of same	2⅔d	2s 8d

[Marginal note in a different hand] 'Md. This of the heires of John Vincent in the bottome of the lease and the next being the first of the next lease are left out in the Duplicate'.

	Rent	Relief
Henry Spoore, ½ farl. in Kingbeare [Kingbear in North Hill]	1s 5d	1s 6¾d
John Reade, ½ farl. there	1s 5d	1s 6¾d
Henry Spoore, ½ of 1/12 of Twelvemennsmoor	2d	2s
[2]id., 3 parts of 1/12 ditto	3d	3s
John Reade, ½ 1/12 do	2d	3s
*Heirs of Nicholas Gennis, 1/12 do	4d	4s
id., 1/12 do	4d	4s
*John Pethen, 1/12 do	4d	4s
*Heirs of John Vincent, 1/12 do	4d	4s
id., 2 parts of 1/12 do	2⅔d	2s 8d
id., 2/3 of 1/12 do	2⅔d	2s 8d
id., ⅓ of 1/12 do	1⅓d	1s 4d

[1] Twelve Men's Moor forms the eastern margin of Bodmin Moor in North Hill parish. Grazing rights over it had been held by twelve tenants, but by the seventeenth century their rights had become much fragmented.
[2] The entries marked with * appear to repeat other entries. If these are discounted, the shares in the Moor add up to twelve. The two copies of the survey differ in the order in which these entries are placed.

	Rent	Relief
Henry Spoore, ¼ of 1/12 do	1d	1s
Arthur Budge, 1/12 do	4d	4s
John Lampen, 2/12 of Twelvemennsmoore	8d	8s
James Bond, 1/12 do	3s 8d	4s
Henry Spoore, 1 ac. C. in Trewortha [in North Hill]	3s 6d	12s 6d
_id._, 1¼ farl. in Whittamore	8½d	3s 10¾d
John Reede, 1 farl. in Kingbeare	1s 5d	1s 6¾d
_id._, 1¼ farl. in Whittamoore	8½d	3s 10¾d
Heirs of Nicholas Gennis, ½ ac. C. in Highouse	3s 4d	6s 3d
_id._, 3 parts of 1 farl. in Trelabe [in Linkinhorne]	1s 8d	2s 3d
John Pethen, 1 farl. in North Bowda [Bowda in Linkinhorne]	1s 8d	3s 1d
Heirs of John Vincent, 1 farl. in South Bowda	1s 6d	3s 1½d
_id._, ⅔ farl. in Odicroft alias Atterigo	1s 6⅔d	2s 1d
_id._, ⅓ farl. in Odicroft	1s 8⅓d	1s 0½d
_id._, ⅔ of a 'landyoke' called Ticke[3]	1⅔d	—
_id._, ⅓ of a 'landyoke'	½d and ⅓ of ½d	
Henry Spoor esq., 1 farl. in Trewortha [in North Hill]	10d	3s 1½d
Arthur Budge, ½ ac. C. in Trewortha	1s 6d	6s 3d
_id._, ½ ac. C. in South Calstocke [Casticke in North Hill]	2s 4d	6s 3d
John Lampen, ½ ac. C. in North Calstocke	2s 4d	6s 3d
_id._, a mess. and corn mill in Measham [_id._ in Linkinhorne]	2s 2½d	4s
Robert Jackman, 1 farl. in Middlewood [in North Hill]	1s 8d	3s 1½d
_id._, ½ farl. there	5d	1s 6¾d
James Bond esq., 1 farl. there	10d	3s 1½d
_id._, 1 ac. C. in Lowrance [Lewarne?] and Combe [Northcombe and Southcombe]	3s 4d	12s 6d
Total rents of assize £4 7s 11½d		& ½ a ¼d

FARMERS BY LEASE OR LETTERS PATENT

John Roberts, by L.P. of 11 March 1626, mess. in Measham and 34 ac. Term: 99 years on lives of Prissilla Roberts (38) and Jane R. (33), daughters of John R., and John Oliver (30), s. of Sampson Oliver of Linkinhorne. Rent 10s. Heriot £3. Imp. val. £10 10s. Exception, etc.; to plant 3 trees yearly. Now growing, 100 trees, worth £13.

William Lawndrie, by L.P. of 21 Feb. 1628, mess. and 19 ac. in Southbotturnell [Botternell in North Hill]. Term: 99 years on lives of Digory Lawndrie (48), Mathew L. (41) and Edward L. (34), sons of William L. Rent 7s 10d. Heriot 13s 4d. Imp. val. £10 12s 8d. Exceptions, etc.; to plant 2 trees yearly.

John Dille, by L.P. of 10 July 1626, ten. and 19 ac. in South Boturnel. Term: 99 years, on lives of John D. (44), Alice (dec.) his w., and John D. (dec.) his

[3] A landyoke was an area of waste land, held at a very small rent; see P. L. Hull, The _Caption of Seisin_, pp. xxxv–xxxvi.

s. Rent 7s 6d. Heriot 20s. Imp. val. £8 12s. 11d. Exceptions, etc.; to plant 2 trees yearly. Now growing, 30 trees worth £4 10s.

John Cotten, by L.P. of 4 April 1627, ten. of Northbotturnell and 30 ac. Term: 99 years, on lives of John C. (dec.), Mary Vewell (36) d. of Margaret Vewell, and Edward Daw (30) s. of John D. of North Hill. Rent 7s 4d. Heriot 20s. Imp. val. £12 12s 8d. Exceptions, etc.; to plant 3 trees yearly. Now growing, 22 trees, worth 4s.
William Smyth has possession by assignment from John Cotten.

Edward Stanton, by L.P. of 11 March 1626, mess. and 36 ac. 2 rods in Northbotturnell. Term: 99 years, on lives of Edward Staunton jn. (41), Edward Stanton (28) s. of William S., Edward Kneebone (38). Rent 7s. Heriot 40s. Imp. val. £14 6s 4d. Exceptions, etc.; to plant 3 trees yearly. Now growing, 70 trees worth £7.

John Kneebone, by L.P. of 11 March 1626, ten. and 39 ac. in Upton. Term: 99 years, on lives of John K. (65), Jane (dec.) his w., and Edward (38) their s. Rent 20s 4d. Heriot 20s 4d. Imp. val. £27 0s 8d. [£27 8s].[4] Exceptions, etc.; to plant 4 trees yearly.
'The Timber trees . . . not sufficient to keep the same in repair.'

Richard Harry, by L.P. of 12 May 1626, mess. and 24 ac. in Upton. Term: 99 years, on lives of Thomas H. (47), Edward H. (dec.) and Katherin (dec.), sons and d. of Richard H. Rent 9s 11d. Heriot 50s. Imp. val. £12. Exceptions, etc. Now growing, 40 trees worth £6. Also one wood, worth £6.

Thomas Budge, by L.P. of 10 July 1626, mess. and 24 ac. in Upton. Term: 99 years, on lives of Thomas B. (50), Thomas Reede jn. (29) of Linkinhorne, and John Cole jn. (26) of St Sampsons (Golant). Rent 11s 1d. Heriot 50s. Imp. val. £12. Exceptions, etc.; to plant 3 trees yearly. Trees insufficient to keep the premisses in repair.

Digery Veale, by L.P. of 1 Feb. 1628, mess. and 21 ac. in Bathpoole [Bathpool in North Hill], with a fulling mill and a corn mill and suit to the corn mill. Term: 99 years, on lives of Mathew (30), John (24) and Joan (32), children of Digery V. Rent 22s. Heriot 26s 8d. Imp. val. £9. Exceptions, etc.; to plant 3 trees yearly.
Lease assigned to Ferdinando Fitz, who is now in possession.

William Daw, by L.P. of 20 May 1626, mess. and 27 ac. 2 rods and 20 perches in Kingbeare. Term: 99 years, on lives of William D. (dec.), William (24) his s., and Richard May (33), s. of Oliver M. of Pellruen [Polruan in Lanteglos by Fowey]. Rent 7s 10d. Heriot none. Imp. val. £11.
John Warne has possession, except a close, by marriage with Thomasin, wid. of William Daw.
John Dill is in possession of the close of 3 ac. 2 rods 20 perches. The rent of 2s included in the above total.
Timber insufficient to keep the premisses in repair.

Thomas Axford, by L.P. of 16 May 1627, mess. and 29 ac. in Boucherdon [Bunchardon in Linkinhorne]. Term: 99 years, on lives of Nicholas (dec.),

---

[4] Figures in brackets are those given in the tabulation [Alphabeticall Rentall], which has not been printed.

Philip (30) and Mary (28), children of Thomas A. Rent 6s 4d. Heriot none. Imp. val. £12 1s 3d. Exceptions, etc.; to plant 2 trees yearly.
Moiety, except houses, gardens and 3 ac., assigned by indenture of 3 Oct. 1635, to William Hooper gent. Rent 2s 8d.
The other moiety with houses, gardens and 3 ac. assigned 23 Jan. 1636, to Robert Jackman. Jackman assigned the houses, gardens and 3 ac. to Jane Dill wid. at a rent of 1s and the moiety to John Budge at a rent of 2s 8d; both assignments dated 12 Dec. 1648.

John John alias Broadlake of Linkinhorne, by L.P. of 10 July 1635, ten. and 16 ac. in Sharisland. Term: 99 years, on lives of John Broadlake (50), Love (42) his w., and Elizabeth (26) his d. Rent 5s 4d. Heriot 40s. [20s]. Imp. val. £3 4s 8d [£3 4s]. Exceptions, etc.; to plant 2 trees yearly. Trees insufficient to keep premises in repair.

Henry Warne, by L.P. of 20 June 1627, mess. caller Nottorre [Notter in Linkinhorne] and 30 ac. Term: 99 years, on lives of Henry (40), Richard (30), and John (28), sons of Henry W. Rent 7s. Heriot 13s 4d. Imp. val. £13 [£13 7s]. Exceptions, etc.; to plant 3 trees yearly.

Thomas Daw, yeoman, by L.P. of 30 March 1626, mess. and 16 ac. at North Kingbeare. Term: 99 years, on lives of Thomas D. (dec.), Edward (30) his s., and Joan (dec.) his d. Rent 8s 2d. Heriot 40s. Imp. val. £7 7s 4d. Exceptions, etc.; to plant 3 trees yearly. Edward D., the only life, is in possession.

William Dingle, by L.P. of 4 April 1628, mess. in Netherton [nr Rilla Mill] and 33 ac. Term: 99 years, on lives of John (dec.), Abell (36) and James (30), sons of William D. Rent 7s. Heriot 20s. Imp. val. £13 7s [£13]. Exceptions, etc.; to plant 3 trees yearly.
Stephen Tanley has possession of 'the most parte of the said tenement and premises in right of his wife whoe was the Executor of the said William'.
Robert Jackman has 3 ac. by assignment by William Dingle.
There are no trees.

John Gooding, by L.P. of 10 July 1635, mess. with 27 ac. in Netherton. Term: 99 years, on lives of John Gooding (dec.), Edward Kempe of Linkinhorne (dec.), and Joan Kempe (41) his w. Rent 8s 4d. Heriot £3. Imp. val. £11 10s 6d. Exceptions, etc.; to plant 4 trees yearly. Now growing, 36 trees, worth £3 12s.
Joan Kempe wid., the only life, now in possession.

John John alias Broadlake, by L.P. of 4 April 1627, mess. and 20 ac. in Netherton. Term: 99 years, on lives of Love (42) w. of John John, Elizabeth (26) and Love (25) their daughters. Rent 8s 4d. Heriot 20s. Imp. val. £11 12s. Exceptions, etc.; to plant 3 trees yearly. Now growing, 20 trees worth £3.

Henry Killigrew of Larracke, by L.P. of 1 Feb. 1621, 2 tenements in Newland and Clinnicombe and 80 ac. Term: 99 years, on lives of Henry K. (dec.), Robert (dec.) s. of Sir Henry Killigrew, and William s. of Sir Robert Killigrew, 'supposed to be alive'. Rent 20s 8d [20s]. Heriot none. Imp. val. £22 14s.

Exceptions, etc.; '. . . to enclose the number of Three Acres and to plant them with Woode as Oake Ash Elme and Apple Tree, And are not to breake up any meadow ground, auncient pasture or greenesward'. No trees growing.
Now in possession of Thomas Budge and Edward Budge by assignment by Henry Killigrew.

John Sheere, by L.P. of 20 June 1627, ten. called Overtrelabe and 113 ac. Term: 99 years, on lives of Jane (54) w. of John Sheere, William (27) and Jane (23) their s. and d. Rent 29s [£1 10s]. Heriot 20s. Imp. val. £20. Exceptions, etc.; to plant 5 trees yearly. There are insufficient trees to maintain the premises.

Richard Foote, by L.P. of 11 March 1626, mess. and 30 ac. at Knolle. Term: 99 years, on lives of John (dec.) s. of Richard Foote, Richard Barrett (dec.) s. of Richard B. the elder, and Richard Foote (32) s. of William Foote. Rent 8s 10d. Heriot 40s. Imp. val. £11 13s [£14 13s]. Exceptions, etc.; to plant 3 trees yearly. No trees growing.
John Foote, s. of John Foote, one of the lives, has possession.

Peter Roberts, by L.P. of 4 Nov. 1627, mess. and 25 ac. in Linkinhorne. Term: 99 years, on lives of Pascha (50) w. of Peter Roberts, John (24) and William (23) their sons. Rent 6s 4d. Heriot 13s 4d [£1]. Imp. val. £9 7s. Exceptions, etc.; to plant 2 trees yearly. No trees now growing.

Sir John Walter, Sir Francis Fullerton, Sir Thomas Trevor, by L.P. of 14 June 1628, mess. with 30 ac. called Crabland. Term: 31 years. Rent 1s. Heriot none. Imp. val. £2 5s [£2 15s].
Assigned 27 March 1628 to Thomas Caldwald; assigned 25 Nov. 1630 by Thomas Colewall (sic) to Edward Kneebone.

Total quit rents	£11 9s 5d [£11 10s 6d].[5]
Total improved value	£280 9s 5d [£271 1s].[6]

COPYHOLDER
Daniel Darley, Nathan Darley, and Mary Darley hold by copy of court roll, dated 20 Sept. 1641, a cottage and 5 ac. in Middlewood for their lives. Rent 3s 4d. Imp. val. £1 6s 8d.
The lives are supposed to be all in being.

'AN ALPHABETICALL RENTALL OF THE FREE TENNANTS' [omitted]
'AN ALPHABETICAL RENTALL OF THE TENNANTS BY LEASE' [omitted]

'THIS MANNOR IS BOUNDED AS FOLLOWETH
This Mannor is devided into divers partes and parcells therefore it cannot be bounded in the whole but distictly as followeth, Viz:
The first parte or plott is bounded from Chipmanns well in the parish of Linkinhorne northward unto Tenn Stones with Crosses called Chimacombe heade. And from thence to another Stone with a Crosse nighe Stanbeare Corner and from that stone to a Combe called Darley Combe. And by the said Combe unto the River Linner on the East. And along by the

---

[5] Neither total is correct; they should be £11 9s 5d [£11 10s 6d].
[6] Should be £275 17s [£280 0s 8d].

said River unto Plishay-bridge unto a certeine hedge there betweene the Lands of Andrewes and Glanvile Esqrs. And soe from the said hedge by a certeine Combe on the south and west until it comes to Chapmann well aforesaid.

The second parte or plott . . . is bounded from the said river of Linner on the east to a certeine lake called Gunnascite which runneth into Linner aforesaid in the parish of North Hill and soe by that Lake unto a little meadow adioyning to Reed Wood on the southside. And by a certeine hedge betweene Botturnell and Treovis in the south unto a certeine close called Alderparke. And from that close by certeine hedges unto Indowne and from thence by certeine hedges unto Blakeombe Ford, and from thence unto a certeine brooke called Whithibrooke, and soe from thence by Withibrooke river betweene Smallacombe And Trewortha unto Trebarth [Trebartha in North Hill] unto a water there on the east and north east which said water runneth into Linner aforesaid.

The third plott is bounded by a certeine water untill it comes unto certeine Stepping Stones which leadeth through the water at a place called Boundes Walls in the north east, And from the said Stepping Stones Westward by Noddon Lane unto Noddon Corner adioyning with Twelve Mennsmoore in the west, And from Noddon Corner unto Marke Woode in the south, and from Marke Woode to a lake called Whittamoore in the south which runneth from North Bowda to Berriow Bridge into the River Linner unto the lands of John Lampen Esq. adjoininge with Linner and called by the name of Hanma. And from thence by the said River of Linner to Bathpoole Bridge and from thence by a certeine foorde on the south side of the said Bridge and from thence to a certeine Stone on the west side. And from the said Stone unto the highway and soe by the Highway in the North unto New Parke Corner being parcell of a Tenement in North Botturnell. And from thence by a certeine hedge unto Rudge Wood and from Rudge Wood by a certeine hedge by the said River Linner unto Gunnascite Water.

The fouerth parte or plott is bounded on the eastside by a certeine white Rocke in Mallett Downe standing betweene the parishes of Linkinhorne and Stoke Clymsland and Southill. And thence by a lake in the South between Linkinhorne and South Hill unto the lands of Richard Courtney esqr within the said parish of Linkinhorne, and thence unto a White Stone on the west side of the church stile in the highway of the said parish of Linkinhorne and from thence by a hedge between the lands of William Beayre gent and Edward Roberts in the west unto sellers Foorde and thence by the highway against Burnedowne in the east and thence by a hedge betweene a tenement of Peter Roberts and Burnedowne unto foote downe and thence to the said rocke in Mallett downe where it began.

The fifth plott being Overtrelabe is bounded with the Mannor of Clymsland Prior on the south east and with the Mannor of Treefrees on the north.

The sixth parte or plott is free land conteyning by estimacion one acre of land Cornish And is bounded by the parishes of North Hill and Linkinhorne.'

CUSTOMS OF THE SAID MANOR

Two courts baron and two courts leet are held yearly. At the Michaelmas court leet one of the leaseholders is presented by the hommage to serve as reeve. His duties are to collect rents, fines and other perquisites, and to account for them at the next audit.

At the same time the hommage presents a tenant to serve as tithingman, 'whose office is to collect of every tennant of the said Mannor the some of three pence which amounts in the whole to the some of sixe shillings of which he is to pay to the bayliffe of the Hundred of East at Michaeltide following foure shillings in discharge of all suites and services that are due from the said Mannor to the Hundred Courte for that yeare which he is tithingman; the other two shillings hath been accustomed to be allowed unto him for serving the said office.' Also chosen are two tenants 'to be sworne Surveyors for the viewing of all the leasehold tenements within the said Mannor and to present the decayes or want of reparacions of any of the said tenements and theire ppurtenances.

. . . if any of the tennants doe want timber for the repaireing of his tenement the Steward upon request is to grant him a lycence under his hand and seale or a warrant to the reeve for the takeing of the same if he have any upon his own Tenement; if not then upon any other tenement as the Steward shall thinke fitt.

And lastly if any the said tennants doe sue another tennant for anything determinable in the said Courtes out of the same Courtes the partie soe offending is upon Conviction (being presented for the same) to pay a fine to the Lord of the said Mannor, which fine is to be collected by the Reeve as aforesaid.'

Fines, amerciaments, heriots and other perquisites amount on average to £5.

'The tennants of the Mannor claime common of pasture in and through all the commons and moores that lye both within this Mannor and alsoe the Mannor of Rillaton and on the moore called Twelvemennsmoore without Stinte.

Md. there are within the said Mannor two mills which claime the suite of multture of the tennants. There is one freehold called Measham Mill now in the possession of John Lampen Esqr. whoe claimeth the suite of all the Tennants by vertue of a deede made by Robert Warrin, Prior of St Stephens of Launceston and the Convent of the same beareing date the 24 May 1474 . . . by which deede there is graunted the said mill with the Course of waterleates and streams and all suites of the Mannor aforesaid.

The other mill being Bathpoole Mill and now in the possession of Ferdinand Fitz (as in the graunte before recited is expressed) claimeth the suite of multure of the tennants by lease which are nearest adioyning to the said Mill, Viz. those who live in Kingbeare, North Kingbeare, Southbotturnell, Northbotturnell, Notter and others which we are informed by oathe did of a long tyme doe theire suite to the said mill untill of late yeeres that the said Mr Lampen did question them for withdrawing their suite from his mill. Now to which of the said mills the said suite eyther in parte or whole doth of right belong Wee leave to your consideracion.'

AN ABSTRACT OF THE PRESENT RENTS, FUTURE IMPROVEMENTS
AND OTHER PROFITS OF THE SAID MANNOR[7]

Rents of assize and perquisites of court	£9	7s 11¾d
Rents of farmers by lease and copyholders	£11	10s 6d
Total	£20	8s 5¾d
Improved rents after expiry of the present grants	£282	1s 5d
Woods and trees on the manor are worth	£41	16s 0d

'Md. that wee have left out of the said totall some of the present rents all such somes which are paid out of the said Mannor. And alsoe that wee have left sufficient houseboote and Timber to keepe the premisses in repaire besides that which we have valued.

This is an Exact Survey . . .'

8   MANOR OF CLIMSLAND PRIOR

DCO S/3; PRO E 317 (C)/9. The manor occupied the western part of the parish of Stoke Climsland, the rest of which formed the manor of Stoke Climsland (no. 38). It belonged to Launceston Priory, and was attached to the Duchy in 1540.

'A Survey of the Mannor of Clymsland Prior . . . retorned [12 November 1649].

The said Mannor for the most parte lyes in the parish of Stoke Clymsland and consisteth of freeholders and farmers by lease and letters pattents.
The Freeholders owe suite and service to the Lords Courtes twice every yeere and eache of them pay a Reliefe according to the custome of the Countrey, viz. twelve shillings and sixe pence for an acre Cornish which is threescore acres English, And so proporconably upon the death or alienacon of every such freeholder according to the number of acres that he holdeth.
The farmers of the foresaid Mannor are by theire severall graunts tied to perform suite and service to the lords courtes and divers other condicions and covenants in the said graunts menconed. All which is more fully discovered in the following parte hereof.

FREEHOLDERS IN THE AFFORESAID MANNOR
Edward Herle esq. freely holdeth to him and his heires for ever Three partes of one Tenement and of forty Acres of land in East Langhargy [in Linkinhorne] paying therefore to the Lord yearely fifteene pence And for a Reliefe upon every death or Alienation   6s 3d.'

	Rent	Relief
John Grills, the other fourth	5d	2s 1d
Heirs of Nicholas Leach esq., ten. and 40 ac. in Noller	1s 6d	6s 3d
id., ten. and 30 ac. in Tresallock [Tresallack in Stoke Climsland]	2s 5d	6s 3d
Pierce Manaton, 4 ac. in Tresallock	10d	10d
Heirs of John Trenoweth esq., ten and 30 ac. in Tresallocke	1s 10d	6s 3d
Total rents	8s 3d.[1]	

[7] Every figure in this abstract is incorrect.
[1] Should be 13s 3d. Edward Herle is omitted from the tabulation on membrane 15 of the manuscript.

FARMERS BY LEASE AND LETTERS PATENT

William Combe, by L.P. of 20 June 1627. Mess. in Caresbrooke [Kersbrook Cross in Linkinhorne]. Term: 99 years, on lives of Walter (52) and James (43), sons of William C, and of Digory (31) s. of William Combe jn. Rent 10s 2d. Fine £72 6s 8d. Heriot 13s 4d. Imp. val. £16. Exceptions, etc.; to plant 3 trees yearly. Now growing, 28 trees, worth £3 10s.

William Congdon, by L.P. of 3 May 1626. Mess. in Tregow alias Tregoiffe [Tregoiffe in Linkinhorne]. Term: 99 years, on lives of William C (50), Elizabeth (dec.) his w., and Lawrence Treheane (20), s. of Stephen T of Southhill. Rent 26s 6d. Fine £140. Heriot 40s. Imp. val. £25. Exceptions, etc.; to plant 4 trees yearly. Now growing, 120 trees, worth £15.

Thomas Axford, by L.P. of 26 May 1628. Mess. called Beneyates and 17 ac. Term: 99 years, on lives of Robert John (42), Elizabeth (dec.) his w., and Walter Brite (dec.) s. of John B of Liskeard. Rent 6s 10d. Fine uncertain. Heriot none. Imp. val. £7. Exceptions, etc.
Lease assigned 20 April 1629 to Walter Harrell, who on 1 July 1630 assigned it to Robert John for 20 years or the life of R.J., with reversion to Edward John his bro., if he should live so long.
Trees insufficient for the repair of the premises. Robert John only living, and in possession.

Henry Stephens, by L.P. of 7 May 1627. Mess. called Trehuste alias Trehingsta [Trehingsta in Stoke Climsland] and 100 ac. Term: 99 years, on lives of H.S. (40), Jane (dec.) his w., and Edward (36) [*sic*] their s. Rent 14s 4d. Fine £40. Heriot 26s 8d. Imp. val. £29 16s 4d. Exceptions, etc.; to plant 4 trees yearly. Now growing, 80 trees, worth £12.

John Hunkin, by L.P. of 17 Nov. 1624. Mess. called Voda alias Woode and 80 ac. Term: 99 years, on lives of Richard Couch (dec.) of Lezant, Margarett (50) his w. and Phillip Cuttie (39) of Stoke Climsland, s. of Sampson Cutty. Rent 12s 2d. Fine £140 7s. Heriot 40s. Imp. val. £24. Exceptions, etc.; to plant 4 trees yearly. Now growing, 160 trees worth £19, and also 11 ac. of coppice wood of 6 years' growth 'worth per Annum now to be sold 12s.' The tenant has the pasture of the said wood, which is worth in toto £6 12s.

John Aunger, by L.P. of 10 July 1626. Mess. in Tregow alias Tregosse [Tregoiffe] and 29 ac. Term: 99 years, on lives of J.A. (dec.), Elena (50) his w. and Henry (30), s. of Sampson Aunger. Rent 8s 2d. Fine £74. Heriot none. Imp. val. £9 8s 3d. Exceptions, etc.; insufficient timber for repairs. Elena Aunger now in possession.

William Hooper, by L.P. of 20 July 1627. Mess. called Nethertrelabe [Lower Trelabe in Linkinhorne] with 28 ac. Term: 99 years, on lives of W.H. (50), Mary (dec.) his d., and William Hender (dec.) s. of Nicholas Hender. Rent 16s 2d. Fine £50. Heriot 26s 8d. Imp. val. £13 4s. Exceptions, etc.; to plant 3 trees yearly. Now growing, 13 trees worth £1 19s.

Robert Stephens, by L.P. of 31 Feb. [sic] 1628. Mess. called Windslade [in Stoke Climsland] with a close called Pound Parke and 40 ac. (including Pound Parke). Term: 99 years, on lives of R.S. (70), and Timothy (39) and Sampson (30), sons of R.S. Rent 12s 8d. Fine £40. Heriot 13s 4d. Imp. val.

£11 14s 9d. Exceptions, etc.; to plant 3 trees yearly. Now growing, 60 trees, worth £3 15s.

Nicholas Leach, by L.P. of 18 Nov. 1624. Two messuages in Sturts and Malletdowne [Tremollet Down in Stoke Climsland] and one in Frogmere with 47 ac. Term: 99 years, on lives of N.L. (dec.), Jenophese (49) his w., and Nicholas (dec.) their s. Rent 20s 3d. Fine £130. Heriot none. Imp. val. £19. Exceptions, etc.; to plant 3 trees.
Md. that the ten. in Sturte 'being Ruinated long tyme before the date of the said Indenture the said Nicholas . . . [is] not thereby tyed or Compelled to repaire or reedifie the same nor to receive any damage or prejudice by any Covenant thereyn Contayned for reparacon thereof'. Now growing 2 ac. of wood of 20 years growth, worth £4 10s and also 660 trees worth £99.

Robert Lobb of Warlegan, by L.P. of 30 June 1626. Mess. in Kerrisbrooke and 30 ac. Term: 99 years, on lives of Robert (30) and Mary (25), s. and d. of R. L., and Sampson Treheane (44) s. of James T. Rent 10s 4d. Fine uncertain. Heriot 10s 4d. Imp. val. £12 1s.
Exceptions, etc.; to plant 4 trees yearly. Lease assigned by R.L. 27 April 1627 to James Trehane, who assigned it to John T. his s., 29 Oct. 1931.
Insufficient trees to maintain the premises.
'One open Quarrie of blue Slaite which may yeeld (if the Lord make use of it)' p.a. £2 10s.

A RENTALL OF THE SAID MANNOR [omitted]
'THE COMON THAT BELONGS TO THE SAID MANNOR
There is a certeine downe or heath belonging to this Mannor as a comon called Mallett [Tremollet] Downe conteyning by estimacion [150 Acres] or thereabouts, and is bounded by the hedges of the severall tenements parcell of this Mannor adioyninge on the west, north and east, and with the Mannor of Stoke Clymsland on the south, where the tennants of this Mannor have free comonage for all manner of beasts without any stint. Divers of the said tennants bordering on the said downe have and doe enclose parte of the said downe and sowe it for one year and then throw it open againe, but whether they do it of right or noe wee cannot certeinely finde out.

THE BOUNDS OF THE SAID MANNOR
This Mannor is devided and bounded in three partes or plotts, distinct and severred from the other by the landes of severall other Lords lying betweene them; each parte is bounded as followeth:
The first parte or plott lyeth in Kerrisbrooke and boundereth with the lands of Sir Richard Vivian Kt and others the Lords of the Mannors of Trefreies on the West, on the north and east with Overtrelabe, parcell of the Mannor of Carnedon Prior and of the annexed Dutchie of Cornewall and on the south with certeine lands called Pengelly and Clampitt, parcell of the Mannor of Rillaton and of the auncient Dutchy of Cornewall.
The second parte or plott lyeth in Tregoiffe and Nether Trelabe and boundereth on the west with the foresaid Mannor of Trefreies, And with the lands of Ambrose Manaton of this and other the lords of Trecarroll [Trecarrell in Lezant] on the north, with the lands belonginge to the Mannor of

Lawhitton, late parcell of the Bishoppricke of Exoncester on the east, with the lands of the said lords of Trefreies and the foresaid Tenement of Overtrelabe, parcell of the Mannor of Carnedon Prior, and on the south with the foresaid lands of Trefreies.

The third plott or parte . . . boundereth with the Mannor of Stoke Clymsland . . . on the south, on the west with the lands of Edward Herle esqr., ·called greate Langhargie and the foresaid Mannor of Trefreies and the said lands belonging to the Bishoppricke of Exon, on the north with the said Mannor of Stoke Clymsland and with the glebe land belonginge to the rectory of Stoke Clymsland on the East.'

THE CUSTOMS OF THE SAID MANOR

Customary tenants in turn to provide a reeve, who is to summon the courts when required to do so by the steward. 'He is also to drive the common belonging to this Mannor at such tyme as he shall find fitt and to take up such estrayes as he shall find there (or shalbe brought unto him) dureing his yeare, and is to enter the same at the next courte and if there come noe owner within a yeare and a day then the lord is to have the apprisement of such estrayes, alloweing for the pastureing of the same.'

The reeve is to collect rents, heriots, fines and perquisites of court, and to pay them 'unto the auditor of the Dutchie at the end of the yeare, where he is allowed by the auditor for the tyme being towards his labor in collecting thereof twenty pence and his Diett. As for other customes (Vide) the severall leases and letters patents by which the said tennants doe enjoy theire estates.'

Fines, heriots, wayfes, strays and perquisites of court amount on average to 16s.

AN ABSTRACT OF THE PRESENT RENTS FUTURE IMPROVEMENTS AND ALL OTHER PROFITS OF THE SAID MANNOR

The present rents	£10 15s 10d[2]
Perquisites of court, fines, etc.	16s
The slate quarries	£2 10s
Improved value of leasehold land	£183 13s 8d
Woods, underwood and timber valued at	£165 6s

'This is an exact survey . . .'

9 BOROUGH OF CRAFTHOLE

DCO S/3; PRO E 317 (C)/10. The borough lay close to the coast in Sheviock parish. It had belonged to the Courtenays, and was attached to the Duchy in 1540.

'A Survey of the Borrough of Crofthole . . . retorned 7 January 1649/50.

This borrough lieth in the parrish of Sheviocke And is bounded on all sides with the Mannor of Sheviocke, being in the time of the Earle of Devonshire

[2] Total rents should be £7 10s 10d. Errors were made in transcribing the rents to the tabulation. The improved value of the leasehold land should be £167 4s 4d. The error appears to have arisen in adding up the figures in the tabulation.

parte of the said Mannor, but by attainder falling to the Crowne, it was by Act of Parliament annexed to the Dukedom of Cornewall.
The Tennants of this Borrough are freeholders and coppie holders. The freeholders hold in free and comon soccage. The coppie holders hold by coppy of the courte rolles for lives as hereafter followeth.

Freeholders within the said Borrough
Jonathan Chapman holdeth in free Soccage to him and his heirs for ever two tenements or messuages with one orchard and meadow by the yearely rent of one shilling sixe pence, and on every death or alienation for a relieffe 3s.'

	Rent	Relief
John Harvey, 3 parts of 4 parts of a mess. or cottage house, curtilage, garden and orchard, and also 3 parts of another mess. or cottage in Combe	9d	1s 6d
Heirs of Brookeing, 'rest of the foresaid premisses and pay an equall parte of the said rent and relieffe'		
Richard Wallis, 7 cottages in 5 burgages of land in Crofthole	4s 1½d	8s 3d
Thomas Smith gent., 3 cottages in 2 burgages	1s 6d	3s
Sir Samuell Rolles, 6 cottages in 1 burgage	2s 6d	4s 6d
id., another mess.	1s	—
Henry Spiller, 3 cottages and a quarter of a fourth part of a house in one burgage	9d	1s 6d
William Jeffrey, quarter of a cottage and 2 burgages	1s 6d	3s
Simon Rowe, a tenement and a burgage	9d	1s 6d
Robert Creefield gent., a cottage in 1 burgage	9d	1s 6d
Edward Moreshed, a cottage in 1 burgage	9d	1s 6d
Phillip Some, a ten in 2 burgages	1s 6d	3s
Alnett Harrie, a cottage and 2 burgages	1s 6d	3s
id., a third part of 2 burgages	6d	1s
Total rents	19s 4½d.	

Copyholders for Lives
John Harrie (36) and Margarett Harrey (35) hold by 'Coppy of Courte Rolle beareing date the 7 August 1612, one little meadow called Willhayes conteyninge by estimacon one halfe acre of land and one little garden and orchard to the said meadow adioyning, with the appurtenances in Crofthole for and dureing the terme of theire lives successively according to the custome of the said borrough.' Fine at the lord's will. Rent 1s 6d. Heriot 3s. Imp. val. £2 10s.

Joan Odihorne [50] wid., 7 Aug. 1612. Ten. in Crafthole built by one Walter Sonne. Term: her life. Fine, as above. Rent 9d. Heriot 1s 6d. Imp. val. 16s.

Elizabeth Spiller (63) w. of William S, Henry (dec.) and George (41) their sons, 26 Oct. 1607; cottage called Bryant Hayes of ½ ac. Term: lives. Fine, as above. Rent 9d. Heriot 1s 6d. Imp. val. £1 5s.

Dorothy Arundell (dec.) w. of Walter A., George (66) and Alexander (50) their sons 7 Aug. 1612, ten. called Highhouse with 2 little gardens and 2 closes of 1 ac. in all. Fine, as above. Rent 9s 4d. Heriot 18s 8d. Imp. val. 50s 8d.

'THE CUSTOMES OF THE SAIDE BORROUGHE

There are kept every yeare within the said Borrough foure courtes Viz: Two Law Courtes and two other courtes to which the tennants both free and coppyholders doe owe suite and service.

The free tennants pay on every death or alienacion a relieffe which is double the rent. Alsoe the coppyholders pay for a herriott and farliew[1] upon the death of every life and upon a Surrender double theire Rent.

The said tennants both free and customary are bound to execute the office of Port Reeve or Mayor, whoe is to collect the Lords rent and to be accountable for the same.

Md. the said rent being [p.a. 31s 8½d] hath not been paid by the said tennants for these last two yeares.

The fines, relieffes, herriotts and other perquisites of Courte comes to, communibus annis, 4s 6d.'

ABSTRACT OF THE PRESENT RENTS AND FUTURE IMPROVEMENTS OF THE SAID BOROUGH

Rents of assize and perquisites	23s	10½d
Rents of copyholders	12s	4d
Total	36s	2½d
Improved value of the copyholders for lives	£7 12s	6d[2]

'This is an exact survey . . .'

10 MANOR OF EASTWAY

DCO S/84; PRO E 317 (C)/11. The manor lay in the parish of Morwenstow, with a small extension into that of Kilkhampton. It belonged to Launceston Priory, and was attached to the Duchy in 1540.

'A Survey of the Mannor of Eastway . . . retorned [7 June 1650].

FREE-TENNANTS OF THE SAID MANNOR

The heires of Sir Nicholas Smith hold freely to them and theire heires for ever in soccage one acre of land Cornish . . . in North Harscott [Herdacott in Morwenstow], Eldowne [Elldowne] and Limsworthy [Lymsworthy in Kilkhampton] for which they pay p.a. 5s 1d.'

Heirs of Richard Browneing gent., 1 ac. C. in Emsworthie [Elmsworthy in Kilkhampton] alias Tilsworthy, 1d; Heirs of Thomas Sheere, 1 farl. in Whitehill, 5d; John Tooker, 1 farl. in Little Millton [Milton in Morwenstow] alias Sprutstard, 1d; John Sherme, 1 farl. in South Harscott, 2s 6d; Heirs of Bennett, 1 ac. in Butborrough [Bottaborough in Morwenstow], 1s 6d.

Total	9s 8d.

---

[1] Or 'farleu', a monetary payment in lieu of a heriot.
[2] Should be £7 1s 8d.

LEASE-HOLDERS OF THE SAID MANOR

Thomas Stanbury, by L.P. of 1 Feb. 1628, 2 tenements in Cleeve [Cleave in Morwinstow] and 95 ac. Term: 99 years, on lives of T. S. (55), Willmett (62), his w., and Thomas (31) their s. Fine at lord's will. Rent 40s. Heriot 30s. Imp. val. £44 0s 4d. Exceptions, etc.; to plant 3 trees yearly.

Timothy Browneing, by L.P. of 27 May 1626, ten. called Holygrove with barn and garden of ¼ ac.; a close called Hilly grove of 13 ac.; a wood called Hillygrove of 12 ac.; a close of pasture 'nigh Gres' of 20 ac.; a close of pasture called Broome Parke of 4 ac.; pasture called two Acre Close of 3½ ac. Term: 31 years. Fine as above. Rent 20s. Heriot none. Imp. val. £29 12s 0d. Exceptions, etc.; to plant 3 trees yearly.

William Langford de Langforde Hill, by L.P. of 1 July 1631, mess. and lands in Eastway alias By Eastway, of 61¾ ac. Term: 99 years, on lives of John (26), William (43) and Elizabeth (28), children of W.L. Fine as above. Rent 31s. Heriot £3. Imp. val. £36 2s. Exceptions, etc.; to plant 4 trees yearly. Now growing trees to the value of £70.

John Walter, Sir James Fullerton, Sir Thomas Trevor, by L.P. of 11 June 1628, ten. called South Harscott of 26 ac. and moiety of ten. called Combe [in Morwenstow] of 23 ac. Term: 31 years. Fine as above. Rent 20s and 10s respectively. Heriot none. Imp. val. £27 8s.
Lease assigned 27 March 1628 to Thomas Caldwell, who assigned it, 20 Feb. 1632 to Thomas Sherme, who in turn assigned South Harscott to his kinsman John Sherme, 7 May 1640, and the moiety of Combe to another kinsman, Abraham Sherme, 20 Jan. 1640.
Thomas Chinge of Morewinstow has a moiety of Combe by assignment from Thomas Caldwell for 31 years, 27 March 1628. Imp. val. £6 7s.

'CUSTOMES OF THE SAID MANNOR

There ought to be kept every yeare for the said Mannor two Courtes Leete to which all the tennants both free and tennants by lease are bound to doe theire suite, and at one of which there is chosen one of the tennants to be reeve whoe is to sumon the courtes and to collect the Lords rents and to be accountable for the same.'
The Reeve also to collect fines and all other perquisites amounting on average to 6s 6d. The free tenants are to pay a relief according to the custom of the country. Leasehold tenants pay a heriot.

AN ABSTRACT OF THE PRESENT RENTS

Rents of assize and perquisites		16s 2d
Rents of leasehold tenants		£6 11s 0d[1]
	Total	£7 7s 2d
Improved value of the leasehold tenements		£147 19s 4d[2]
Trees and woodland are worth		£70.

'This is an exact survey . . .'

[1] Should be £6 1s.
[2] Should be £137 2s. 4d.

11   MANOR OF FENTRIGAN

DCO S/3; PRO E 317 (C)/12. The manor lay in the parishes of Warbstow and Treneglos.
It formerly belonged to Tywardreath Priory, and was attached to the Duchy in 1540.

'A Survey of the Manor of Fentrigan . . . retorned 28 May 1650.

FREE TENNANTS OF THE SAID MANNOR
Peter Wakeham holdeth freely to him and his heires for ever in soccage one
messuage called Treneglosse alias Corneglos (Treneglos) with certeine
land thereunto belonginge for which he payeth p.a. 14s.'
Samuel Gilbert: mess. and land in Fentrigan, rent 6s 8d;   Abell French
gent., Warbers Parke, 1 farl., 3s;   Stephen Rouse, lands in Warpstowe
(Warbstow) Church Towne, nil;   Heirs of John Cole, ten. in Treserrie
[Tregerry in Treneglos], 2d;   John Hixt, ten. called Trefrie, 1s 3d;   Heirs
of John Hender, lands in Netherhext, 2s;   Mr Phillipps, lands in
Netherhext, 1s;   Abell French and John Salteren, lands called Whitchell
alias Snowhill, 4s;   Edward Murth, lands in Treneglosse, 2s.

Total   £1 14s 2d.[1]

LEASE-HOLDERS OF THE SAID MANOR
Thomas Joll, by L.P. of 16 June 1628, ten. in Fentrigan of 62 ac. Term: 99
years, on lives of T.J. (dec.), John Grigg (43) of Warbstowe, and Margarett
(41) his w. Heriot 13s 4d. Rent 12s. Imp. val. £26 5s. Exceptions, etc.; to
plant 2 trees yearly.

John Grigg of Trenaylas, by L.P. forementioned, ten. in Tretherappe
[Tredarrup in Warbstow] of 30 ac., occupied by Richard Sibley. Term: 99
years, on lives of Thomasine (dec.) w. of J.G., John (26) and James (23)
their sons. Heriot 13s 4d. Rent 9s. Imp. val. £17 16s 6d. Exceptions, etc.; to
plant 2 trees yearly.

Nicholas Avery, by L.P. forementioned, ten. in Fentrigan of 62 ac. Term: 99
years, on lives of N.A. (dec.), William (31) and James (25) his sons. Heriot
13s 4d. Rent 12s. Imp. val. £29 7s.

'BOUNDES OF THE SAID MANNOR
This Mannor is bounded on the north with the lands of Samuel Gilbert
gent., on the west and south west with the lands of Mr Berrie; from thence
by the highway that leadeth from Canerie water [Canworthy Water] to
Tregrie Lake [? Tregay] on the south and east, and from thence by the lands
of Mr Speccott on the north east.

CUSTOMES OF THE SAID MANNOR
There ought to be kept two Law Courtes and two Courtes Barrons within
the said Mannor yearely; at one of the Corte Leetes there is chosen and
sworne one of the tennants to be reeve of the said Mannor whoe is to collect
the lords rents and answere the same.
Alsoe the said reeve is to gather and seize all such erriottes, ayfes, estraies

---

[1] Should be £1 14s 1d.

and other perquisites of courte which doe happen within the said Mannor and which will amount unto, communibus annis, 6s 8d.

The free tennants of this Mannor pay on every death a relieffe according to the custome of the countrey . . . The customary tennants pay a herriott as is expressed in theire severall leases.'

AN ABSTRACT OF THE PRESENT RENTS . . .

Rents of assize and perquisites of court		£2 0s 10d
Rents of leaseholders		£1 13s 0d
	Total	£3 13s 10d
Improved value of the leasehold lands		£73 8s 6d

'This is an exact survey . . .'

12   FISHING OF THE RIVER FOWEY

DCO S/3; PRO E 317 (C)/13, 14. Part of the ancient possessions of the Duchy. The surveyors were evidently not aware that these rights belonged to the Duchy, and they were surveyed only in 1656, after information had been given by Anthony Rowse. There are two copies in the PRO in addition to that in the Duchy Office.

'A survey of certeine fishing lying and being within the County of Cornewall parcell of the revenue belonging to the late King Charles.

All that the fishing of the water, watercourses or river of Fowey with the royaltie thereof within the County of Cornwell, running neare the Castle of Restormell, extending itself from the port of St Galdeor alias St Saviour [in Polruan] unto the bridge called or knowne by the name of Reprembridge, alias **Reprymbridge** [**Respryn Bridge** in Lanhydrock and St Winnow parishes], and soe farr as two oxen yoaked can goe and pass: together in the said water belonging with the severall fishings, and libertie of fishing within the river or waters aforesaid at all tymes and seasons which we value to be worth p.a. £5.

Dec. 2 1656   The premisses are the discovery of Anthony Rowse esq. and in present possession of the honorable the trustees.

[Sd] Hugh Webb   Ron. Brasbridg   Will. Mar
Examined by Will. Webb, Surveyor General'

[The second copy in the P.R.O. has not been counter-signed by the Surveyor General.]

13   BOROUGH OF FOWEY

DCO S/68; PRO E 317 (C)/15. The borough was created by charter granted by the Prior and monks of St Andrew's, Tywardreath, which continued to exercise rights over it until the Dissolution. In 1540 these rights were transferred to the Duchy.

'A Survey of the Borroughe of Foy alias Fowey . . . retorned 12 Feb. 1649/50.

FREE TENANTS

John Trefrie esq. holdeth freely to him and his heires . . . certeine Tenements within the said borroughe . . . in a streete called the North Streete . . . Rent 3s.'

Heirs of John Joseph ditto, 9d;   Oliver Saule, tenements in the said borough, 1s 3d;   Thomas Peters, clericus, tenements in North Street, 1s 3d;   John Rashley, ditto, 1s 3d;   Robert Rashley, do, 1s 3d;   The Lord Mohun, a ten. in North Street, 6d;   John Rashley, do, 4d;   Jonathan Rashley, certain tenements, 3s 9d;   Robert Rashley of Combe, a ten., 3d;   Philip Mayo, certain tenements, 6d;   Heirs of Thomas Colquoite, certain tenements, lately Goodales, 1s 10d;   Robert Rashley, certain tenements, 2s;   John Trefrie esq. and Robert Morris, certain land, 9d;   Thomas Peters, Clerke, certain tenements, 1s;   *id.*, a ten., 3d;   John Rashley, a ten., 2d;   Robert Rashley, a ten., 1d;   John Rashley, a ten., 9d;   Lewis Colquoite, certain tenements 'neere Cemiter', 3s;   John Rashley, a ten., 6d;   John Lord Roberts, certain tenements, 1s;   John Rashley, a ten., 2d;   Robert Rashley, certain tenements, 1s;   John Rashley, a ten., 4d;   Philip Goodale, a ten., 6d;   Robert Rashley of Combe, certain tenements, 2s;   Heirs of Hore, a ten., 2d;   Heirs of Joseph, a ten., 9d;   Heirs of Smyth, a ten., 6d;   John Trefrie, a ten., 4d;   Philip Goodale, a ten., 2d.

'These tennants hereafter named pay onely a quitt rent and owe noe suite to the courte nor pay on death or alienacion a relieffe:' The heirs of Wallacombe, ten. in Mixtoe [Mixtow in Lanteglos by Fowey], 6d;   Jonathan Rashley esq., ten. in Mixtoe, 6d;   Henry Hawkin, ditto, 6d;   Reginald Michell, ditto, 6d.

Total [Blank in PRO. copy; added in a later hand] 33s 4d.

'LANDES BELONGINGE TO THE LORD OF THE SAID
BORROUGHE AND IN HAND

All that one tenement within the Borroughe aforesaid conteyninge one burgage with a garden to the same adioyning late in the tenure of one John Clotworth but now held at the will of the lord by one Edes, and lying betweene the tenements heretofore of John Smyth on the south, of Robert Boniface on the west and north and the highway on the east . . .' Rent 1s. Imp. val. 9s.

'All that one garden, lately Michall Williams, but now in the Lord's hand.' Worth p.a. 18d. [Marg. note] 'This to be valued.'

'All that on parcell of wastland adioyning with the lands of John Treffry and by him held at the will of the Lord' Rent 8d. Worth p.a. besides the rent 10d. [Marg. note] 'This also to be valued.'

'The port reeve of the said borroughe is to collect the lords rents and perquisites of courte which are groweing and arising out of the said burroughe and doe amount to communibus annis' [blank; added in a later hand 12d]

The improved value of the severall tenements in hand is in toto p.a. 11s 4d.

This is a perfect survey . . .'

14   MANOR OF GREADY

DCO S/3; PRO E 317 (C)/16. A widely scattered manor, most of which lay in the parishes of Lanlivery, Cardinham and Luxulyan. It had belonged previously to Tywardreath Priory, and was attached to the Duchy in 1540.

'A Survey of the Mannor of Gredioe . . . retorned 4 July [1650]

FREE-TENNANTS OF THE SAID MANNOR

Walter Kendall esq. holdeth freely to him and his heires for ever in soccage one acre of land Cornish in Lanlivery [*id.*] for which he paieth p.a. 5s 1d,; *id.*, lands in Gredioe [Greadow in Lanlivery], 2s 3d; *id.*, a mill called Redwith Mill, 2s 6d; *id.*, 2 tenements and 1 farl. in Lanlivery, 12s; *id.*, 1 ac. C. called Carminowe in Luxillian [Luxulyan], 4s; *id.*, lands in Luxillian, 1s 8d; Joseph Bastard esq., lands in Tregantell [Tregantle in Lanlivery], 4s 6d; *id.*, 1 farl. in Peegsbeanie, 3s; *id.*, lands called Crast, alias Pelin Parke [Pelyn in Lanlivery], 6d; *id.*, 1 farl. in Gome, 3s; John Lord Roberts, 1 farl. in Carren (Carne in Luxulyan), 12s 6d; *id.*, 2 farl. in Luxillian, 5s; Loveday Herle, wid., ½ ac. C. in Aurean Vean, 6s 2d; *id.*, ½ ac. C. in Lostowen [Lestoon in Luxulyan], 4s; Robert Saule, 1 ac. C. in Lawreanelas, 8s 10d; Richard Kendall, 1 farl. in Gomme in Resculian, 4s 8d; Nicholas Sawle, a mill called Rilleden Mills, 16s; Charitie Richards, 1 ac. C. in Tremabin [Tremabyn in Lanivet], 8s; Richard Kendall, 1½ farl. in Resculian, 4s 6d; John Trenance, lands in Resculian, 1s 4d; Oliver Turney, lands there, 6s 8d; John Scott, lands there, 5s; William Mineheire, lands there, 2s 1d; Richard Harper, lands there, 2s 1d; William Couch, 1 farl. in Tretherrape [Tretharup in Luxulyan], 2s; Thomas Hoblin and William Carlyon, 3 farl. in Penrosse [Penrose in Luxulyan], 14s 4d; Thomas Killiow, 1 ac. C. in Grediow, 8s; Edward Polsew, land there, 2s 6d; Walter Trubody, land there, 7s 6d; Richard Luxton, land there, 8s; Jonathan Rashleigh, land in Gredioe the Nether, 2s 3d; John Pendell, land in Gredioe, 2s 3d.

Total rents of assize   £8 11s 4d.

LEASE-HOLDERS OF THE MANOR

Richard Harper of Tretharrape, by L.P. of 24 Nov. 1627, ten. in Tretharrapp of 13½ ac. Term: 99 years, on lives of R.H. (58), Mary (56) his w. and Thomas (26) their s. Fine at lord's will. Heriot 13s 4d. Rent 6s. Imp. val. £9 14s. Exceptions, etc.; to plant 3 trees yearly.

Sir John Walter, Sir James Fullerton and Sir Thomas Trevor, by L.P. of 14 June 1628, in trust for the late King, ten. called Lady Vale, held by Hugh Flamancke, of 5 ac. Term: 31 years. Fine at Lord's will. Rent 4s. Imp. val. 16s 4d.
Lease assigned 24 March 1628, to Thomas Coldwald esq., who assigned it to Richard Langford, who 20 Feb. 1645 assigned the residue of the lease to Hugh Rowe of Cardinham.

William Pierce, in right of his w. Jane, claims a ten. called Le Hay and 28 ac. on the lives of Jane (50) and of Martha Squire (48) and Edward S. (42) her sister and bro. Rent 18s 6d. Imp. val. £18 17s.

Edward S. 'is gone to sea and supposed to be alive'. Md. W.P. 'produces no evidence to make good his claim'.
[Marg. note] 'This graunt to be produced.'

William Parker late Archdeacon of Cornewall, by indenture of 30 April 1622: water or corn mill of Cardinham with 2 meadows of 2 ac. and 'suite of Multure'. Term: 99 years, on lives of James P. (50) s. of w. P.; Katherin (44) his w. and Katherin (dec.) their d. Fine at Lord's will. Rent 26s 8d. Imp. val. £5 18s. Exceptions, etc.; to plant 2 trees yearly.
Lease assigned to James Parker, who in turn assigned it to William Henwood [no dates given].

'BOUNDES OF THE SAID MANNOR

This Mannor of Grediowe lieth dispersed in severall parishes Vizt. the parishes of Luxullian, Lanlivery and Cardinham soe that the same cannott be bounded.

CUSTOMES OF THE SAID MANNOR

The freeholders of this Mannor owe suite to the lords courtes of the said Mannor which are two courtes leete and two courtes barron and alsoe pay a relieffe on every death or alienacon accordinge to the custome of the countrey . . . .'

AN ABSTRACT OF THE PRESENT RENTS AND FUTURE IMPROVEMENTS

Rents of assize and perquisites of court	£9 1s 4d
Rents of leasehold tenants	£2 15s 2d
Total	£11 16s 6d[1]

[1] The Abstract is missing from the D.o.C. copy. In the PRO. copy the total is incorrectly given as £11 15s 6d.

15   MANOR OF HELSTON

DCO S/5; PRO E 317 (C)/17. This was an ancient manor of the Duchy. It covered most of the southern half of the large parish of Helston in Kerrier, and included parts of the neighbouring parishes of Stithians, Cury and Breage.

'A Survey of the Mannor of Helston . . . retorned [10 May 1650].

There is onely one acre of wood in a tenement within the said Mannor called Cost Post the fallinge whereof belongeth to the Lord of the Mannor and is worth now to be sould 40s.
The tennant of Cost Post claimeth the herbage and the underweedings of the said woode to be a parte of his customary estate soe that the Lord hath onely the falling of the woode as aforesaid which will be worth p.a. 2s.

FREE-TENNANTS OF THE SAID MANNOR

William Pendarves by the death of Samuell P. his father holdeth freely to him and his heires for ever in soccage tenn acres of land Cornish in the

Mannor of Helston aforesaid, For which he is to performe suite to the Lords Courtes at two termes onely in the yeare: *secta curiae tantummodo.*'
[—], ½ ac. C. in Trefannow [Treevarno in Sithney], *ditto*; Lady Grace Greenevile wid., d. and heir of Lady Grace Smith wid., moiety of 5 ac. C. in Trehile [Trelill in Wendron]; Richard Erisy esq., a quarter, and John Vivian, by the d. of John Vivian his f. the other quarter, *ditto*; John Penrose of Manackan [Manaccan], moiety of 2 ac. C. in Naffan [? Nanfan in Cury]; Richard James, a quarter; Thomas Betty, the other quarter, *ditto*; [—], 3½ ac. C. in Trelaston alias Trelascon, *ditto*.
Richard Vivian Kt, by d. of Francis V. his f., 1 ac. C. in Brownewoone, 3d.
John Lord Roberts, by d. of Richard Lord Roberts his f., moiety of 2 ac. C. in Boskerwen [Buscoverran in Crowan]; John Sentawbin esq., the other moiety, 4s.
William Keygwin and William Lawelis gent., a moiety in Cardue [Carthew in Wendron]; [—] Pointer, the other moiety; John Lord Roberts, 2 parts in 3 in Tregois [Tregoose in Wendron or Mawgan], and John Sentawbin, the third part of 2 ac. C. in Cardue and Tregois 5s 6d.
John Prideaux esq., by d. of Zenobia P. wid., moiety of land in Brodowennicke; William Bolitho, the other moiety. William Pointer esq., by d. of William P. gent., lands in Treweldres; in all 2 ac. C. in Trevoldres, Brodericke and Brodowennicke. Also 4s for a hoggaster[1] and 'on the first day of May being the feast of Philip and Jacob one shilling', in all 5s.
John Oliver, in right of his w. by d. of John Trevennoe, 1 ac. C. in Bodilley [in margin: veor] [Bodilly in Wendron]; William Pendarvis, by d. of Samuell P. esq., 7 ac. of land in Pembro; Thomas Arundell of St Collombe and the heirs of Thomas Rece, land in Poglas (Polglase in Wendron), Cardillian and Wickingou, in all 4 ac. C., 8s.
John Lord Roberts, moiety of 2 ac. in Tremanhere [Tremanhere in Wendron]; John Prideaux by d. of Zenobia P., the other moiety, 5s.
John Hill, 2 ac. C. in Trevethnicke, rent 4s and 1s for a hoggaster, 5s.
Francis Godolphin, moiety of 1 ac. C. in Penhale; [—] Hugo wid., late w. of Tyracke Hugo, the other moiety, rent 2s. Hoggaster and 6d, [as above] 2s 6d.
John Trefusis esq., 1 farl. C. in Parkehambley nigh St Michaels Church [the parish church of Helston], 8d.
John Sentawbin, by d. of John S. his f., ⅓of a moiety of 1 ac. C. in Trewitta alias Gwelmayoue; John Penrose esq., by d. of Thomas P. his f., rest of the said land, 3s.
John Vivian, by d. of John V. his f., a moiety of ½ ac. C. in Tresprison [*id.* near Helston]; Thomas Glinn the other moiety, 1s 6d.
Francis Godolphin, 2 ac. C. in Degemma, rent 16d and hoggaster [as above], 4d, 1s 8d.
John Lord Roberts [as above], a moiety of land in Trewalls [? Tregolls in Stithians]; John Sentawbin [as above], land there; John Penrose of Mannacken esq., a moiety in Lestraywortha; John Penrose of Penrose [Penrose, near Porthleven], by d. of Thomas P. his gdf., the other moiety; John Lord Roberts, land in Resuggan; in all 3½ ac. C., 7s.
Thomas Glyne esq., by d. of Mary his m., ½ ac. C. in Tresprison, 1s 6d.
John Cooke esq., by d. of John C. his f., a moiety of a fourth part of 1 ac. C. in

---

1 A hogget, or young sheep.

Tolcarnewolas [Tolcarne in Wendron]. John Hill gent., by purchase, the
other moiety, rent 8d, and Hoggaster [as above], 2d, 10d.
John Cooke [as above], 2 ac. C. in Tolcarnewartha [Tolcarne in Wendron],
rent 16d, and Hoggaster [as above], 4d, 1s 8d.
John Lord Roberts, 1½ ac. C. in Trewayves alias Trewaves [Trewavas in
Wendron], rent 3s, and Hoggaster [as above], 1s, 4s.
Thomas Glyn gent., 1/6 of 1 ac. C. in Porthkellis [Porkellis in Wendron];
John Ennis gent., in right of his w. Winifride, ⅓; William Pendarves by d.
of Samuell P. his f., the residue, rent 2s, and Hoggaster [as above], 1s, 3s.
John Hunkin, by d. of Thomas Talskethy, 1 ac. C. in Trelabas alias
Trelabaswolas [Trelubbas in Wendron], 2s.
John Gervas, 1 ac. C. in Egglosderry, 'for which he paieth noe Rent But is
onely to finde a nett or Sagen to draw in Loo Poole [The Loe] against the
comeing of the Lord to Helston.'
Richard Vivian Kt. by d. of Francis P. his f., ½ ac. C. in Belloysacke, 6d.
Richard Grissey [Erisey?] esq., 1 ac. C. in Gonnehille, 3s.
William Keigwin, by the d. of John K. his f., ½ ac. C. in Trevennyn 2s.
                                            Total   67s 6d.

'CONVENTIONARY TENNANTS OF INHERITANCE WITHIN THE SAID MANNOR
Henry Leonard gent., by the surrender of William Leonard holdeth in free
Conventionary to him and his heirs for ever from Seven yeares to Seven
yeares Two Messuages and Thirty Acres of land English in Wortha Treneere, late in the tenure of William Beuchamp gent. for which he paieth p.a.
9s 0d.'

John Greenevile Kt., by d. of Lady Grace Greenevile his m., ¼ of a piece of
land in Helstoncoith Wolas of 56 ac.; Agneta Robinson sp. holds a fourth;
Nicholas Trevethian jn. by d. of William T. his f. holds ¼ and 1/8; Paule
Wearne, by d. of Christian Warne wid., an eighth. No fine. Rent 6s 8d.
The same tenants hold a quarter of a piece of land in Helstoncoith Wolas in
the same proportions, rent 6s 8d; the same hold a quarter of another piece of
land there, rent 3s 4d; the same hold a quarter of another piece of land
there, rent 5s.
John Greenevile, by d. of Lady Grace Greenevile his m., by d. of Bevill
Greenwile, by surrender of Lady Grace Smith and others [as above],
quarter of a piece of land there; Agneta Robinson, a quarter; Nicholas
Trevethan, a quarter; Paule Warne, an eighth. No fine, rent 3s 8d.
John Greenevile [as above] and the others in the same proportions, a
quarter of another piece of land there. No fine, rent 4s.
The same persons and fractions there. No fine, rent 4s; ditto, rent
2s 8d; ditto, rent 3s 4d.
Francis Robinson gent., by surr. of Thomas Robinson, 'all that whole
village of Nanslogreese [Nansloe]. No fine, rent 46s 8d.
William Code, in his own right, 'the whole village of Rastin alias Roselin' of
80 ac. No fine, rent 22s.
Richard Michell alias Perce, by d. of Elizabeth his m., mess. and land in
Coroskerne [Crasken in Wendron]. No fine, rent 7s 6d; *id.*, the same, rent
7s 6d; *id.*, the same, rent 7s 6d; *id.*, the same, rent 7s 6d.
John Greenevile Kt. and others [as above], land in Helstoncoith wolas, in
the same proportions. No fine, rent 5s 10d.

Henry Leonard, by surr. of William L. gent., quarter of the village of Fiscor; Benedict Perce, by d. of John P. his f., ¼; Henry Leonard [as above], ¼; Richard Trisillian gent., by surr. of Edward Williams, the residue. No fine, rent 4s.

William Pendarves esq., by surr. of Peter Roscrowe, ¼ ac. 'in the Lords waste' in Fiscor and 'one Mill there called a Knocking mill and a Scoffe mill[2] lately built with a Course of Water thereunto belonging'. Fine 8s, rent 2s.

Henry Leonard [as above], ⅔ of the village of Newhoneghan [Newham in Helston]; Richard Michell, in his own right, the other third. No fine, rent 13s 4d.

Thomas Bodilley alias Trelobas alias Thomas, by d. of Elizabeth his m., the village of Bodillyvighan. No fine, rent 19s.

id., 'one Mill heretofore a Knocking Mill but now a Grist mill and knowen by the name of Bodillie Mill'. Fine 13s 4d, rent 3s 4d.

id., in his own right, 'Two Mills one of which is called a Stamping Mill, the other a Craseing Mill,[3] lately built by Michaell Bodilley with a Course of water from Treneere Bridge to the foresaid Mills'. No fine, rent 3s 4d.

Jane Trelowarth wid., by surr. of Henry Leonard, the village called Trelowarth [? Treloar in Wendron]. No fine, rent 8s 10d.

Alice Hill alias Carbillocke wid., by d. of Thomas H. alias C. her hbd, the whole village called Crowsy [Crowsey] alias Crowgey. No fine, rent 8s 6d.

Thomas Flamancke gent., by surr. of William Nicholas, mess. and 16 ac. in Laytie [Laity in Wendron]. Fine 3s, rent 7s.

Thomas Alexander gent., by surr. of Thomas Glynn gent., 2 messuages with 'certeine land thereto belonging' in Nanslowartha [Nansloe in Helston]. No fine, rent 20s.

John Eva, in right of Thomasin his wife, the village of Tregassicke. No fine, rent 16s.

Thomas Cooke, by d. of John C. his f., land in Gwelangeare. No fine, rent 23s 4d.

James Penhaluricke gent, in his own right, a pasture close called Parke Derinith nigh Holskoite, of 2½ ac. No fine, rent 5s.

John Mooreton gent., by d. of Oliver Mooreton his f., ten. called Costpost. No fine, rent 8s.

Edward Thomas, by d. of Joan T. his m., ten. called Covanghanvighan. No fine, rent 14s.

id. [as above], mess. and 15 ac. 'lying betweene the Tenement of Covanghangvighan and the village of Trehinquethicke. Fine 18s, rent 4s 6d.

Ralphe Jane, in his own right, three parts of four parts of a moiety of ten. called Trehinquethicke; Jenkin Jane, by surr. of R.J., quarter of said moiety. No fine, rent 5s.   *id.*, three parts of four parts of the other moiety, Jenkin Jane [as above], the other quarter. No fine, rent 5s.

Thomas Prickman, by d. of Florentine his m., ten. called Trevenethicke [Trenethick in Wendron]. Fine 112s, rent 28s.

Thomas Shepheard, by surr. of John Tregiswan, moiety of ten. called Tregiswin; Balthazar Burges merchant, the other moiety. No fine, rent 27s.

2 A knocking mill was used for reducing large lumps of ore to a size suitable for the stamping mill, and a scoffe or stoffe mill to prepare ore of a very high quality (per Mr Leslie Douch).
3 A crazing mill reduced the small lumps of ore to a fine powder, using millstones similar to those in a flour mill.

Beatrix Trewin wid., by d. of William T. her hbd, a mess. in Pencoise, formerly Robert Rossiter. No fine, rent 14s.

id. [as above], moiety of mess. and land belonging in Pencoise; James Penhalueruke, the other moiety. No fine, rent 9s.

Beatrix Trewin [as above], moiety of another mess. and land in Pencoise [Pencoose in Wendron]; James Penhaluericke, the other moiety. No fine, rent 10s.

Pascatius Auda, by d. of James A. his f., ten. called Polkistan. No fine, rent 10s.

Mayor and burgesses of Helston, a curtelage, formerly John Lanmarth, 'which fell as an Escheate to the Lord in the said Towne'. No fine, rent 9s 10½d;   *id.*, 300 ac. waste known as Goemoyne, rent 6s 8d.

Walter Trevetham, by surr. of Darnell Bedford, moiety of a mess. and lands belonging called Trewennicke [Trewennack in Wendron] and John Thomas, by surr. of Richard Michell, the other moiety. No fine, rent 13s 4d.

Richard Michell alias Pearce, by d. of Elizabeth his m., moiety of mess. and land in Trewennicke; John Thomas, the other moiety. No fine, rent 18s 4d.

John Trevethan jn., by surr. of Richard T. his f., third of a mess. and piece of land in Talvemeth; Samuell Pearce, in his own right, a third, and also, by d. of Richard P. his f., 3 parts of the other third; Henry Gregor, in his own right, the residue. Fine 44s, rent 11s.

id. [as above], third of another mess. and land in Talvelmeth; Samuell Peirce, a third and 3 parts of the other third; Henry Gregor, the residue. Fine 44s, rent 11s.

John Trevethan, by surr. of his f., ⅓ mess. and land in Trewelmeth; Samuell Pearce, another third, and also, by the d. of his f., 3 parts of the last third; Henry Gregor, in his own right, the residue. Fine 44s, rent 11s.

Henry Leonard, by surr. of William L., a corn mill in Trenerewolas [Trenear in Wendron] lately held by John Jenkins. No fine, rent 12s.

id. [as above], 1 ac. in Trenerewolas 'with a house called a Blowing house[4] lately built on the same land'. No fine, rent 2s.

John Richard alias Carwerry jn., by surr. of John Richards alias Carwerry his f., a mess. in Corwerry. No fine, rent 7s.

John Moorton gent., by d. of Oliver M. his f., 'one peece of ground upon which is scituated six bloweing Mills' in Polmarth [*id.* in Wendron]. No fine, rent 1s.

John Penrose esq., by d. of Agneta P. wid., land in Pentire 'nigh Gonehusband'. Fine 3s 4d, rent 3s 4d.

George Collins merchant, by d. of Elizabeth Bedford wid., piece of land in Castlewaine. No fine, rent 10s.

id. [as above], piece of waste in Castlewaine [in marg.: Castlewaire]. No fine, rent 10s.

Beatrix Trewyn wid., by d. of William T. her hbd, ten. called Carnbane [Carnebone in Wendron]. No fine, rent 10s.

William Pendarves, by surr. of Peter Roscrow: 1 ac. in Carliniowe 'on which there is built a Stampinge Mill'[5]; William Trewin, by surr. of

---

[4] A blowing house was a smelting house for tin, in which the blast was provided by bellows worked by a waterwheel.

[5] A stamping mill was intermediate between a knocking and a crazing mill.

William T. his f., a piece of waste land there of 100 ac. Fine (for mill only) 4s, rent 4s.

William Trewin [as above], 'one Stamping Mill lately built with the moiety of 100 ac. of waste land in Carlinow. No fine, rent 12s.

Paule Baswarthacke, in his own right, ten. called Tresprison. No fine, rent 20s.

Richard Tregeare and Marie his w., in right of said Mary, mess. and 25 ac. in Carillie. Rent 9s.

Richard Tresillian and Mary his w., mess. in Chianhale. No fine, rent 7s.

Richard Tregeare and Marie his w. [as above], mess. and 25 ac. in Carillie. No fine, rent 10s.

John Williams, by surr. of William W. and Joan his w., mess. and 16 ac. in Trewoen. No fine, rent 10s.

Henry Nance esq., by d. of John N. his bro., 'one bloweing house and a Knocking Mill in Mooreknapp'. No fine, rent 3s 4d.

William Trewin, by surr. of William T., ⅓ part of the village called Lesgree alias Lesserrey; Michaell Peirce, in his own right, another third (except a fortieth); John Trelower, in his own right, the said fortieth and a quarter; Blaunch Symons wid., by d. of John S., fourth of a twelfth part, and also, by said death and also surr. of John Parkin, a third and a 1/24 of a twelfth; Anne Jenkins wid., by d. of Thomas J. her hbd, the residue. No fine, rent 15s.

Thomas John, in right of Elizabeth his w., 2 parts of 3 parts of the whole village of Castarell alias Givelltree; Thomas Cooke, by d. of John C., the other third. No fine, rent 6s.

Hunt Greenewoode gent., by d. of Susan G. his m., a close in Castarell [Casterills in Wendron] called Cardoe [Cardroe]. No fine, rent 1s.

Joshua Palmer gent., by surr. of John Hill sen., moiety of 50 ac. 'in one Landyoke in Castrell alias Gwellanford alias Gwelleanford'; Agneta Alexander wid. by d. of John A. jn. her hbd, moiety of the said land. No fine, rent 37s.

John Hill gent., in his own right, a mess. and 48 ac. and 2 ac. of meadow in Treworwall [Treworlas], rent 20s.

Nicholas Biscowen esq., by surr. of Oliver Dunstone, piece of land in Halvewither 'where was heretofore a bloweing Mill with liberty of Digging and seeking lez sinders[6] 'in the said ground and any where nigh'. No fine, rent 1s 4d.

id. [as above], 'one Moore of land Wast in Halvewither for the digging of Turfe and Cannburend'. Rent 1s 4d.

Barbara Warne wid., by d. of Henry W. her hbd, 2 parts of 3 parts of a mill and 40 ac. in one parcel and 20 ac. in 3 parcels in Trewossell alias Trewessell; Michael Trussell, in his own right, the residue. No fine, rent 2s.

Hunt Greenewoode, by d. of Susan G. wid., a corn mill called Melincoss Mill. Rent 16s.

John Penrose esq., by the surr. of John Trefuiss esq., 'the fishing of the Water of Looe' [The Loe]. Fine 6s, rent 2s.

Stephen Polkinhorne, in right of Elizabeth his w., 1 part of 3 of a mess. and 60 ac. in Medlin [Medlyn in Wendron]; Ralphe and Elizabeth Jane,

---

[6] i.e. the cinders left from earlier smelting operations, capable of being reworked for the sake of the tin left in them.

another third; the said Ralphe, in his own right, the other third; Nathaniell Randall, in his own right, 1 ac. and a mill built on it. No fine, rent 4s 6d.

Maderne Penhaluricke, in his own right, a piece of waste land in Nanslogregorie [? Nansloe in Helston]. No fine, rent 13s 4d.

id., another piece of waste in Nanslogregorie. No fine, rent 13s 4d.

John Wearne, in his own right, a toft and 160 ac. 3 perches and 3 parts of a rood of land in Retannowe, previously Richard Johns. No fine, rent 10s 6d.

Henry Leonard, by surr. of William L. gent., a stamping mill in Trenere Wolas. No fine, rent 3s 4d.

Humphrey Pascoe, by surr. of Martin P., moiety of Hallowbesecke alias Halebesset (except a close called Scurvymoore of 14 ac. and 1/8 of the said ten.); Thomas Pascowe, in his own right, the other moiety; Henry Bath, by surr. of Edmond B., Scurvymoore close. No fine, rent 15s.

Zenobia Sentawbin sp., by d. of Thomas S. esq., ten. of Nanslowolas [Lower Nansloe in Helston]. No fine, rent 28s.

Henry Nance, by d. of John Nance his bro., 3 messuages and 200 ac. in Talfennecke alias Calvenecke. Rent. 23s 4d.

Henry Bath, by surr. of Edmond B., 2 'mills called Stamping Mills' and 10 ac. in Calvennecke' with a course of Water to the said Mills belonginge'. No fine, rent 6s 8d.

Elizabeth Gillard, by d. of William G. her hbd, $\frac{1}{4}$ of piece of land in Halwen; Henry Urin, by surr. of Sampson Urin, 1/8 of the same; Elizabeth Pascowe, by d. of Alarve Pascowe, $\frac{1}{3}$; William Francis alias Trewallecke, by surr. of Dorothie Thomas wid. alias Cornebone by surr. of William Francis alias Trevallecke, residue. Fine 24s, rent 6s.

Hunt Greenewoode, by d. of Susan G. wid. his m., $\frac{1}{4}$ of pasture of 36 ac. in Engais alias Goangoze [Engoyse in Wendron], Coistonth and Nansuwone, being 3 pieces; William Penhaluricke, by surr. of William Trewin, 1/8 and 1/16 of the same; John Eva jn. and Thomasin his w., $\frac{1}{3}$; James Penhaluricke, in his own right, 1/8 and 1/16; Richard Eva in right of Anne his w., 1/8 of said pasture. Fine 17s 4d, rent 4s 4d.

Thomas Hunkin, by surr. of Thomas Talskedy, 7 ac. in Henstwast. Fine 8s, rent 2s.

Henry Leonard, by surr. of William L. 'one mill called a Scoffe Mill lately built by Robert Trewere'. Fine 8s, rent 2s.

Zenobia Sentawbin sp., by d. of Thomas S. arm., a piece of 'waste Moore ground' in Goenhusman. Fine 16s, rent 4s.

Humphrey Pascowe, by surr. of Martin P., $\frac{1}{4}$ of a piece of land in Rame [Rame in Stithians] of 300 ac.; John Warne, by surr. of William Leonard, $\frac{1}{4}$ and 1/8 of the same; Henry Vincent jn., by surr. of William Lillyreape, $\frac{1}{4}$; Tristram Moore, by surr. of Edmond [—], 1/8. Fine 12s, rent 3s.

Mayor and burgesses of Helston, piece of land called Nansmoreon. Fine 16s, rent 4s.

Tristram Moore gent., in his own right, $\frac{1}{4}$ of 104 ac. in Kernekey [Carnkie in Wendron]; John Thomas jn., by surr. of William T. his gdf., a moiety; William Thomas, by surr. of William T. his f., $\frac{1}{4}$. Fine 16s, rent 4s.

Zenobia Sentawbin sp. [as above], 16 ac. of waste in the forest of Nanswithian. Fine 6s, rent 1s 6d.

Heirs of Henry Carnarthan and others, Creucknorthgan. Fine 28s, rent 7s.

Richard Pendarves gent., in his own right, ten. in Polemarthe. Fine 16s, rent 4s.

William Roscrow jn., by surr. of William Rosecrow his f., ten. of Menalue [Menerlue in Wendron]. Fine 8s, rent 2s.

Sampson Bloy, by surr. of Peter Halamore, ten. of Ball Polemarthe. Fine 8s, rent 2s.

Henry Crowgey, by surr. of Henry C. his f., ten. of Carvenneth with a mill. Fine 13s 4d, rent 4s 4d.

John Trefusis, piece of land called Cornebonelis [Carnmenellis in Wendron]. Fine 4s, rent 1s.

John Oliver, by surr. of William Jenkin, piece of land in Proserewith. Fine 6s, rent 1s.

James Bath, by surr. of Edmund Bath, piece of land called Mawherrian. Fine 4s, rent 1s.

Blaunch Simons wid., by d. of John S. her hbd, piece of moore called Caervenneth [Margin: Goencarvenneth] of 40 ac. Fine 20s, rent 5s.

William Pendarves, by surr. of Samuell P., 2 messuages and 200 ac. in Polmarth. Fine 36s, rent 9s.

Blaunch Simons wid. [as above], mess. and 15 ac. in Carethvyham. Fine 9s, rent 4s 6d.

Nicholas Boscawen, Kt., by surr. of Oliver Dunstone, a toft of 25 ac. and 3 tofts totalling 110 ac. in Lancarren. Fine 43s 2d, rent 10s 9½d.

id. [as above], 15 ac. of land and 1 ac. meadow and 'all the land of Pencoys'. Fine 5s, rent 9s.

Henry Naunce esq., by d. of John N. his bro., ten. of 40 ac. called Knapp. Fine 19s, rent 4s 9d.

John Penrose, by grant at the last Assession 'the royaltie of Hawkinge, Huntinge and Fowlinge'. No fine, rent 2s.

'Md. wee have certified the value of the Tolle Tynn of this Mannor in grosse with the Lease thereof herewith returned [See No. 16].

THE BOUNDES OF THE SAID MANNOR

This Mannor of Helston is not to be bounded but in divers parcells because that the lands of other men doe Interveene and sever the Lands of the said Mannor. And therefore we have bounded it as followeth (Vizt):

The one part of this Mannor which lieth within the parish of Wendrone is bounded on the east with the parish of Constantine, on the north with the parish of Stithians, on the west with the parishes of Crowan and Sythenie [Sithney], and on the south with the parish of Maugan [St Mawgan in Meneage], unto the parish of Constantine where the bounds began.

Another part of this Mannor (Vizt) Costpost lieth in the parish of Stithians and is bounded on the west with the lands of John Lord Roberts, on the south with the lands of Sir John Arundell kt, on the east with the lands of William Pendarves esq. and on the north with the lands of John Beachampe gt.

One other part or parcell of the said Mannor (devided into three tenements and known by the names of Tregeswin, Polkiskan and Colvenneth) lieth in the parish of Cury, and is bounded on the east, north and west with the lands of John Lord Roberts and the lands of John Penrose esq., and on the south with the lands of John Hele esq.

The last part or parcell lieth within the parish of Breage and is devided into two tenements one of which (Vizt) Trewane, is bounded on the south and east with the lands of Francis Godolphin esq., on the north with the lands of Edward Trelawney esq., and on the west with the lands of Polkinhorne. The other tenement (Vizt) Carworie is bounded on the East with the lands of Godolphin, on the south with the lands of Penrose, on the west with the lands of Walter Kestle esq., and on the north with the lands of John Glin gt.

Md. there lieth within the bounds of the said Mannor the Borrough of Helston which was heretofore parte of the said Mannor, but by Charter granted to the burgesses thereof by Henry the Eight it was made a free borrough, and the rents and other profitts arising out of the same for which they pay a certaine rent to the Crowne was graunted to them in fee farme for ever.

COMMONS

There are divers large Wastes and Marrishes that lie within the said Mannor in which the tennants thereof claime right of pasture unstinted, and for which they pay a certeine Rent yearely as for theire customary estates, it being by them held in free convenconary as theire other tenements, and by them taken and the rent thereof paid in grosse with theire respective tenements.

OFFICERS WITHIN THE SAID MANNOR

There ought to be a steward within the said Mannor whoe is to keepe the courtes thereof (Vizt) a courte barron which is kept every three weekes and a courte leete which is held twice every yeare, The privileges whereof is to arrest by body (for any some of money) any person within the bounds of the same Mannor, and also to sue any tennant for any trespasse or other Action which is determinable by the steward and a jurie of the said Mannor.

At one of the courte leetes there is presented by the homage a fitt person to be reeve whoe is to sumon the courtes and to call them and to retorne juries or two sufficient men whoe are called Islers,[7] and those two are to choose a sufficient jury to themselves. Alsoe the said reeve with the assistance of the tithingman is to arrest within the said Mannor.

There is also presented by the said homage two men (at the said leete) to be viewers of reparacions whoe are sworne to present what houses within the Mannor are out of repaire and to give notice to the tennants thereof to repaire the same by the tyme appointed them by the Courte.

Alsoe there is presented by the said homage one of the tennants to be a tithingman who is by his office to assist the reeve and the constables of the parish.

Lastly there hath beene time out of minde a bayliffe chosen and appointed by the Lord of the Mannor to collect the Rents thereof and alsoe to seize and gather up all such wayfes, estraies, felons goods, herriotts, fines and other casualties and perquisites or courte within the Mannor, which said perquisites and casualties will amount unto, communibus annis, £8.

CUSTOMES OF THE SAID MANNOR

There ought to be kept every seventh yeare an assession courte for the said Mannor unto which every customary tennant is to repaire for to take or

[7] i.e. 'elizors' or choosers (per Mr Leslie Douch).

render his estate in his customary tenement, not that his former estate doth then determine but that the lord may thereby know who are his present tennants, there being divers surrenders made within the tyme of seven yeares by which surrenders there happens to the Lord a new rent (vizt) double the rent and fine of such tenement or part of tenement that is surrendered betwixt every assession, and is called new knowledge money and is paid by the present tennant besides his present rent and fine, and within three yeares next after such assession and not otherwise, which said new knowledge money will amount unto, communibus annis, £2 10s.

Also the said assessions are kept that the way of payinge the lords rents and fine may be the better observed for that the tennants are to pay theire rent and the sixth parte of theire fine every yeare for the first six yeares after every assessione yeare and in the seventh yeare rent onely.

All the tennants of this Mannor as well free as customary are bound to do suite and service to the lords courtes every three weekes and as often as they shalbe thereunto sumoned, except such of the free tennants whoe by theire severall holdings are onely bound to do suite to the courte but twice in the yeare.

The customary tennants of this Mannor are to serve the offices of reeve, beadle and tithingman within the Mannor when they shalbe thereunto elected by the homage. And alsoe to keepe theire respective tenements in good and sufficient repaire at theire owne chardges.

The free Tennants pay on every death or alienacion a relieffe according to the custome of the countrey . . .

The customary tennants pay upon every death a best beast for a herriott for every tenement that they hold and die seized of.

Alsoe a customary tennant dying seized of a customary estate his wife (if he have any) is to enjoy the same during her widowhood and after her marriage or decease it presently descends to his next heire whether male or female, and if it be a female the estate is not to be devided by coparcinerie but to remayne in the eldest sister.

Lastly a customary tennant cannot forfeite his customary estate for any action by him done, but may set out any parte thereof to whom he pleaseth or for what time he pleaseth so that the same exceede not the number of six yeares, because he ought to be present tennant when any Assession is holden. Alsoe he may sell and surrender his said estate to whom he will, neither cann the steward refuse to take such surrender, the same being made within the Mannor. But if the steward shall refuse to doe it, the reeve, tithingman and two other tennants of the Mannor may take such surrender. And the same is and wilbe as effectuall as if it had beene taken by the steward, Which surrender is to be entered by the steward in his courte bookes and to receave for his fee six pence for every such surrender.'

AN ABSTRACT OF THE PRESENT RENTS AND OTHER PROFITS OF THE SAID MANOR

Rents of assize and perquisites of court	£11 7s 7d
Rents of the conventionary tenants	£48 8s 9d
Fines paid by the conventionary tenants	£4 13s 9¼d
	and a seventh of 6 farthings

Old recognition money paid by the same   2s $0\frac{1}{2}$d
      and a seventh of $\frac{1}{2}$d
New recognition money paid by the same within 3 years after
  each assession, average   £2 10s $0\frac{1}{2}$d
Improved value of the acre of woodground at the Lord's disposal   2s 0d
           Sum total of the present rents   £66 14s $2\frac{1}{4}$d
The wood now groweing on the foresaid Acre of Woodground
  is worth now to be sould   40s.

'This is an exact survey . . .'

16   A RETURN OF TOLL TIN OF THE MANOR OF HELSTON

DCO S/5; PRO E 317 (C)/19. The toll tin, or royalty on the tin mined in these manors, was part of the ancient perquisites of the Duchy of Cornwall.

'A Returne made of the tolle tynn of the Mannors of Helstone in Kerrier, Tywarnhaile and Tewington, being parte of the auntient Dutchy of Cornewall (and lett to farme by letters pattents of the late King Charles for twenty and two yeares) . . .

The late King Charles by his letters pattents under the greate seale of England beareing date at Westminster 13 June 1628 . . . (upon speciall trust and confidence and to his owne use and benefitt) did graunt to Sir John Walter Kt., Sir James Fullerton Kt. and Sir Thomas Trevor Barronett theire executors, administrators and assignes (amongst other things) all that tolle of tynn or tolle tynn happeninge or groweinge within the Mannor of Helston in Kerrier, Tywarnayle and Tewington, parcell of the possessions of the Dutchie of Cornewall, habend' for and dureing the terme of twenty and two yeares to comence and begin immediately from and after 25 March 1637 . . . redd' inde to the bayliffe or reeve of the premisses for the tyme being the yearely rent of £20 6s 8d.'
The lessees assigned the lease 17 March 1629 to Thomas Caldwall for the remainder of the term. The said Caldwall assigned the lease 10 June 1634 to Sir David Cunningham Kt., 'in consideracon of the some of one hundred pounds five [sic], for the residue of the term. Sir David Cuningham by deed of 25 May 1638, 'in consideracon of the some of £175', assigned the lease to Roger Sleeman of Sithney for the residue of the term. 'Which said tolle tynn . . . ariseing and groweing within the Mannor . . . was valued to be worth upon improvement in the year 1641 (besides the present rent) p.a. £20.

Md. that the present tennant Mr Sleeman doth Complaine that some of the tinners of Tewington and Helston . . . aforesaid have and doe refuse to pay the tolle tynn due from them soe that thereby he can hardly make the rent he paieth for the same.'

'Signed . . .'

17   MANOR OF HELSTONE IN TRIGG

DCO S/5; PRO E 317/(C) 18. This manor lay mainly in the parish of Michaelstow, but extended into St Tudy, Lanteglos by Camelford, Tintagel, Davidstow and Advent. It was one of the ancient manors of the Duchy, and included the important Park of Helsbury.

'A Survey of the manor of Helstone in Trigge . . . retorned [12 July 1650].

There is not any mannor or mansion house within the said mannor but the demeasnes land belonginge to the foresaid mannor and lett in lease are as followeth:
All that parcell called and knowen by the name of the Deere Parke of Lanteglosse, lately disparked and devided into severall inclosures of meadow, pasture and arrable ground conteyning one hundred twentie six acres.
All that other parcell of land knowen and called by the name of Helsbury Parke alsoe lately disparked and devided into severall enclosures . . . conteyning by mensuracon [306 ac.].'

Sir Richard Buller kt, by L.P. of 5 May 1627, the disparked parks of Lanteglosse [Lanteglos by Camelford] and Hellesbury [Helsbury in Michaelstow]. Term 99 years on the lives of John Buller (dec.), Anthony (25), and William (24), sons of Richard Buller. Rent £10 13s 4d. Imp. val. £126 8s 8d. Exceptions, etc.; to keep premises in good order and to plant 12 trees yearly.
'The timber trees, pollards and sapplins in Lanteglosse Parke are valued to be worth . . . £13 2s 6d.
Md. that there hath beene cutt out of Lanteglosse Parke by Mr Buller or his assignes six acres of coppice wood which he sould for five poundes the acre which amounteth to in the whole £30.
The timber trees, sapplins and pollards groweing in the hedge rowes and other partes of the Parke of Helsebury are valued to be worth . . . £82 10s.
The under woodes groweing in the said parke being 18 acres amongst which are valued divers sapplins and timber trees is valued to be worth . . . £180.

FREEHOLDERS OF THE SAID MANNOR

The heires of John Nicoll esq. hold freely to them and theire heires for ever in free soccage two acres and a halfe of land Cornish in Pendulgate [Bodulgate?] for which they pay' p.a. rent 7s 6d, relief 31s 3d.
id., 6½ ac. C. in Trewarledge Downe and elsewhere, rent 19s, relief 81s 3d;   Phillip Spry gent., 3 ac. C. in Hendra Walls [Hendrawalls in Davidstow] and elsewhere, rent 6s 3d, relief 37s 6d;   Heires of John Davis, 3 ac. C. in Treclogow [Treclugo in Advent] and a head-weir there, rent 5s 6d, relief 37s 6d;   *id.*, mill called Hagrish Mill, rent 6d;   *id.*, 3½ ac. C. in Camelford Werrings and elsewhere, rent 7s 7d, relief 40s 9d; Anthony Nicoll esq., 1½ ac. C. in Penhale alias Bowithicke, rent 1s 3d. relief 15s 9d;   William Scawen esq., ½ ac. C. in Penhale, rent 1s 6d, relief 6s 3d;   Hugh Boscawen esq., 1 ac. C. in Michaelstow Church Town, rent 4s, relief 12s 6d;   John Billinge esq., of the Manor of Polrade [Polroad in St Tudy], 1 ac. C. in Trewanion, 'which said Mannor holdeth in soccage of

this Mannor payinge therefore', rent 2s, relief 12s 6d; William Glynn esq. with the heirs of Sir Richard Carnsew kt, 1 ac. C. in Polroade, rent 2s; Warwicke Lord Mohun, ½ ac. C. in Fontonadle [Fentonadle in Michaelstow], rent 7½d, relief 6s 3d; *id.*, head weir for Knights Mill, rent 6s; Thomas Bullocke, ½ ac. C. in Fontonadle, rent 7½d, relief 6s 3d; Elizabeth Mattis, 1 ac. C. in Tregrewwill [Tregreenwell], rent 1s, relief 12s 6d; William Jack gent., 1 ac. C. in Tregrewwill, rent 2s 6d; relief 12s 6d; John Kernicke gent., and John K. jn., 1 ac. C. in Tregrewwell, rent 2s, relief 12s 6d; Robert Roll, 3 ac. C. in Trethia [Trevia nr Camelford], rent 9s, relief 34s 6d; Heirs of Sir Richard Carnsew, 1 ac. in Trecarne [in Advent], rent 2s 7d, relief 12s 6d; William Glynn esq. and heirs of Sir Richard Carnsew, 1 ac. C. in Trenoweth [Trenewth in Michaelstow], rent 2s 7d, relief 12s 6d; Heirs of Hender Moulsworth esq., John Mullis and Nicholas Hender, 1 ac. C. in Trefrew [*id.* in Lanteglos], rent 4s 8½d, relief 12s 6d; George Carew gent. and Richard Shorte, 1 ac. C. in Trefrew, rent 2s 7d, relief 12s 6d; George Carew and William Glynn, 2 ac. C. in Tregarth [Tregath in Lanteglos], rent 4s, relief 25s; William Glynn and heirs of Sir Richard Carnsew, 1 ac. C. in Penpethy [in Tintagel], rent 1s 3d, relief 12s 6d; Alice Hickes wid., 1 farl. in Pendulgate, rent 9d, relief 3s 1½d; Heirs of Carminow, meadow and a head weir in Trevennicke, rent 5s 2d; Tavenor Langford jn., 2 'headweares which cometh to Kerkeene and one little meadowplott', rent 6d; 'The Rector of the Rectory of Lanteglosse', a headweir, rent 6d.

Total   £4 18s 0½d.

'CUSTOMARY TENNANTS OF INHERITANCE

John Colman in the right of Barberie his wife holdeth to him his heires and assignes for ever in free convenconary from seven yeares to seven yeares according to the custome of the Mannor one third parte of the moiety of one messuage or tenement in Forda [Treforda in Lanteglos] and the eighth parte of another moiety. John Seccombe by the surrender of William Seccombe holdeth . . . one seventh parte of a moiety; Christopher Sloggett by the surrender of John Seccombe holdeth . . . one close and a house; Digory Seccombe by the surrender of John Cowlinge and Henry Cowling holdeth . . . foure closes, two lanes and one house and a garden being one fouerth parte William Taylor, Andrew Burgesse and Agnes Cowlinge wid. hold . . . the residue for which they pay in toto' 15s.

Elizabeth Arundell wid., by d. of John A. her husband, a mess. in Forda, rent 15s, fine 31s 6d.
Mary Dannon, by d. of Hugh Dannon, 2 parts of 3 parts of a mess. in Trewia [Trevia in Lanteglos]; John Cocke gent., by d. of H.D. the other third, rent 10s 4d, fine 20s.

George Carew gent., by surr. of Hugh Hockin gent., 3 mess. in Trewia, rent 31s, fine 60s.

Richard Hambley, in right of his w. moiety of mess. in Trewia; Humphrey Milward, in right of Mary his w. by surr. of Richard Ibell, moiety of the other moiety; Richard Bond, by surr. of Digory Bond his f., the residue, rent 10s 3d, fine 20s.

Richard Hambley, in right of his w., $\frac{1}{4}$ of mess. in Trewia and a close called Lower Welly Parke of $2\frac{1}{2}$ ac.; Anne Weringe wid., in her own right, residue of mess. except 2 closes called the Bowe Towne and New Parke, with 2 houses. Thomas Sandeys, in right of Jane his w., the said land and houses, rent 10s 4d, fine 20s.

Christopher Moyle, in his own right, moiety of ten. in Tregoddell [Tregoodwell in Lanteglos]; Simon Carne, Thomas White and Christopher Colman jn., the residue, rent 8s, fine 20s.

Constance Hore wid., by d. of William Hore her hbd, mess. in Tregoddell, rent 8s, fine 20s.

John Hoare, by d. of Mary his m., 2 closes called West Parke and Turne Meade of 6 ac., part of another ten. in Tregoddell; John Hodge, in his own right, a close called Gilbarte alias Gilberte of 1 ac.; Christopher Colman, Austance Hoare, John Marten, Thomas White, Wilmott Landry and John Pearce, the residue, rent 8s, fine 20s.

Alice Pearce, moiety of ten. in Tregoddell; John Bearne, in his own right, the other moiety, rent 8s, fine 22s.

Christopher Colman, by d. of Mary his m., ten. in Tregoddell, rent 8s 8d, fine 26s 8d.

John Hoare, by d. of Mary his m., close of $1\frac{1}{4}$ ac., part of another ten. in Tregoddell; John Pearne, in his own right, close called the Higher Close of $3\frac{1}{2}$ ac. and another close in the right of Anne his w., being 1/8 of the said ten.; William Joll in right of his w., William Blacke and Caleb Bennett in right of his w., the residue, rent 8s, fine 26s 8d.

Richard Hambley, in right of his w., ten. in Tresinne [Tresinney in Advent], rent 7s, fine 22s.

George Burgesse, by surr. of Andrew Burgesse his f., 1/8 of ten. in Tresinne; Stephen Sloggatt, by surr. of John Edwards jn., by surr. of John Edwards sn., 1/6; John Gaire and Digory Seaccombe, the residue, rent 7s, fine 22s.

John Rawles jn., by surr. of Stephen Sloggatte, moiety of ten. in Tresinne; John Batten, by surr. of William Hocken, 2 closes called Little Parke and Little Meadow, of 3 ac. being 1/6 of the other moiety; Nicholas Harris, by surr. of Richard Hambley, 1/5; Christopher Doubte, by surr. of John Crabb, 1/23; Digory Congdon by d. of Thomas Congdon, 2 closes called Home Downes; Stephen Sloggatt, by surr. of Digory Seaccombe, the residue, rent 7s, fine 22s.

John Trethwy, in his own right, 1/6 of ten. in Helston; Digory Seccombe, in his own right, 1/8; John Thorne, in his own right, $\frac{1}{4}$; Alice Basterd wid., Richard Basterd and John Battin, the residue, rent 6s 8d, fine 6s 8d.

John Horndon gent., by surr. of John H. sn., his uncle, moiety of ten. in Helston; Elizabeth Hordon w. of John H. jn., by surr. of Anthony H., the other moiety; the said John H., by the same surr., moiety of another ten. there; the said Elizabeth H., the other moiety, in all rent 9s 2d, fine 20s 6d.

John Thorne, in his own right, ten. and 10 ac. in Helston, rent 3s 4d, fine 8s.

Azias Hickes wid., moiety of ten. in Helston; Thomas Tiner, by surr. of John Cocke, the other moiety, rent 6s 8d, fine 11s.

Samuell Wallis in his own right, ten. and 15 ac., 1 in Helston, rent 5s, fine 8s; *id.*, in right of his w., mess. and 10 ac. in Helston, rent 3s 4d, fine 8s.

Digory Seccombe, John Saunders, Thomas Shorte, Thomas Shearme, Alice Basterd and Richard Basterd, ten. in Helston, rent 6s 8d, fine 10s.

Thomas Shearme, William Parson, John Lawrence in right of his w., Richard Basterd, Thomas John, Azias Hickes wid., Thomas Tinner, John Symons and Anthony Symons, ten. in Helston, rent 10s, fine 20s.

John Hickes, by d. of Jane Pawle his gdm., ten. in Fentenwansera [Fenterwanson in Lanteglos], rent 10s, fine 20s.

Azias Hickes wid. by d. of Henry H. her hbd, moiety of ten. in Fentenwansera; James Tremble, by surr. of Margarett Tremble, 1/16 of the other moiety; Andrew Burgesse in his own right, another 1/16; Roberth Cocke in his own right, another 1/16; George Basterd, the residue, rent 10s, fine 24s.

Azias Hickes, as above, 5 ac. of waste in a piece of land called Watislake in Fentenwansera, rent 2s 4d, fine 3s.

Henry Cocke in his own right, moiety of ten. in Hendra [*id.*, near Camelford]; John Cocke by d. of Agnes his m., the other moiety, rent 6s 8d, fine 14s.

Christopher Cocke, by surr. of Richard Cocke, ten. in Hendra, rent 6s 8d, fine 14s.

George Carew, by surr. of Hugh Hocken gent., moiety of ten. in Trethian; Elizabeth Kever wid. by d. of William K. her hbd, the other moiety, rent 7s, fine 12s.

id., by the same surr., mess. in Trethian, rent 6s 8d, fine 15s.

Francis Calmady, by surr. of George Lethbridge, ten. in Overtregavenna, rent 8s 10d, fine 22s.

Vincent Calmady esq. by surr. of [—] Calmady his w., ten. in Overtregavenna, rent 8s 10d, fine 22s.

John Keane, by surr. of Tristram K. his f., ten. in Michaelstow, rent 10s, fine 20s.

William Mullis, by surr. of Katherin M. his m., moiety of ten. in Michaelstow; Katherin Mullis, by d. of John M. her hbd, the other moiety except a close of 2 ac.; Joan Nicoll, by d. of Richard N. her hbd, the said close, rent 8s, fine 20s.

William Autridge, Phillip Autridge, Robert Poolely, Richard Watts in right of his w., and John Pearce, ten. in Nethertregenna, rent 10s 6d, fine 24s.

Lawrence Kendall, in right of his w., and Hugh Autridge, ten. in Nethertregenna, rent 5s 11d, fine 24s.

Nicholas Hender w., in his own right, ten. in Trefre gent., [*id.*, in Lanteglos], rent 10s, fine 15s.

John Dagge, by surr. of John Chaple, 1/12 ten. in Trenalder [Trewalder in Lanteglos]; Thomas Jory jn., by d. of Arthur Jory, a moiety except 1/12; Peter Martin, in his own right, 1/16; Richard Basterd, in right of Armineble his w., ¼ and 1/12; Michael Rush, in right of Jane his w., 1/8; Thomas Jory jn. by d. of Arthur J., the residue, rent 12s, fine 16s.

Thomas Sloggatt, by surr. of Elizabeth S. his m., 2 ten. in Trenalder, rent 24s, fine 32s.

Digory Sloggatt, by d. of Elizabeth S. his m., garden and house, part of another ten. in Trenalder, 'which said house was lately built', Joan Illary, by d. of John I. her hbd, 1/3 of residue of said ten.; Richard Basterd by surr. of William Phillippes, another third; Stephen Adams, in his own right, another third except a meadow, garden, house and mowhay; Elizabeth Martin, by surr. of Peter Martin, said meadow; Martha Crowdacate alias Williams, said house, garden and mowhay, rent 6s, fine 7s.

John Dagg gent., by surr. of John Chapple, ¼ and 1/16 of ten. in Trenalder; Richard Basterd, in right of Armineble his w., close called the Meadow under the Redmore of 1 ac.; John Ellerie and John Trethewie clk., in right of Alice his w., the residue, rent 12s, fine 15s.

Agnes Crowdecott wid., by d. of Bartholomew C. her hbd, ten. in Trenalder, rent 12s, fine 16s.

Jane Rush, Thomas Jore, John Rush and John Thorne, moiety of ten. in Trenalder, rent 6s, fine 8s.

Thomas Bridge, by surr. of John Tattershall, ten. in Trevigean [Treveighan in Michaelstow]; rent 11s 6d, fine 22s.

John Parson, in his own right, ten. in Trewigean, rent 10s 6d, fine 20s.

John Mullis, by surr. of Grace Blerett his m., ten in Trivegean, rent 11s, fine 22s.

James Fowler, in his own right, moiety of ten. in Trewegean 'except one house with a little garden and backside to the said house belonginge', Joan Edy, by d. of George E. her hbd, the said house, garden and backside. John Parson, in his own right, ¼ and 1/8; John Mullis, by surr. of Grace his m., 1/8, rent 11s, fine 22s.

Francis Calmadie gent., by surr. of George Lethbridge, ¼ ten. in Trevigean; John Parsons, in his own right, 1/8; Phillip Parson wid., by d. of William P. her hbd, residue except 1/8; Walter Morris, by surr. of said William Parsons, the said 1/8, rent 11s 6d, fine 20s.

Roger May sn., by surr. of Mary Pearce, moiety of ten. in Trewigean; Roger May jn., by surr. of Roger M. sn., ¼; Florence Hockin wid., by d. of William H. her hbd, the other ¼, rent 11s, fine 22s.

Richard Olver, by d. of Thomas Olver his bro., moiety of ten. in Trewigean; John Barson in his own right, the other moiety, rent 11s, fine 22s.

Thomas Gidley in his own right, 3 parts of 8 of ten. in Trewigean; John Mullis, by surr. of John Werringe, 1/8; Christopher Mullis, in his own right, 1/16; Richard Marke and John Barson, the residue, rent 11s, fine 22s.

William Lower gent., in right of Anne his w., ten. on Tregreenwin [Tregreenwell in Michaelstow], rent 6s 8d, fine 14s.

Mary Mullis wid., by d. of Henry M. her hbd, 9 ac. in one piece in Tregreenwin, rent 2s 10d, fine 4s.

id., by the same, ¼ ten. in Tregreenwin; Florence Hocken, by surr. of Henry Mullis, the residue, rent 6s 8d, fine 12s.

id., by the same, 9 ac. in one piece of waste land in Tregreenwin, rent 2s 6d, fine 2s.

id., by the same, ten. in Tregreenwin, rent 7s 8d, fine 12s.

William Lower gent., in right of Anne his w., ten. in Tregreenwin, rent 5s, fine 10s.

Digory Seccombe, in right of Phillippa his w., ten. in Tremagennow [Tramagenna in Lanteglos], rent 7s 6d, fine 15s.

John Horndon jn., by surr. of John Hore sn., 1/8 ten. in Tramagennow; Elizabeth Horndon, by surr. of Anthony Horndon, 1/8; James Hockin, by surr. of Christopher Rooby, 2 closes called the Barr and the Slade Parkes and 2 houses, being ¼ of the whole; Digory Seccombe, Thomas Paule and Maria Robins, the residue, rent 7s 6d, fine 15s.

James Hockins, by surr. of Christopher Robby, moiety of ten. in Tremagennow; Margarett Robby wid. by d. of Christopher R. her hbd, the other moiety, rent 7s, fine 15s.

John Horndon jn., by surr. of John Hore sn., ¼ ten. in Tramagennow; Elizabeth Horndon, by surr. of Anthony H., ¼ except a house and 2 gardens; Katherin Edwards, by d. of William E. her hbd, the said house and gardens; Margarett Rooby, by d. of Christopher R. her hbd, ¼; Digory Seccombe by d. of Walter Hele alias Hey, 1/8; Thomasin Trease wid., by d. of Michael T. her hbd, 1/8, rent 7s 6d, fine 11s.

Robert Beere gent., in right of Margerie his w., ¼ ten. in Camelford, rent 2s.

Christopher Worthyvale esq., Joan Chapman and John Horndon, divers parcels in Camelford, rent 4s 11d, fine 6s.

Edward Seccombe, moiety of ten. in Trewenna [Treween in Lanteglos], rent 3s 4d, fine 16s 8d.

Roose Breist wid., by d. of Thomas B. her hbd, ten. in Trewenna, rent 6s 8d, fine 13s 4d.

John Pearce jn., Christopher Cocke and Nicholas Werringe, ten. in Trewenna, rent 6s 8d, fine 13s 4d.

Christopher Cocke and Anne Pearse, ten. and moiety of another in Trewenna, rent 10s, fine 20s.

John Willcocke, by d. of Joan his m., ten. in Castlegoffe [Castlegoff in Lanteglos], rent 4s, fine 8s.

John Bennett alias Rawling, by surr. of John Collins, ten. in Castlegoffe, rent 4s, fine 8s.

Mary Pope wid., by d. of Thomas P. her hbd, divers ten. in Fentonnadle, rent 27s, fine 31s 9d.

Richard Symons, by d. of John Symons and surr. of Hugh Symons, moiety of ten. in Fentonnadle; John Giddy, by d. of John G. her hbd, 1/3 of the other moiety; John Werringe, by d. of John W., another 1/3; Richard Symons, by surr. of Hugh Symons, ¾ ac. in the Hare Parke; Elizabeth Keene wid., by surr. of Richard Symons, house and garden, part of said Hare Park; Richard Symons, by surr. of Hugh his f., orchard and mowhay; Elizabeth Owen wid., by d. of John O. her hbd, house and garden; Humphrey Symons, by surr. of Hugh Symons his f., house adjoining the mowhay, rent 5s 5d, fine 8s 8d.

John Werring, by d. of John W. his f., part of 2 ten. in Fentonnadle, rent 4s, fine 5s 9d.

Henry Cullis, by surr. of Tristram Keene, moiety of ¾ of ten. in Trevellicke [Trevillick in Michaelstow]; Robert Pooly and Barnard Nankevile, by surr. of Thomas Bullocke, the residue, rent 10s 6d, fine 25s.

Barnabas Nankevile, by surr. of Thomas Bullocke, ten. in Trevellicke, rent 12s, fine 23s 4d.

Florence Hocking wid., by d. of William H. her hbd, divers tens. in Tretherrape, rent 13s 2d, fine 36s 8d.

id., as above, 3 ac. of waste land called Whitelight in Tretherrape, rent 3s, fine nil.

John Batten, by surr. of John B. his f., ten. in Kennistocke [Kenningstock in Advent], rent 12s, fine 7s.

Florence Hocking wid., by d. of William H. her hbd, 7 ac. of waste land called Colegrave in Tretherrape, rent 6s, fine nil.

Nicholas Hender in his own right, 2/3 of ten. in Trefrew alias Netherdowne; Francis Gorland, by surr. of Richard Isbell, the residue, rent 5s, fine nil.

John Lethebridge, ten. in Trenwithdowne, rent 7s, fine 6s 8d.

Mary Mullis, 4 ac. of waste lane in Tregenwin Downe, rent 1s, fine 3s.

Christopher Worthyvale esq., by surr. of John Batten, 2 corn mills called Kennistocke Mills, rent 40s, fine 4s.

Grace Trefrie wid., by d. of John Leane, 7 ac. of waste land in Cornedowne alias Werrings Parkes, rent 1s 3d, fine nil.

Nicholas Hender, by surr. of John Sergeant, 24 ac. of waste in Trefrew alias Midledowne, rent 7s 6d, fine nil.

Joan Wade wid., by d. of Thomas W. her hbd, ¼ of 7 ac. of waste in Odwill Parke; John Banden jn., by d. of John B. his uncle, moiety; Grace Trefrie, by d. of John Leane her hbd, residue, rent 1s 6d, fine nil.

Andrew Burges and George Burges, 4 ac. of waste in High Staps, rent 6s, fine nil.

Christopher Worthyvale esq., by surr. of Nicholas Cooke, 2 corn mills called Camelford Mills, rent 40s, fine 20s.

Mary Pope, by d. of [—] P. her hbd, parcel called the Out Woodes alias Fentonadle Woodes, rent 2s 8d, fine nil.

Nicholas Hender in his own right, 20 ac. of waste in Trefrew alias Overdowne, rent 6s 8d, fine 4s.

John Bawden, by surr. of John Bawden his uncle, a close called Beadlakesmeadow, part of a ten. in Penekrow; Agneta Bawden in her own right, the residue, except a house and garden held by John Cole by surr. of Philip his m., rent 7s 3d, fine 26s 8d.

id., by the same surr., ten. in Penekrow, rent 7s 3d, fine 6s.

John Parson, by surr. of Henry Cocke, moiety of 27 ac. of waste in Helesbury Downe; Elizabeth Arundle wid., by d. of John Arundell her hbd, the other moiety, rent 3s 4d, fine 1s 8d.

Florence Hockin wid., John Keene, Katherin Mullis and John Pooley in right of his w., 27 ac. of waste in Helesbury Downe, rent 3s 4d, fine 1s 8d.

John Bearst in his own right, moiety of 7 ac. of waste in Colland; John Honny, the other moiety, rent 2s 6d, fine 1s.

William Lower gent., in right of his w., piece of waste called Browneditch near Helesbury Downe, rent 2s 6d, fine 5s.

William Jory, by surr. of Thomas J., 12 ac. of waste in Wide Wall, rent 6s, fine 8d.

Johan Wade, by d. of Thomas W. her hbd, 26 ac. of waste in Pickwalls alias Poole Walls, rent 3s, fine 6s.

'The Reeve of the Mannor for the tyme being taketh for the use of the tennants of the said Mannor every seventh yeare divers moores vizt Corndowne alias Coledowne, Coylehill, Goosehill and Goosehill [sic] wherein the tennants depasture what cattle they please and for which there is paid by the Reeve . . . the yearely rent of £3 3s 4d.

Christopher Worthyvale esq., 'at the will of the Lord from year to year . . . the royaltie of fishinge, fowleing, hawkeing and hunting within the said Mannor'. Rent 3s 4d.

'THE BOUNDES OF THE SAID MANNOR

The said Mannor is bounded on the south and south east with the Mannor of Hamatethy, being the lands of John Billinge esq., Anthony Nicoll esq., Humphrey Lower gent., [—] Escott gent., Thomas Lower esq. and [—]; Waller gent; on the east with the lands of John Trevillian esq. and thence with the lands of [—]; on the north with the lands of Richard Hockin gent.; from thence by the lands of John Lampen esq., from thence by the Barton of Worthevale being the lands of Christopher Worthyvale esq.; from thence with the lands of Hender Moulsworth; from thence with the lands of William Glynn esq. and Christopher Worthyvale esq.; from thence with the lands of Anthony Nicoll esq.; from thence on the north west with the Mannor of Tintagell parcell of the auntient Dutchie of Cornewall, and from thence by the Mannor of Trebarra being the lands of [—] Harrington esq.;

from thence with the lands of William Scawen esq.; on the west with the lands of the heires of John Nicoll esq.; from thence with the lands of John Davis esq. and Thomas Lower esq.; thence with the lands of John Chappell; thence with the lands of the heires of John Nicoll esq.; thence with the Mannor of Newhall being the lands of John Lord Roberts; thence with the lands of John Nicoll esq.; thence with the lands of Tavenor Langford; thence with the lands of Warwicke Lord Mohun; thence with the lands of Tavenor Langford gent.; thence with the lands of Carminow esq.; on the south with the Mannor of Polroade being the lands of Warwicke Mohun; thence with the Barton of Hengar beinge the lands of John Billing esq.; thence with the lands of the heires of John Davis esq. untill the foresaid bounds come to the Mannor of Hamatethy where the same did begin'.

COMONS WITHIN THE SAID MANNOR

There are divers large and spacious downes belonginge to the said Mannor, knowen by the names of Corndowne alias Coledowne, Coytehill, Goosehill and Goosehill [sic], in which the tennants claime right of comon, it being taken as theire other customary estates for which there is paid a yeerely rent by the Reeve as it appears in theire customary takeinge.'

CUSTOMS OF THE SAID MANOR

An Assessions Court is held every seven years, its purpose being the payment of rent, fine and new knowledge money and to record changes in tenants. A Court Baron is held every three weeks and a Court Leet twice a year. A relief is paid on the death of every free tenant and a heriot on that of each customary tenant.

OFFICERS BELONGING TO THE SAID MANOR

The Lord chooses a Steward to keep the courts.

At the Michaelmas Court Leet the homage nominates a tenant to serve as Reeve, whose duties are to summon the courts, collect rents and account for them, to seize heriots, waifs, etc. and to collect heriots and fines.

The homage also presents at the same time fit persons to be viewers of 'reparacions' and also a tithingman whoe is to assist the Reeve and Constable of the said Mannor'.

AN ABSTRACT OF THE PRESENT RENTS, FUTURE IMPROVEMENTS AND OTHER PROFITS OF THE MANOR

Rents of assize and perquisites of court		£14 2s 6½d
Rents of customary tenants		£44 12s 11d
Fines paid by customary tenants within six years of each Assession [Old Knowledge Money]		£9 9s 6¼d
		and a seventh of ¼d
New Knowledge Money		£3 15s
Rent of land in lease		£10 13s 4d
	Total	£83 3s 9¾d
		and a seventh of ¼d
Improved value of the lands in lease		£126 8s 8d
Timber, woods and underwoods, worth		£275 12s 6d

'This is an exact survey . . . [Sd].'

18 MANOR OF KILLIGARTH

PRO E 317 (C)/20. The manor lay in the parish of Talland. It was in the possession of the Crown, having been seized on account of the debts of its former owner, Sir James Baggs.

'A Survey of the Mannor of Killigath alias Killigarth heretofore parte of the possessions of Sir James Baggs Kt and afterwards extended by a writt out of the Exchequer for and to the use of Charles Stuart late King of England And hath soe continued for about these fouerteene yeares last past, But is now setled on Trustees for the use of the Comon Wealth . . . retorned [12 Feb. 1649/50].

THE SCITE OF THE MANNOR OR MANSION HOUSE

The said house consisteth of one hall, one parlour, one butterie, one kitchen, one wash-house, with tenn chambers over them and divers other roomes fallen to the ground. Without doores there is one stable with three lodging roomes for servants, one empty dovehouse and one barne fallen to the very foundacion. All which foresaid premisses are out of repaire, the materialls being not worth the takeing downe or carrying away. The scite whereof consisteth of one square corte with a garden thereunto adioyning and conteyning about one halfe acre of land. Alsoe three faire orchards consisting of tenn acres and a halfe, all which scite (after it is cleered of the said decayed house and outhouses) with the said garden and orchards are worth (ultra repriss'), p.a. £10

DEMEASNES LAND BELONGING TO THE SAID MANSION HOUSE

All that peece of arable land comonly knowen and called by the name of Sandhill conteyning by admeasurement 37 acres.'
Higher South Downe, arable, 24½ ac.;   Lower South Downe, pasture, 28¾ ac.;   Gressome, arable, 8 ac.;   woodland, 3 ac.;   Headwell, pasture, 36 ac.; Bridles, 4 pieces of pasture, 35 ac.;   The Meadow, meadow, 20 ac.; Upper Parke, Cutts Parke, arable, 5½ ac.;   Nether Cutts, arable, 5 ac.;   The Warren, heretofore used as a cony warren, pasture, 35 ac.
'All which foresaide parcells . . . are commonly . . . called by the name of the Barton of Killigarth and conteynes . . . 237½ ac. and is worth p.a. £160 13s 10d. The timber trees, saplins and other greate trees now standing and groweing . . . being in number 699 are worth in ready money . . . £79 5s.

FREE-HOLDERS OF THE SAID MANNOR

John Lord Roberts holdeth freely to him and his heires for ever certeine lands in Poole Parke for which he paieth p.a. 1s.'
id., lands in Newton [*id.* in Lansallos], 1s;   Mr Moth, in knight service lands in Menedow [Menadue in Lansallos], 12s;   Mr Hix, lands in Pleiton, 6s 8d;   Thomas and Elizabeth Wash, heirs of John Wash, lands in Polkerries, 1s;   John Couch, lands in Motha, 1s 1d;   Certeine tenements in Palpadon pay to the lord, 4s 6d.

Total quit rents   £27 3s.

'LEASE-HOLDE TENEMENTS BELONGINGE TO THE SAID MANNOR AND IN HAND

Pleton Farme

All that parcell of pasture ground commonly called . . . the Upper Brent conteyning by mensuracon, 2½ ac.'

The Middle Brent, pasture, 3 ac.; the Lower Brent, arable, 7 ac.; the Upper North Brent, pasture, 5½ ac.; Nether North Brent, arable, 4½ ac.; Westhill, arable, 4 ac.; Midlehill, arable, 2½ ac.; Easthill, arable, 6½ ac.; the Above home, pasture, 3½ ac.; the Meadow, meadow, 1 ac.; Stone Parke, pasture, 5½ ac.; two other parcells of pasture ground belonging thereto, 6¾ ac.

'All which . . . doe conteyne . . . 52¼ ac., the farme house whereof is wholely decayed and ruined, and it is worth at an imp. val. £31 2s.'

Robysicke Farme

The Hill, arable, 8 ac.; Barkes Hill, arable, 4¾ ac.; the Barne Parke, pasture, 5¾ ac.; West Hill, pasture, 8½ ac.; Little Meadow, meadow, 2½ ac.; Greate Meadow, meadow, 4½ ac.; Hare Parke, pasture, 3½ ac.; Abovehome, pasture, 4¼ ac.; Two other parcels of arable, 6½ ac.

'The farme house belonging thereto and used therewith is utterly ruined; all the forecited particulars thereof conteyning in the whole 48¼ ac., and it is worth at an imp. val. £27 3s 4d.

Bound Farme

Pigge parke, arable, 3½ ac.; The parke, pasture, 5¼ ac.; The High . . ., pasture, 2½ ac.; the Bedle, pasture, 2½ ac.; the Meadow, meadow, 1 ac.; Rash Parke, arable, 3¾ ac.; Pound Hill, pasture, 3 ac.; Pound Hill furse, arable, 4½ ac.; two closes of arable adjoining, 6 ac.

'The farme house belonging thereto is wholely ruined. All the foresaid particulars conteyning in the whole 32 ac. worth at an improved value p.a. £21 10s.'

Trehurst Farme

Way Parke, pasture, 2½ ac.; Midle Parke, arable, 2 ac.; Little Close, pasture, 1½ ac.; Nether Long Parke, arable, 1¾ ac.; Upper Long Parke, pasture, 1¼ ac.

'The homesteede is wholely ruined, the scite whereof conteynes about ¾ ac. This tenement is in the possession of one Wills whoe holdeth it by licence from the Sheriffe . . . by the yearely rent of foure pounds. The severall particulars whereof conteyne in the whole by mensuracon tenn acres. All which is worth (with the said rent included)' p.a. £6 14s 6d.

LEASE-HOLD TENEMENTS BELONGING TO THE SAID MANOR

Trehurst: Trehurst Park, pasture, 2 ac.; Best Parke, arable, 4¾ ac.; North Parke, pasture, 5 ac.; Cox Hill, arable, 4¼ ac.; North Hill, pasture, 6¼ ac.; Under Home, pasture, 6¼ ac.

Now in the possession of Reginald Hawkie, who claims to hold by assignment of one Hele, who had it assigned to him by one Gregorie, who held it by deed from Sir Bevill Greenevile, 'but produced neither assignment or deede to make good his title'. Rent 40s, a hen and a harvest journey. Total area, 28½ ac. Worth with the homestead at an improved value besides the present rent £15.

Trehurst [sic]: North Hill Parke, pasture, 3¾ ac.; Long Combe Hill, arable, 5½ ac.; Long Parke, arable, 1¼ ac.; Meadow, 2 ac.; Under Home, pasture, 1 ac.; Shutt Parke, arable, 2¼ ac.; Best Parke, 3¼ ac. In total 18½ ac.; occupied by George Richards by deed of Sir Bevile Greenevile of 20 Jan. 1631, for 99 years on lives of G.R. (46) and Margerie (40) his w., d. of Simon Dear of Lansallos. Rent 26s 8d., and 'one plough iorney at wheateland and two capons at Christide.' Imp. val. £14 15s 9d. G.R. owes suit to court and mill and is not to 'let out any of his farme without lycence of the Lord . . . .and alsoe to repaire all the premisses at his owne chardges and that without doeing any wast or cutting downe any oake. ash or elme before licence had for the doeing thereof.'

The moiety of a tenement called Trelay [*id.*] in the parish of Plinte [Pelynt] belongs to the lord of this manor, but is intermixed with the lands of Sir John Trelawney. It consists of:
the Bell Hay, pasture, 9 ac., moiety 4½ ac.; Higher Meadow, meadow, moiety 1 ac.; Midle Meadow, meadow, 1¾ ac., moiety 15/16 ac.[1]; Longe Meade, meadow, 3 and 11/28 ac., moiety 1½ & 5/14 ac.[2]; Tuley Gutter [sic], arable, moiety 2½ ac.; Rood Parke, pasture, moiety 4 ac.; Greene Parke, pasture, 5 3/8 ac.; Ashen Crosse Parke, arable, 7¼ ac.; Piece of ground on which the house stood, moiety ¼ ac.
The whole is in the occupation of Sir John Trelawney. The moiety, 28¼ ac., which forms part of the manor of Killigarth was let to him by deed of 10 May 1632 by Francis Buller of Treggarricke who had the same granted to him for 21 years following the 'deathe, surrender forefeiture or other deter-minacon of the estates of ' Thomas Hambley (dec.) and Emme (dec.) his d. (who had the same graunted to them for terme of their lives). Rent 56s 8d. and 4 capons. Imp. val. £15 12s 10d.
The last of the lives, Emme, 'died and was buried about the sixth day of May 1643, soe that seven yeares (wanting one quarter) of the one and twenty is expired.'

Polperra [Polperro]: Jerome Withers, by indenture of 1 July 1603 granted him by Francis Mannor, ten. with a meadow and 2 gardens adjoining in Polperra, for 99 years on the lives of Elizabeth, Phillippa and John Withers, children of Jerome. 'Lives are all in being' and aged between 40 and 50. Heriot 4s 4d. or a best beast. Rent 10s. Imp. val. 30s.

Polperra [sic]: Edward Sprie of Polperra, by indenture from Sir Bernard Greenevile of 20 Dec. [blank], house lately occupied by John Axford 'with one stich of land thereunto belonginge situate . . . in Polperra . . . bounded with Brent Hill on the east, the lands of Henry Abraham on the west, the lands of John Walton gent. on the north, and by the sea on the south.' for 99 years on the lives of Edward S. (60), Marie Sprie (dec.) and Anne Sprie (30). Rent 5s. Imp. val. 15s.

Polperra [sic]: Christopher Calcott, by indenture from Francis Mannor. of Killigarth of 20 July 1603, mess. or ten. and a grist mill with 2 closes, a moor and an orchard in Polperra, for 21 years beginning after the expiry of a lease granted 13 April 1580 by William Bevill to Elenor Marten. Rent 33s 4d and 2 capons. Imp. val. £2 6s 8d.

[1] The text gives '¾ 1/8 1/16', which together make up more than a moiety.
[2] The moiety here is less than half of the meadow.

'The said mills have been heretofore worth besides the present rent ten pounds p.a., but since the lord of the mannor hath not lived within the same and that the tennants thereof have decreased, it is worth noe more than ut supra.
Md. that Joan Marten hath possession . . . by vertue of an assignment made . . . unto her by the said Calcott for and during the residue of the said terme granted to him in reversion, whereof there is already expired nine years soe that there remaynes twelve yeares behind and to come of the said one and twenty yeares.'

Polperra: John Carne (dec.), by indenture of Philip Bevill of Killigarth dated 16 Feb. 1612, had granted to him, Petronell (60) his w. and Peter (dec.) his s., 'all that peece of old walls . . . in Polperra . . . between the lands of Mr North gent. on the east, of Leonard Baylie gent. on west and the High Way on south and north sides' for lives. Rent 2s. Imp. val. 5s.

Polperra: Achem Clements, by indenture of Sir Bernard Greeneville of 1 Dec. 1625, 'one quellet of land conteyning . . . about 30 yards uppn condicon that he shold build one house thereon' for 99 years on lives of Bernard (28), Silvester (27) and Mary (30), children of A.C. Heriot 1s. Rent 2s. Imp. val. 8s.

AN ALPHABETICAL RENTAL OF THE SAID MANOR [omitted]
'The said Mannor is thus bounded viz on the west side with a certeine brooke called Long Coombe, on the south by the sea, on the north and north east with the lands of Sir John Trelawney kt, and on the east by a little brooke that runneth into the sea.

Md. this Mannor did heretofore belong to Sir James Badge kt; since his decease one Marsom pretended a right unto it (as we are informed) by purchase, but, the said Sir James Badge being indebted to the late King, the said Mannor was after the deceasse of the said Badge extended by a writt out of the Exchequer, and soe continued untill the time when the King deserting the Parlyament, kept courte at Oxford where the said Marsome, compounding with the said King, had the said Mannor graunted unto him in fee farme for one thousand yeares, which composicon being made at Oxford in the tyme aforesaid, the Comittee of the Revenew accounted of noe validitie, but continued the old extent in force as it was formerly, soe that the said lands have beene under the said extent for about these fouerteene yeares last past, by which meanes the said lands ly (as it were) utterly wast. The woodes thereon are spoyled, and the houses fallen utterly to decay, which we have reprised in the value thereof. This is the truest state of the said Mannor as it now stands and as wee could possibly be informed in the country.'

AN ABSTRACT OF THE PRESENT RENTS AND FUTURE IMPROVEMENTS
WITH OTHER PROFITS OF AND BELONGING TO THE MANOR

Rents of Assize	£1 12s 3d
Rents of leasehold tenants	£8 8s 8d
Value of workdays	2s 6d
Value of 'churchetts'	16s 8d
Total	£10 15s 1d.

The Barton and several leasehold tenements are now in hand and at the lord's disposal worth p.a. £57 2s 8d
Improved value of tenements in lease p.a. £49 2s 3d
Timber and other trees on the Barton at the lord's disposal, worth £70 5s.

'This is an exact survey . . .'

19 MANOR OF LANDREYNE

DCO S/4; PRO E 317 (C)/21. The manor, the bounds of which are not given in the survey, lay in the parish of North Hill. A Courtenay manor it was attached to the Duchy in 1540.

'A Survey of the Mannor of Landreyne . . . retorned [30 Nov. 1649].

This mannor consisteth of free-holders and coppy-holders. The free-holders hold in free soccage and pay yearely to the Lord a quitt rent, and upon every death or alienacon a relieffe certeine. They alsoe owe suite and service to the Lords Courtes.
The coppy holders hold by coppy of courte rolle and owe suite and service to the Lords Courtes as often as they shalbe thereunto called which are accustomed to be foure tymes in the yeare.

FREE-HOLDERS

The heires of Robert Trencricke and William Fountayne hold to them and theire heires for ever certeine lands in Penhole [in North Hill] for which they pay to the lord . . .' relief 3s 1½d, rent 2s 8d.
Heirs of John Reade, land in Penhole, relief 3s 1½d, rent 2s 8d;   heirs of Thomas Hender, land in Penhole, relief 3s 1½d, rent 4s;   heirs of William Wevell, land in Penhole, relief 3s 1½d, rent 1s 4d.

Total   10s 8d.

'COPPIEHOLDERS FOR LIVES ARE AS FOLLOWETH

Henry Spoore esq. and Henry his sonne hold by coppy of courte rolle [of Oct. 31 1627] one close of land called Noddon, namely a third parte of three partes of one tenement called Westberriow [near Berriowbridge in North Hill] . . . conteyninge by estimacon [34 ac.] for and dureing the terme of theire lives successively paying therefore yearely to the Lord the some of 3s 4d. And it is worth besides the present rent p.a.' £3 6s 8d.
Fine, at the lord's will. Heriot, a best beast. The said lives are both in being: Henry Spoore 50; Henry his s. 23.

John Masters [56] and Ferdinando [29] his s. by copy of Oct. 31 1627, 2 parts of 3 parts of Westberriow (except the foresaid close called Nodden), in all 28 ac. For lives. Fine at the lord's will. Heriot a best beast. Rent 6s 8d. Imp. val. £10 3s 4d.

Henry Spoore (50), Richard S. and George S., sons of Richard Spoore esq., dec., by copy of 28 Aug. 1612, a cottage and curtelage of land and a garden lying near Colsa Bridge, for lives. Fine and heriot, as above. Rent 10d. Imp. val. 5s 10d.

Phillippa Warren, wid. of Edward W., by her widow's estate, mess. and 10 ac. in Westremella [West Tremollett in North Hill], for life. Fine and heriot, as above. Rent 2s 6d. Imp. val. £7.

John Fudge (48), by copy of 12 May, 1607, mess. and 10 ac. in Westremolla, for life. Fine and heriot, as above. Rent 2s 6d. Imp. val. £7.

Mary Harvey wid. (60) and Robert (19) her s.,[1] by surr. of John Reade and Walter Paplestone, by copy of 17 Oct. [2], mess. in Landren [Landreyne in North Hill] and 40 ac., 'paying therefore yearely to the Lord of the said Mannor 5s 9d, to the Lord of the Mannor of North Hill 9d and to the Lord of the Mannor of Launceston 7s 2d.' For lives. Fine and heriot, as above. Rent 13s 8d. Imp. val. £20.

Elizabeth Willis (110) [sic], wid. of Edward W., by her widow's estate, mess. in Landrine and 40 ac. for life. Fine and heriot, as above. Rent 5s 9d, 9d to the Manor of North Hill and 7s 2d to the Manor of Launceston: total 13s 8d. Imp. val. £20.
E.W. is said to be aged 110 years.
'Reversion said to have been granted to John Billing and Margaret his sister, but no copy produced' [margl. note 'This coppy to be produced within the tyme permitted']. J.B. 'is affirmed to be in the Army in the Parlyaments service and by the tennants on oath to have a coppy.'

William Masters (60) claims to hold a mill for the lives of himself and of William (24) and Henry (22) his sons, but the copy was not produced [margl. note 'This copy to be produced']. Fine and heriot, as above. Rent 8s. Imp. val. £3 10s.

THE CUSTOMS OF THE MANOR

A copyholder's widow to continue to hold the tenement during her widowhood, but if she marries again the tenement to pass to the next heir.
If a tenant die without any life in reversion, the tenement falls into the lord's hands, but any child of the last tenant 'ought to have the refusall of such tenement'.
No tenant may cut timber without licence of the Steward, and then only for the repair of his own property. If he has insufficient timber he may with licence cut on the tenement of any other copyholder in the manor.
Tenants owe suit of mill. Copyhold tenants to serve as reeve in turn.
Free tenants to pay 3s 1½d as a relief on each death or alienation, and copyholders a best beast as a heriot, which, with fines and other perquisites, amount on average to 10s.

[1] The text also refers to him as Henry H.
[2] The text gives 23 James I. There is no such date.

AN ABSTRACT OF THE PRESENT RENTS AND FUTURE IMPROVEMENTS

Rents of assize and perquisites of court	20s 8d
Rents of copyhold tenants	52s 8d
Paid out of this to the Manors of North Hill and Launceston	15s 10d
Total rents	£2 16s 8d
	[Should be £2 17s 6d]
Improved value of copyhold tenements	£8 8s 6d.

'This is an Exact Survey . . .'

20   MANOR OF LANDULPH

DCO S/4; PRO E 317 (C)/22. The manor occupied approximately the parish of the same name. It had belonged to Henry Courtenay, Marquis of Exeter, and was annexed to the Duchy in 1540.

'A Survey of the Mannor of Landulph . . . retorned [30 Oct. 1649].

This Mannor consisteth of severall villages, viz. Collogat [Colloggett], Kings Mill [Kingsmill], Grove [*id.*], Penyoke [*id.*], parte of Landulph, and Grigmoore.
There belongs to this mannor certaine freeholders which owe suite and service . . . and free customarie tennants who hold by coppy of courte rolle for terme of life, whoe owe like suite and service.

FREEHOLDERS IN THE MANNOR OF LANDULPH ARE AS FOLLOWETH
Sir Nicholas Lowre Kt, holdeth one messuage or tenement conteyninge by estimacon eight acres for which he payeth . . . a quitt rent . . .' 2d.
John Hornedon, mess. and 9 ac., 1d.
'Edward Ameredith, present Rector of Landulph and succeeding rectors halfe of the fishinge and fowlinge in the river of Goodlake as a privileg belonging to the said rectory, 4d.

COPPIE HOLDERS FOR TERME OF LIFE ARE AS FOLLOWETH
Copyholders in Collogatt [Colloggett]
John James (33) by coppy of courte rolle (beareing date Sept. 14 1612) one messuage or tenement with certaine lands contayning by estimacon 30 acres for terme of his life and is worth at an improved value p.a.' £16 10s. Fine at the lord's will. Heriot a best beast. Rent £1 11s 6d. [15s 11d in rental].

John Emmett (23) and Francis E. (21) his bro., by copy of 29 Jan. 1633, mess. and 30 ac. for lives. Fine and heriot, as above. Rent 14s 1d. Imp. val. £16 10s.

John Oxenham (28) and Margarett (29) his w. by copy of 15 Jan. 1638, mess. and 30 ac. for lives. Fine and heriot, as above. Rent 15s 11d. Imp. val. £16 10s.

Robert Bray, by copy of 1 Jan. 1639, mess. and 30 ac. for lives of R.B. (62),

Joan (33) his d. and Alexander (30) his s. Fine and heriot, as above. Rent 13s 11d. Imp. val. £16 10s.

Francis Emmett, by copy of Sept. 3, 1617, mess. and 30 ac. for lives of F.E. (56) and Joan (50) his w. Fine and heriot, as above. Rent 13s 11d. Imp. val. £18 10s.

Henry Pengellie, by copy of Sept. 1, 1630, mess. and 30 ac. for lives of H.P. (37) and Thomasin (33) his w. Fine and heriot, as above. Rent 16s 1d. Imp. val. £16 10s.

John P. (14) their s. has the reversion by copy of 22 April 1646.

'Md. These premisses were formerly the demeasnes of the Mannor but have been time out of minde converted into coppyhold as it now stands.'

COPYHOLDERS IN LANDULPH

Mary Bache, by copy of 3 Sept. 1617, mess. and 30 ac. for lives of M.B. (43) and Samuell Hole (36) her bro. Fine and heriot, as above. Rent 18s 4d. Imp. val. £18.

John Bray jn., by copy of 7 July 1627, mess. and 30 ac. for lives of J.B. (35) and Joan (35) his w. Fine and heriot, as above. Rent 18s 4d. Imp. val. £18.

Joane Bray wid. by copy of Sept. 23 1639, mess. and 40 ac. for lives of J.B. (70), Roger B. (34) her s. and Joan (33) his w. Fine and heriot, as above. Rent £1 11s 3d. Imp. val. £24.

Joane Rayne wid., by copy of July 25, 1633, mess. and 8 ac. for lives of J.R. (34) and John (15) her s. Fine and herriot, as above. Rent 9s 9d. Imp. val. £5.

William Webb, by copy of Oct. 10 1637, mess. and 18 ac. and one water grist mill, for the lives of W.W. (40) and Elizabeth (30) his w. Fine and heriot, as above. Rent 22s 3d. Imp. val. £22.
Md. The mill is valued on improvement at £11 'if the custome of the coppyhold tennants be continued unto it; if not that then there is to be reprized to the purchaser . . . £2 10s. And then the imp. val. thereof will be but £8 10s.

Katherin Elliott (78) by copy of April 6 1572, mess. and 28 ac. for her life. Fine and heriot, as above. Rent 8s 9d [8s 11d in Rental]. Imp. val. £11. Thomasin Webb (36) d. of K.E. was granted the reversion, 23 Sept. 1617 for life.

COPYHOLDERS IN GROVE

William Piper (40) and Katherin (34) his sister by copy of Aug. 21 1612, 2 mess. and 14 ac. for their lives. Fine, as above. Heriot 3s 4d for a best beast. Rent 21s 4d. Imp. val. £8 8s.

Edmond Edgecombe by copy of Oct. 21 1633, mess. and 8 ac. for lives of E.E. (33) and Katherin (35) his w. Fine and heriot, as above. Rent 8s 8d. Imp. val. £4 16s.

Rebecca Reynolds (45) by the name of Rebecca Oxenham, by copy of Aug. 21 1612, mess. and 6 ac. for life. Fine at the lord's will. Heriot 3s 4d. Rent 14s. Imp. val. £3.

Francis Emmett (56) and his s. Richard (18) were granted the reversion Feb. 17 1641.

Francis Emmett, by copy of Feb 1 1620, mess. and 12 ac. in Penyock for lives of F.E. (56) and Samuell (29) his s. Fine and heriot, as above. Rent 12s 8d. Imp. val. £7 4s.

Thomas Gunnett (56) by copy of Sept. 16 1602, cottage and 2 ac. for life. Fine and heriot, as above. Rent 3s 6d. Imp. val. £2.
Agnes (37) his w. has the reversion by copy of April 23 1629.

John Champlin (70) by copy of Oct. 23 1576: cottage and 2 ac. for life. Fine and heriot, as above. Rent 2s 10d [3s 6d in Rental]. Imp. val. £2.
Mary (33) his d. has the reversion by copy of Sept. 27 1630.

John Markes by copy of Sept 7 1620, cottage and 2 ac. for lives of J.M. (65) and Thomasin (60) his w. Fine and heriot, as above. Rent 2s 10d. Imp. val. £2.

Luce Skelton (35) by copy of 27 Feb. 1641, cottage and 2 ac. for life. Fine and heriot, as above. Rent 5s 9d (3s 6d in tabulation). Imp. val. £2.

Grenvile Beile (35), cottage and 4 ac. for life. 'His coppy not seene' (Margl. note 'This coppy is to be produced'). Fine and heriot, as above. Rent 5s 9d. Imp. val. £2 4s.

'Md. Henry Pengellie and John Emmett hold the other halfe of the fishing in the river of Goodlake and is comprised in theire severall coppies.'

A RENTALL OF THE FREE AND COPPY-HOLD TENNANTS [omitted]

THE BOUNDS AND BUTTS OF THE MANNOR OF LANDULPH
The said Mannor is bounded from Kings Mill to Penyoake with the sea being the south and east side of the said mannor, and on the north and west with the lands of Sir Nicholas Lower kt, Francis Buller esq. and William Webb.'

THE CUSTOMS OF THE SAID MANOR
1.   Four courts to be held yearly, i.e. two courts leet and two courts baron. No tenant may sue another elsewhere for any matter determinable therein.
2.   No tenement may be let to a stranger unless refused by the tenant, his executors and administrators.
3.   Most copyhold tenants owe a best beast as a heriot; some a monetary payment. Each tenant pays 20s as a 'farleiue' [sic] on surrender of his tenement.
4.   After the death of a tenant his executors are to hold the tenement until Michaelmas following; if none, then the next life is to hold the tenement, paying 4d as acknowledgement to the lord.
5.   When a house has to be repaired or rebuilt, the tenants may with permission cut timber on their tenements for the purpose. If there is insufficient timber they may cut on another tenement. Unauthorised cutting to be presented at the next court.
6.   A tenant may cut timber on his tenement for making and repairing old gates, bars and stiles.

7.   A tenant may let his tenement or part of it for a period of five years with the permission of the steward and on payment of 4d. If for a longer period, a further payment is necessary.
8.   Tenants owe suit of mill.
9.   Six tenants to serve in turn as reeve, and nine in turn as tithingman. Those who serve as reeve are included in the nine for tithingman.

An Abstract of the present Rents and future Improvements of the said Manor

Rents of assize and perquisites		£1 5s 7d
Rents of copyhold tenants		£13 14s 5d
		[£13 15s in tabulation]
	Total	£16
Improved value of copyhold tenements		£230 12s

'This is a true and exact survey . . . [Sd].

21   HONOUR OF THE CASTLE OF LAUNCESTON

PRO E 317 (C)/23. The Duchy Office retains only a copy which, from its style appears to have been made in the latter half of the sixteenth century. It is copied, along with other surveys, into a bound book, S/68. The Honour consisted of the castle of Launceston and of the obligations of knight service and castle-guard that were due to it. The Honour was part of the original endowment of the Duchy.

'A Survey of the Honor of the Castle of Launeston alias Dunhevid . . . retorned [10 Sept. 1650].

'Launceston Castle alias Dunhevitt Castle

The said castle is built of lime and stone but much out of repaire, the hall and chappell quite levell with the ground; there is onely now standing one old tower in resaonable good repaire, the same being soe kept by the County for a prison. The lead that covered it was taken away by the soldiers in the time of warr. Besides the said tower there is noe parte of the castle but the gate house remayning habitable in which one John Sorrell, the present Constable of the castle liveth, which said house conteynes two roomes in reasonable good repaire. The courtes of the said castle and the ruines thereof within the walls conteyne about three acres.

The scite of the said castle without the walls vizt the castle ditches, conteyneth one acre and a halfe, in partes of which ditches towardes the towne are divers dwelling houses and gardens with other necessary houses which are in the possession of divers persons whoe hold the same for and dureing the naturall life of the foresaid John Sorrell by a certeine yearely rent which is as followeth:
Robert Warnell holdeth there one garden for which he payeth p.a. 1s.'
Edward Ball, one house, 1s; John Hixe, one house, 1s;   William Jose, one house, 1s;   George Jackson, a brewhouse with a 'cotte', 1s;   Digorie Martin, one house,1s;   George Jackson, one stable, 1s;   John Gin, Nicholas Gumes, Juda Pearce, Roger Willcocke, Mary Drew and Thomas

Courtice, 'certeine sheds lately built and alsoe divers gardens', 6s; Richard Perne, one house, 1s; Thomas Bolithoe gent., one house, 1s; Prudence Seymoore, one house, 1s; Richard Pawley, one house, 1s; Thomas Bolithoe, a stable, 1s; Sampson Soper, one house, 1s; Richard Kingdon, a stable, 6d; James Hoskin, a garden, 1s; Oswell Kingdon, a stable, 4d; Thomas Bolitho, a garden, 1s; Richard Pawley, a garden, 1s; Priscilla Noble, a stable, 1s; Thomas Wenner, certain houses and gardens, 3s.

'Which said castle and premisses with the rents for the same are claimed and enjoyed by John Sorrell, Constable of the said Castle by vertue of Letters Pattents produced and seen by us beareing date at Westminster [May 23 1607], whereby the said office of constableship is graunted unto him as alsoe the office of Feodary and Escheater of all the honors, mannors, lands, tenements and all other the possessions . . . appurtaining to the Dukedom of Cornewall within the said Countie of Cornewall and the Countie of Devon [To hold] . . . from the date of the said Letters Pattents for and dureing the term of the life of him the said John Sorrell. All which said castle and ditches with the foresaid are valued with the rents upon improvement £20.

Launceston Park
All that parcell of ground adjoyning the castle known as Launceston Parke conteyninge [30 ac.] the agistement of which is sett to Thomas Trewen esq. by assignment of ' [17 April 1641] from Roger Palmer, who held it by lease from the late King when Prince of Wales, dated 19 August 1624, for 31 years. Rent 33s 4d. Imp. val. £18 18s.

Thomas Bullocke gent. by L.P. of 9 June 1626, ten. and 30 ac. in a farl. C. in Hele near Lostwithiell, for 99 years, on the lives of Thomas B. (dec.) and George B. (28), sons of Richard B. of Lannevit [Lanivet], and John B. (dec.) s. of John B. of Lanlivery. Rent 8s 8d. Imp. val. £10 13s 4d. Exceptions, etc.; 3 trees to be planted yearly. All 'bootes' allowed. Trees now growing worth £25 8s.[1]

Sir John Walter, Sir James Fullerton and Sir Thomas Trevor, by L.P. of 14 June 1628, 2 gardens in Tregony, for 31 years. Rent 1s 2d. Imp. val. 19s. Trees now growing worth 35s.[1]
Lease assigned 17 March 1629 to Thomas Caldwall esq., who assigned 31 Oct. 1630 to Richard Langford gent., and 'since by divers meane conveyances they are come into the hands of Stephen Cocke who now enjoys them'.

'There is collected by Thomas Gewen esq. feodary and escheater of the said Honor for certeine lands in the Countie of Cornewall that are held of the same Honor the yearely rent of £18 7s 8½d out of which the said Feodary (holding a place by pattent) claimeth to have for his fee yearely for collecting the said rent the some of £9 2s 6d, soe the said rents doe amount unto de claro p.a. £9 4s 2½d.[2] [This should be £9 5s 2½d.]

---

[1] Omitted from copy at the Duchy of Cornwall Office.
[2] The DCO copy gives £9 4s 0½d, but see the abstract at the end of this return.

Md. Gewen did not produce the said L.P. [Margl. note: 'to be produced'.] 'There hath beene alsoe paid yearely out of the said Honor for respite of Homage' p.a. £15.

Md. 'that the said respite of Homage hath not been paid since the vote for putting downe the Court of Wardes'.

FREE-HOLDERS OF THE SAID HONOUR

The heirs of Denham hold knight service of the Honour . . . 72 knights fees 'in Cardinham and the members thereof' in both Cornwall and Devon, 'for which they are to find in time of warr at theire owne costs for fortie daies seventie one [sic] men well armed for the custodie of the said castle (every fee shall keepe his garrett) and if it shall be necessary that the said men shalbe kept longer, then the said men shalbe kept at the Lords chardge. And when the said heires shall die theire heires if within age shalbe in ward to the lord, but if they be of full age the Lord shall have in his hand (by reason of his prerogative) all his lands and tenements and of them receave all the profitts and incomes untill the said heires shall doe homage. And the said heires shall give for every knights fee held in mortmaine five markes and no more for a 'relieffe.'

Heirs of Mohune, Courtney and Lower, 6 fees in Polrade.
Heirs of the Earl of Huntingdon, 12½ fees in Worthsale Penhele and Botrus Castle [Boscastle].
Heirs of Peter Edgecombe esq., 4 fees in Recradecke.
Heirs of Cuttisheade, 3 fees in Trehake.
Heirs of John Arundell of Trerise, of Trewinnard, and of Trevillan, 1½ fees in Hallett.
Heirs of Tregian, 1 fee in Trenowth.
Heirs of Peter Edgecombe, 3 fees in Tremodrett and three parts of another fee there.
Heirs of Hedenow, 1 fee in [blank].
Heirs of [blank], 10 fees in Midleland.
Heirs of Greenefield, 5 fees in Heylton.
Heirs of George Tubbes, 1 fee, except an eighth part in Farington.
Heirs of [blank], 7 fees in Aldeston, Heanteasbeare and Bray, all in Devon.
Heirs of Henry Beamond kt, 1/8 fee in Farington.
Heirs of [blank], 1 fee in Raddon in Devon.
Heirs of John Danvers esq. and Sentawbin, 1 fee in Stratton.
Heirs of [blank], 1 fee in Wadfast in Devon.
Heirs of John Arundell of Trerise, 1 fee in Ellforde [Efford in Bude].
Heirs of John Vivian, [—] Kendall and [—] Kempthorne, 1 fee in Trevrys.
Heirs of [blank], 1 fee in Holtwell.
Heirs of Christopher Coppleston, ½ fee in Penrosse.
Heirs of Lord Brooke, 2 fees in Hempston in Devon.
Heirs of George Bassett, 1 fee in Trehaddy [Tehidy in Illogan].

'Md. that the foresaid relieffes of this Honnor are lett with the relieffes of the Honnor of Trematon and Bradnych [Bradninch] unto Rebecca Bird wid. by L.P. of the late King (not produced unto us) under the yearely rent of £7. And wee value the said relieffes together with all rights . . . to be worth upon improvement', on average, £16.

Md. [in a different hand] that the said £16 p.a. 'is intended to be the value of the reliefes only, there not having been any courte kept for about this forty yeares last past, where by we could not value the foresaid royaltys.'

AN ABSTRACT OF THE PRESENT RENTS, FUTURE IMPROVEMENTS AND OTHER PROFITS OF THE SAID HONOUR

Rents collected by the Feodary and Escheator		£9 4s 0½d
For respite of hommage		£15
Rents of leaseholders		£2 3s 4d
	Total	£28 7s 4½d
Improved value of leasehold lands		£50 10s 4d
Improved value of reliefs		£16
Tree now growing worth		£27 3s.

'This is an exact survey . . . [sd].'

22 MANOR OF LEIGH DURANT

DCO S/4; PRO 317 (C)/24. The manor lies entirely within the parish of Pillaton. It formed part of the lands of Henry Courtenay, Marquis of Exeter, and was annexed to the Duchy in 1540.

'A Survey of the Mannor of Leighdurant . . . retorned [12 Nov. 1649].

This Mannor lyeth in the parish of Pillaton . . . and consisteth of freeholders and coppyholders.
The Freeholders hold in free soccage and owe suite to the court twice a yeare. The coppyholders hold by coppy of courte rolle for terme of life and owe suite to the courte foure times a yeare.

FREEHOLDERS OF THE SAID MANNOR

Sir Christopher Wrey kt holdeth in free soccage by fealty one messuage called by the name of Trewolst alias Wolsdon [Wallaton?] with certeine lands belonginge thereunto and conteyninge by estimacon [60 ac.] and paieth yearely' 1d.
Anthony Rouse esq., ten. and lands, 2d.
John Hore of Landulph, by indenture of sale of Oct. 22 1625 between him and Francis Sampson and Ambrose Monniton, a mess. called Foorde alias West forth [Ford in Pillaton], 3s.

COPYHOLDERS

Edward Webb, by copy of 16 July 1634, mess. and 48 ac. on lives of E.W. (40), Joan (40) his w. and Vortiger (15) their s. Fine, at the lord's will. Heriot, a best beast. Rent 12s 4d. Imp. val. £14.

John Trenaman (30), by copy of 20 May 1641, mess. and 24 ac. for life. Fine and heriot, as above. Rent 7s 4d. Imp. val. £6 10s.

Henry Cloake, by copy of 30 April, 1641, mess. and 24 ac. on lives of Mary (35) his w. and Dorothy (11) his d. Fine and heriot, as above. Rent 6s. Imp. val. £6 10s.

Francis Herringe, by copy of 26 March 1634, mess. called Treehill [Trehill in Pillaton] and 160 ac. on lives of F.H. (30) and Arthur H. (37) and William H. (27) his brothers. Fine and heriot, as above. Rent 24s 6d. Imp. val. £32.

John Hodge, by copy of 2 March 1632, mess. in Brison [Briston in Pillaton] and 20 ac. on lives of J.H. (40) and Edward H. (30) his bro. Fine and heriot, as above. Rent 5s 3d. Imp. val. £9.

Edward Webb, by copy of 30 Sept. 1641, mess. called Prestondowne and 30 ac. on lives of Edward W. (11) and William W. (10) his sons. Fine and heriot, as above. Rent 6s 10d. Imp. val. £9.

Annis Dodge, by copy of 25 March 1619, mess. and 30 ac. on lives of A.D. (50) and John D. (30) her s. Fine and heriot, as above. Rent 8s 10d. Imp. val. £15 10d.

Francis Herringe, by copy of 9 Sept. 1640, mess. and 30 ac. on lives of F.H. (30) and Dorothy (27) his w. Fine and heriot, as above. Rent 8s 5d. Imp. val. £17 12s.

Nicholas Bole (63), by copy of 7 Dec. 1586, mess. in Leigh [Leigh Farm in Pillaton] and 50 ac. for life. Fine and heriot, as above. Rent 15s 4d. Imp. val. £20.

John Bole (36) has reversion by copy of 16 Sept. 1633.

Samuell Line, by copy of 16 Sept. 1633, mess. and 40 ac. on lives of S.L. (45) and Richard L. (36) his bro. Fine and heriot, as above. Rent 15s 4d. Imp. val. £16 5s.

Richard Lucas (60), by copy of 20 Oct. 1600, mess., 2 corn mills and 4 ac. 3 roods belonging thereto, for life. Fine and heriot, as above. Rent 17s 6d. Imp val. £11.
Reversion granted 5 Sept 1645 to Nicholas Bole (27) and Elizabeth (24) his w. for their lives.

Grace Spiller wid. (45), by copy of 22 Aug. 1612, mess. and 40 ac. for life. Fine and heriot, as above. Rent 15s 4d. Imp. val. £19.

Anthony Toazer, by copy of 15 Sept. 1628 and in right of Joane [35] his w., mess. and 80 ac. Fine and heriot, as above. Rent 17s 4d. Imp. val. £22. Reversion granted to said Anthony T. (34), 7 Sept. 1640.

Christopher Herringe (32), by copy of 26 May 1633, mess. and 40 ac. for life. Fine and heriot, as above. Rent 11s 8d. Imp. val. £19.

George Vincent (46), by copy of 2 Oct. 1640, mess. and 40 ac. for life. Fine and heriot, as above. Rent 10s 8d. Imp. val. £19.

Henry Cloake, by copy of 9 Nov. 1611, cottage called Island yeate and 20 perches of land, for lives of H.C. (36), Mary (38) and Charity (20) his sisters. Fine, at the lord's will. Heriot 6s 8d. Rent 12d. Imp. val. 6s 8d.

Total quit rents	£9 6s 10d
Total improved value	£236 13s 8d

'A RENTALL OF THE SAID MANNOR [omitted]

BOUNDS OF THE MANNOR

This mannor is bounded on the north side with the lands of William Corriston esq., on the south side with the lands of William Courtney gent., on the east with the way that leadeth from Duxpoole to St Mellion, and on the west with the highway that leadeth from Deanes Bridge [Dean's Bridge in Pillaton and Botus Fleming] to High Kernicke [Kernock].'

CUSTOMS OF THE MANOR

1. Two law courts and two 'by' courts held yearly. No tenant is to sue another out of the courts for any matter that is determinable in them.
2. Tenants are to maintain their tenements and houses in repair.
3. Timber may be cut for necessary repairs with the Steward's permission.
4. On the death of any tenant his executors are to hold the tenement until the Michaelmas following. If no executors have been appointed, the next heir is to hold. A heriot is payable on each death and 20s as a farliew on each alienation. This amounts with perquisites to 20s yearly.
5. Tenants owe suit of mill.
6. Tenants are to serve as reeve.

ABSTRACT

Rents of assize and perquisites of court		£1	3s	3d
Rents of copyhold tenants		£9	3s	7d
	Total	£10	6s	10d
Improved value of copyhold land		£236	13s	8d

'This is a true and exact survey . . . [sd].'

23   MANOR OF LISKEARD

DCO S/5; PRO E 317 (C)/25. The manor was essentially the parish of Liskeard, with the exception of the town, which was an incorporated borough. The castle of Liskeard, which lay within the town, was however part of the manor. The Manor of Liskeard was one of the ancient possessions of the Duchy.

'A Survey of the Mannor of Liskerett alias Liskerd . . . retorned [7 December 1649].

The Mannor or Mansion house was heretofore the Castle which is much ruined and in decay, the materialls about it being not worth the takeing downe. And it is now in the possession of one John Harris esq. whoe holds it at the will of the Lord as will hereafter more plainely appeare.

The scite of the said Castle consisteth of ninety sixe pearches of land within the ruined walls thereof, within which walls there now standeth one old house comonly used for scholehouse, where alsoe the Courte is usually kept for the said Mannor. And it is bounded on the east with certeine lands belonginge to the tennants of the said Mannor, on the south with the lane leadeing out of the towne of Liskerd unto the church, on the west side with a

streete comonly knowen by the name of Prick Streete, and on the northside
with a lane leadeing out of the said towne into certeine grounds neare
adioyning.

There is alsoe one garden conteyning eight pearches and lyeth on the west
side of the said castle and is enclosed with a stone wall which said scite and
garden is at the disposall of the lord and is worth p.a. £3.

DEMEANES

The demeasnese belonging to the lord of this Mannor is in lease and held by
severall persons as followeth:

Sir Warwicke Heale kt by lease of 15 June 1619, 'all those tenements houses,
buildings, edifices, lands, meadowes, feedeings, pastures grounds, fishings
. . . scituate . . . within . . . the scite of the late disparked Parke of Liskerrett
. . . comonly called . . . Lodge Parke alias New Parke' for 99 years, on lives
of Dame Margarett Hele (dec.) w. of Sir Warwicke H., John Hele (dec.) s.
of Sir Francis Hele kt, and Warwicke Hele (37) s. of George H. gent. Rent
£20. Exceptions, etc. 'all mines and quarries . . . with liberty of ingresse,
egresse, regress and passage from time to time . . . for and concerneing the
said mines and quarries, and the digging, carrying, useing and disposeing
thereof.'

Sir Warwicke Heale has for £400 'all timber trees and all kinde of woodes in
and upon the premisses with liberty . . . to fell, roote up dispose of and carry
away the same.'

Md. He is 'to keep all buildings in good repair' as well as ways, hedges,
ditches. He is not 'to eare or plough up any of the land above the space of
foure yeares and then to let it rest five yeares. Neither is he to let alien, sell or
assigne the premisses or any parcell thereof for longer tyme then three
yeares without speciall lycence or consent first had or obtayned in writeing.

There is now on the premisses one messuage or house comonly knowne by
the name of Lodge House, which is very much in decay and consisteth of
one hall and three other roomes below staires. Over the said hall there is one
chamber and over the other roomes there is three little lofts. Opposite the
said house there is one kitchin and a roome used for a brewhouse, one old
ruined stable, one large barne and other out houses, alsoe one garden and
one orchard, the scite whereof doth conteyne by estimacon one acre.

All the foresaid premissès are within one hedge, noe other ground intermix-
ing, and lieth in the parish of Liskerett . . . within the Mannor aforesaid,
and is thus bounded vizt from the Lodge Gate by a lane that leades to a
bridge called Trussells Bridge [Trussell Bridge] on the east and from thence
by the lands late John Markes and Jonathan Rashleys esq. on the southside;
from thence by the lands of Richard Bayly and the lane leadeing from Duloe
towards Bosent neare to the Beaton House on the west side; from thence by
divers closes belonging to the customary tennants of the said Mannor to the
grounds belonging to Bodnell [Boduel] and Newhouse [*id.*] and soe to the
water running from Lamelin [Lamellion] Bridge on the north west, and
from thence by Lamellian grounds and the lane that leadeth from thence to
the Lodge Gate on the north and east. All which lands with the scite of the
foresaid house conteynes in the whole by admensuracon [580] acres. And it
is worth at an improved value besides the present rent' p.a. £90.

Walter Hele esq., executor of Sir William Hele is in possession.

WOODS IN LEASE

John Cunliffe gent. of London, by L.P. of 20 Feb. 1628, woods called Highwoode of 32 ac.; Lady Parke Wood of 22 ac.; Doble boys [Doublebois] Wood of 45 ac.; Connings Wood of 26 ac. Term 31 years. Rent: for Highwood, 27s; for the rest, £3 6s. Total £4 13s. Exceptions; all timber trees, saplins and oak fit for timber and sufficient staddels in every acre, according to the statute.

Md. The lessee may cut only once in ten years 'and that onely when the woodes ought to be cutt or fallen, and upon every such cutting or fallinge are to leave sufficient standells in every acre of woode ground accordinge to the Statute, and after such cutting are to fence the same with mounds and hedges and to preserve the said woodes from biteings, treadings and other hurt by beasts which might hurt or hinder the groweth of the woodes or springs thereof.' Thomas Avery, by assignment of 15 May 1631 has Lady Parke and Connings Woods for remainder of term at a rent of 33s. Value at the expiry of the lease p.a. £6.

Hugh Abraham, by assignment of 31 Oct. 1635 has High Woode at a rent of 27s. Value at expiry of the lease £4. The said Hugh has not paid the rent for the last 3 years 'whereby we conceave the assignement to be void and the premisses to be in hand.'

Nicholas Grosse claims Dobleboys Wood by assignment (not produced) from John Cunliffe, at a rent of 33s. Its improved value £5 2s 6d.

Thomas Major gent. of London, by L.P. of 8 June 1642 has a coppice wood called Cleaver Woodes, of 32 ac., and the coppice wood called Knilly Wood, of 8 ac. Term 31 years. Rent 12s. Exceptions: 'out of the said graunt all timber trees, sapplins fitt for timber and also sufficient staddells on every acre . . . accordinge to the Statute.'

Premises assigned 20 Jan. 1644 to Richard Langford of Liskeard for remainder of term. Their improved value £4 16s.

FREE-HOLDERS WITHIN THE MANNOR

The feoffees of the parish of Liskerett, ½ ac. C. in Lamitton alias Lansetton [Lametton in St Keyne]. Rent 3s 10d.

Walter Hele esq., heirs of Henry Beckett and Galfride Clerke, ½ ac. C. called Lowisland, 2s; *id.*, a water leat near Heathisland, 1s 8d; *id.*, a piece of land called Sanctuary, 2d; James Markes gent. and Hunt Greenewood, a piece of land called Flower Croft in Longbinhay, once David Poulestoughs, 6d; *id.*, heirs of Thomas Cooke mercht, Richard Hunkin and John Beere gent., 1 farl. 'in one peece called Piperland', 8s 6d; Thomas Fudge, a garden there, 6d; John Vosper of Redruts gent., Thomas Piper and Nicholas Bescowen esq., 1½ ac. C. in Kethway, Lentoma [Lantoom in Liskeard] and Loomill [Looemills], 13s; Hunt Greenewood, land called Wadeland, 1d; John Connocke esq., 1 farl. in Hoggesbinghay, 6d; Heirs of Stephen Medhope Clerke, 1 farl. in Hathmoreland, 1s 2d; *id.*, 1 farl., previously John Rescarrockes, 8d; John Harris esq., ½ ac. C. in Lanreast [Lanrest] previouly Richard Kendall, 2s; John Kendall esq., 'fishing of the water of Lowe sometyme Robert Crockheards, 13s 4d; Heirs of Samuell Rolle kt, 1 farl in Pennant, 4s 9d; Heirs of Henry Jennings gent., 'one Bedam Mill of Scowen' [Scawns], 6d; Heirs of John Markes, ½ ac. C. in

Bromboite [Brimboyte], 1s 6d; Thomas Fiudge, land in Kingsmill, 3d; John Connocke esq., land called Hassockes Parke, 6d; Richard Hunkin gent., 'a close near Hassockes land', 9d; John Connocke esq., 1 farl. near Heathland, 1s; _id._, 'holdeth certeine lands neare Hassocks Parke', 9d; **Heirs of Samuell Rolle kt**, of John Kendall esq., [—] Bray and [—] **Code, 3 ac. C.**, 1s 8d and 3 grains of pepper; **Heirs of Samuell Rolle kt**, **land called Fursdowne, 3d**; John Lord Roberts and [—] one Bedam Mill called Lamellyn, 2s; Walter Hele esq., one Bedam Mill called Pinnockes Mill, 6d; John Connocke esq., land called Made Parke neare Heathland, 3d; Peter Speccott esq., Richard Keast and William, Code, ½ ac. C. in Bottkinnowe, 1s 6d; John Connocke, land in Longbinghay, 4d; John Lord Roberts, 2 ac. C. 'by the service of going to meete the Lord of the said Mannor at Polston Bridge'.[1]

The Reeve of the Manor of Rillaton pays to this manor 'for a Molletto',[2] 4s.

Total rents £3 3s 5d and 3 grains of pepper

From Rillaton 4s

CONVENTIONARY TENANTS OF INHERITANCE

John Couch, ten. in Torr with 22 ac. in ½ ac. C. and 2 ac. of waste, formerly William Edwards. Heriot a best beast. Fine 46s 8d. Rent 5s 8d.

Richard Oliver, close called Thorne Parke of 6 ac. Heriot as above. Fine 10s. Rent 3s.

John Russell, ten. in Treheere of 6 ac. in 3 farl. Heriot as above. Fine 47s 2d. Rent 11s 6d.

John Russell sn., ten. with 34 ac. in 1 ac. C. in Treheere. Heriot, as above. Fine 66s 8d. Rent 15s.

'There is one messuage or tenement called Trehidland with 24 acres of land Cornish which is divided into divers partes by surrender. And it is held in free convenconary by the severall persons as followeth':[3]

John Sergeant, 1/8 of a moiety; Christopher Boddy, 1/8 of a moiety, and ¼ of 1/3 (except the two eighth parts of the foresaid moiety); Johan Towssey wid., another third part of ¼ of a 1/3, except the 2/8 part of the foresaid moiety; Elizabeth Towsey, 2 parts of 3 parts of 2/5 and a moiety of a 1/5 part of 2/3 of the appurtenances (except two eighth parts of the foresaid moieties); _id._, 1/5 and a moiety of another fifth part of two-thirds of the appurtenances (except the 2 eighth parts of the foresaid moieties); Peter Short, 1/3 of 2/5 of the appurtenances and a moiety of a fifth part of 2/3 of the appurtenances, 'except the 2 eight partes of the foresaid moieties'; Christopher Boddy, 1/5 of 2/3 of the appurtenances, except the 2 eighth parts of the foresaid moieties, and also a mess. there, for all of which they pay a heriot for every part severally.

Fine 62s. Rent 8s 3d.

'There is one other messuage or tenement in Trehidland and 27 ac. in 1 ac. C. 'likewise devided in divers parts' and held by:

---

[1] Polson Bridge on the River Tamar, which here formed the boundary between Cornwall and Devon.

[2] Molletto not identified.

[3] The Manor of Liskeard is noteworthy for the extreme subdivision of its assessionable tenements, not paralleled on any other manor of the Duchy in south-western England. It would appear that some form of partible inheritance prevailed here.

Thomas Vincent, a moiety and 1/3 of the other moiety, except 1/16; Peter Short, the said 1/16 of a moiety; Margarett Hanncocke, ¼ and 2/3 of a moiety, except the said 1/16; William Jory, 1/30 of 2/3 of a moiety, except the said 1/16; Jane Watts wid., 2/3 of 2/3 of a moiety except the said 1/16 of a moiety and the said 1/30 for all which parts they pay: Heriot, as above. Fine 64s. Rent 8s 3d.

Another ten. with a mill called Penquite Mill and 13 ac. in 1 farl., 'likewise devided into severall partes and is by the persons undernamed held in free conventionary by surrender . . .':
John Hoskin, moiety and 1/3 of a quarter; Thomas Hoskin, the other moiety and 1/3 of a ¼; Thomas Vincent, 'onely a fouerth parte'. Heriot, as above 'to be paide by eache of them theire respective partes'. Fine 6s 8d. Rent 14s.

John Harris esq., in his own right, ten. called Stearte and 26 ac. in ½ ac. C. Heriot, a s above. Rent 52s 10d. Rent 8s.

Henry Marke, ten. called Bromboite and 30 ac. in ½ ac. C. Heriot, as above. Fine 40s. Rent 9s.

Margarett Cowling wid., ten. in Trevelmond [*id.*] and 46 ac. in 3 farl. Heriot, as above. Fine 53s 4d. Rent 11s.

id., another ten. there and 34 ac. in ½ ac. C. Heriot, as above. Fine 31s 8d. Rent 5s.

Arthur Manaton gent., ten. in Trevelmond and 19 ac. in ½ ac. C. Heriot, as above. Fine 27s 11d. Rent 3s 4d.

John Cowling, in his own right, ten. there and 19 ac. in ½ ac. C. heriot, as above. Fine 27s 11d. Rent 3s 4d.

'There is in Trevelmond . . . one other ten. and 19 ac. in ½ ac. C. which is devided into severall partes and is held by severall persons':
Thomas Cowling, moiety of ¾ of a third; Richard Bickley, the other moiety of ¾ of a third; Thomas Cowling, ¼ of a third; Thomas Finch, in right of his wife, moiety of ¾ of another third; *id.*, as above, another moiety of ¾ of the said third; Anthony Manaton cler., ¼ of a third; John Bickton, in the right of his w., 2/3 of a moiety of a third; Reginald Cole, 1/3 of a moiety of said three parts; Digory Eadgcombe, ¼ of said 3 parts; Anthony Swigg, in right of his w., moiety of 4 parts of said 3 parts; *id.*, another moiety of 4 parts of the said 3 parts.
Heriot a best beast to be paid by each. Fine 35s 4d. Rent 8s.

Another mess. in Trevelmond and 19 ac. in ½ ac. C. 'devided into like severall partes as aforesaid and held by the forementioned Thomas Cowling, Richard Bickley and the rest in free convenconary by surrender'. Heriot a best beast for each part. Fine 46s 8d. Rent 8s.

Another mess. there and 11 ac. in 1/6 ac. C. divided similarly. Heriot, as above. Fine 13s. Rent 3s 4d.

Another mess. there and 23 ac. in ½ ac. C. divided similarly. Heriot, as above. Fine 13s. Rent 4s 8d.

John Cowlinge, in his own right, a corn mill in Trevelmond called Trevelmond Mill. Heriot, as above. Fine 6s 8d. Rent 10s.

Magarett Cowling, mess. and 14 ac. in 1 farl.; heriot as above. Fine 19s 8d. Rent 5s.

'There is alsoe a pasture of heathland called Cliver in the wood of the Lord, divided by surrender into divers partes' and held by:
Thomas Cowling, moiety of a third; Anthony Swig, in right of his w., moiety of a moiety of a third; Richard Bickley, another moiety of a moiety of the said third; Thomas Finch, in right of his w., moiety of a third, and another moiety of the same; John Bickton, in right of his w., another moiety of a third; Digory Eadgcombe, ¼ of said third; Anthony Swigg, in right of his w., another moiety of ¼ of said third; *id.*, another moiety of ¼ of said third. Fine 1s. Rent 4s.

Margarett Cowling wid., 15 ac. of waste, previously William Grevill's and then Henry Gartha's. Fine 4s. Rent 4s.

Mess. in Knilly and 28 ac. with pasture of a wood called Knilly Wood, divided by surrender and held by:
Roger Wills, moiety and ¼; Thomas Hoskin, moiety of ¼; John Hoskin, moiety of a ¼. Heriot a best beast from each. Fine 30s. Rent 4s 6d.

A ten. in Landazer [Landazzard] and 30 ac. in ½ ac. C. divided into parts by surrender and held by:
Dorothy Hore, ¼; John Tipper, third of ¼ of a moiety, except a 1/15; *id.*, 1/15 and ¾ of a moiety; William Byland jn., 1/8 of a moiety; William Byland sn., 1/8 of a moiety; Thomas Hancocke, ¼. Heriot as above. Fine 44s 7d. Rent 6s 8d.

Thomas Mounce gent., 7 ac. 2 rods in ½ ac. C. in Luxcroft. Heriot as above. Fine 60s. Rent 2s.

There are 7 ac. 2 rods and 1/20 of a rood in 1 farl. in Luxcroft divided and held:
John Hill, a moiety; John Carpenter, in right of his w., 2/3 of a moiety; Richard Markes, in right of his w., 1/3 of a moiety. Heriot as above. Fine £4 2s. Rent 2s.

There are 4 ac. and a rood 'in a certeine croft called Whiteland', divided as follows:
Theodore Bennett, a moiety; Francis Hodge, in right of his w., the other moiety. Heriot as above. Fine £1 19s. Rent 2s.

The same persons hold an acre in a waste called Northwoode. Fine nil. Rent 2s.

John Crabb, 16 ac. in 1 farl. in Whiteley. Heriot as above. Fine £3 1s 11d. Rent 3s.

James Marke gent., 15 ac. in 1 farl. Heriot as above. Fine £3 1s 11d. Rent 3s.

Edward Bowell esq. in right of his w., 12 ac. in 2 parts of ½ ac. C. in Heathland near Lamellyn. Heriot as above. Fine £2 17s 9d. Rent 5s 1d.

id., 6 ac. in ½ ac. C. No heriot. Fine £1 10s 9d. Rent 2s 6d.

Philip Trenaman: 'one peece of land English in a certeine garden called Whiteash' in Hidland. Heriot as above. Fine 1s. Rent 1s.

A mess. in Tempello and 20 ac. in ½ ac. C. divided:
Dorothy Cloake wid., ¾; John Harris esq., ¼. Heriot as above. Fine £2 12s. Rent 6s 8d.

A mess. there and 24 ac. in ½ ac. C. divided:
Dorothy Cloake, a moiety; John Harris esq., the other moiety. Fine £2 8s. Rent 6s 8d.

Henry Lawrence, by surr. a piece of waste called Blicke 'nigh the old gate there and lying betweene the comon highway leadeing towards the north and on the south and nigh to one parte leadeing towards the west'. Heriot as above. Fine nil. Rent 3d.

A mess. in Tremabe West and 32 ac. in ½ ac. C. divided:
John Marke s. of Phillip Marke in right of his w., moiety; Philip Marke sn., the other moiety. Heriot as above. Fine £1 11s 8d. Rent 4s 5d.

Mess. in Tremabe West and 32 ac. in ½ ac. C. divided:
Henry Lawrence, moiety of 1/8; Philip Benninge, 1/8; John Roos, moiety of ¼; John Bickton, in right of his w., ¼; John Roos, moiety of ¼; Phillip Marke jn., moiety of ¼; John Howsey, 1/8 and 1/16. Heriot as above. Fine £2 4s 10d. Rent 5s.

Robert Hickes, moiety of a mess. and 60 ac. in Tremabe. Heriot as above. Fine £1 15s 6d. Rent 2s 10d.

The other part of the said mess. and 20 ac. are divided:
Jane Langford wid., a moiety and the other moiety of the mess. aforesaid [sic]; Robert Hickes, the other moiety. Heriot as above. Fine £1 15s 6d. Rent 2s 10d.

Mess. in Leane and 42 ac. in 1 ac. C. divided:
Thomas Wills, a moiety; John Jane, moiety except 1/6 of a moiety; Johan Burrell wid., 1/6 of a moiety. Heriot as above. Fine £1 18s 7d. Rent 15s.

John Jane, 1 ac. 'in one peece of land in Clicker [Clicker in Menheniot] neare the Lewland'. Heriot as above. Fine nil. Rent 3d.

Mess. in Leane and 69 ac. in 1½ ac. C. divided:
Peter Nottle, the whole except 1/20 and 1/8; Philip Russell, 1/20; John Couch, 1/8. Heriot as above. Fine £1 11s. Rent 15s.

Mess. in Fursdowne and 27 ac. in 3 farl. divided:
William Wills, ¾ except one thirtieth; Thomas Wills, the said thirtieth of three-quarters; Beniamin Vincent, moiety of a ¼; Philip Russell, moiety of ¼. Heriot as above. Fine £2 0s 3d. Rent 9s 9d.

Mess. in Dobleboys [Doublebois] and 34 ac. in ½ ac. C. divided:
Dorcas Coyler, a moiety; John Prinn, the other moiety. Heriot as above. Fine £2 6s 6d. Rent 7s.

Mess. and 30 ac. in Doblebois divided:
Wilmott Robins wid., a moiety; John Quoyler, the other moiety. Heriot as above. Fine £1 14s 6d. Rent 5s 2d.

Another mess. there and 126 ac. divided:
Johan Scobel wid., 2 mess. [sic] and 84 ac.; Nicholas Grosse gent., a mess. and 42 ac. except 1/5 of the said mess.; Hugh Colmer and Elizabeth Grosse, 1/5 of said mess. Heriot as above. Fine nil. Rent £1 10s.
Also 65 ac. in 1 ac. C. divided:
William Grosse, ten. and 32 ac.; Nicholas Grosse, 33 ac. Heriot as above. Fine 16s. Rent 16s 6d.

Richard Robbins, mess. and 28 ac. in Twywalwood peece [mgl. note: 'in Doblebois']. Heriot as above. Fine £1 6s 8d. Rent 3s 4d.

Mess. in Penhale [*id.* in Liskeard] and 39 ac. in ½ ac. C. divided:
John Cole, in right of his w., 2/3; John Bickton, 1/3. Heriot as above. Fine £3 4s. Rent 5s 2d.

Jane Parkin wid., a pasture called Redmore. Heriot as above. Fine nil. Rent 2s.

William Berry, mess. and 16 ac. in 1 farl. in Well. Heriot as above. Fine £5. Rent 12s.

id., mess. and 21 ac. in ½ ac. C. in Well. Heriot as above. Fine nil. Rent 2s 10d.

John Bickton gent., in right of his w., mess. and 18 ac. in ½ ac. C. in Slad [Slade]. Heriot as above. Fine £1 1s, Rent 3s.

James Marke gent., mess. and 31 ac. in ½ ac. C. in Woodehill. Heriot as above. Fine £1 12s 4d. Rent 2s 8d.

Mess. and 30 ac. in ½ ac. C. called Old Parke divided:
James Marke gent., moiety and 1/8; John Crabb, ¼ and 1/8. Heriot as above. Fine £2 5s 6d. Rent 10s 1d.

Mess. and 30 ac. divided in Old Parke:
Henry Hicks, ¼ except a 1/5 of 4 parts; Henry Lawrence, said fifth of 4 parts; John Crabb, ¼ except ¼ of a fourth part;[4] William Hobb, ¼ of a fourth; John Crabb, 1/8 of a moiety; Sampson Kitt, ¼ and 1/8 of a moiety. Heriot as above. Fine £1 12s 8d. Rent 10s 1d.

Mess. and 30 ac. in Old Parke divided:
James Markes gent., a moiety; John Crabb, a fourth; Thomas Avery, 2/3 of a quarter; John Hunter gent., 1/3 of a quarter. Heriot as above. Fine £1 12s 6d. Rent 10s 1d.

Another mess. there and 30 ac. divided:
James Markes, ¼; John Crabb, ¼ except 1/15 of a fourth; Henry Lawrence, the said 1/15; John Rundell, a moiety. Heriot as above. Fine £1 16s 6d. Rent 10s 1d.

---

[4] The text (DCO) gives 'except a fouerth a fouerth of a fouerth parte'.

Mess. in Benetheway [Beneathway in Liskeard] and 18 ac. in $\frac{1}{2}$ ac. C. divided:[5]
John Score, a moiety of 2 parts of 3 parts; Richard Score, moiety of 2/3 except 1/8; Wilmott Robbins wid., 1/8 of the moiety of said 2/3; John Coyler, 1/3. Heriot as above. Fine £2 2s 5d. Rent 3s 4d.

Another mess. there called Hoggeswell alias Doblewell [Dobwalls] and 23 ac. in $\frac{1}{2}$ ac. C. and 4 ac. in $\frac{1}{2}$ ac. C. and 4 ac. in 1/9 farl.
Divided: Peter Browne, all except 1/5; Mathew Antrum, the said 1/5. Heriot as above. Fine £1 6s 8d. Rent 3s 4d.

Mess. and 28 ac. there in $\frac{1}{2}$ ac. C. divided:
Thomas Cole, a moiety; Anthony Buckler sn. and Anthony B. jn., other moiety. Heriot as above. Fine £2 1s. Rent 3s 4d.

There is a piece of waste of 12 ac. in 1 Landyoke called Goensparke divided:
John Harvey, a fourth; Christopher Moore, a fourth; Jane Parkin wid., a moiety. Heriot as above. Fine 2s. Rent 4s 6d.

John Anstice, mess. called Trembrass [Trembraze] and 26 ac. 3 roods in $\frac{1}{2}$ ac. C. Heriot as above. Fine £2 10s 9d. Rent 8s 6d.

Thomas Mounce gent., Robert Hicks and Sampson Tupper, mess. and 39 ac. in $\frac{1}{2}$ ac. C. in Trembrasse. Heriot as above. Fine £2 14s 11d. Rent 8s 6d.

id., 1 ac. waste called Troys Putt. No heriot. Fine 1s. Rent 1s.

Mess. in Trembrass and 29 ac. in $\frac{1}{2}$ ac. C. divided:
Walter Austice, all except 1/8; Richard Thorne, the said 1/8. Heriot as above. Fine £3 14s 3d. Rent 5s 4d.

John Bickton in right of his w., $4\frac{1}{2}$ ac. C. in Heath. Heriot as above. Fine 10s. Rent 1s.

Thomas Lucas, mess. and 26 ac. in $\frac{1}{2}$ ac. C. called Little Heath. Heriot as above. Fine £1 6s 6d. Rent 5s 4d.

Mess. in Rosenune [*id.* in Liskeard] and 24 ac. and 3 parts of a rood in 3 farl. C. divided:
Walter Pookey and Jane Pookey, 1/5 of a moiety; George Vuch in right of his w., residue. Heriot as above. Fine £3 8s 2d. Rent 6s.

Another mess. there and 32 ac. in 3 farl. C. divided:
Rosea Vuch wid., $\frac{3}{4}$; John Russell and Richard Parkin, $\frac{1}{4}$. Heriot as before. Fine £2 9s 2d. Rent 6s.

Another mess. there and 26 ac. divided:
Robert Newton, a moiety; Walter Pookey, a moiety. Heriot as above. Fine £2 6s. Rent 8s.

There are 16 ac. in Roseland subtus Highwood divided into 2 equal parts:
Edward Viwell [Vowell in rental] in right of his w., and John Tipp, a moiety each. Heriot as above. Fine 4s. Rent 3s.

Thomas Mounce gent., Robert Hicks and Sampson Tipp, mess. and 29 ac.

---

[5] This very awkwardly phrased division can be written:
$\frac{1}{3} + [\frac{1}{4} - \frac{1}{4}(\frac{1}{4})] + \frac{1}{4}(\frac{1}{4}) + \frac{1}{3}$

in ½ ac. C. called Kastwill alias Castle. Heriot as above. Fine £3 13s 3d. Rent 7s 6d.

There is a mess. called Newhouse [in St Cleer] and 40 ac. of which 21 ac. are waste in ½ ac. C., divided:
Jane Parkin wid., a moiety; Peter Parkin, 2/3 of a moiety; Ezekiell Parkin, 1/3 of a moiety. Hariot as above. Fine 14s. Rent 5s.

Mess. called Bodnell South [South Boduel] and 19 ac. in ½ ac. C. divided:
Nicholas Penquite in right of his w., ¼ of a moiety; Christopher Moone, 2/3 of a moiety; John Henry, a moiety. Heriot as above. Fine £1 1s 11d. Rent 2s 3d.

Thomas Penlyne, mess. and 27 ac. in ½ ac. C. in Bodnell South. Heriot as above. Fine £1 4s 11d. Rent 3s.

A mess. in Bodnell North [North Boduel] and 30 ac. in ½ ac. C. divided:
John Parklin [sic], third of a moiety except a fifth; John Bickton gent. in right of his w., 2/3 of a moiety; John Row, 1/8 of a moiety, except an eighth part; John Gilbert, the said eighth of an eighth; Christopher Moone, a fifth of a moiety; John Parkin, third of a moiety except a fifth part and the eighth of a moiety; Peter Smyth and Sibill his w., 2/3 of a moiety 'with the members belonging to a moiety except a fifth parte and an eighth parte belonginge to the moiety'; Peter Smyth, two-thirds of a moiety of a moiety except a fifth part and an eighth part belonging to a moiety; John Bickton in right of his w., fifth of moiety. Heriot as above. Fine £2 3s 6d. Rent 5s.

Another mess. there and 34 ac. in 3 farl. divided:
Richard Parkin, moiety and an eighth; John Parkin jn., an eighth; Richard Parkin, a fourth. Heriot as above. Fine. £2 0s 3d. Rent 5s.

Mess. in Loo Mill [Looemills] and 16 ac. divided:
John Harris esq., a sixteenth; William Beyle, residue. Heriot as above. Fine £1 10s 4d. Rent 5s.

William Beyle in his own right, mess. and 20 ac. in Looedowne [Looedown in Liskeard]. Heriot as above. Fine 3s 3d. Rent 4s 2½d.

John Bickton gent., in his own right, mess. and 8 ac. of waste in Woodland. Heriot as above. Fine nil. Rent 1s 3d.

Mess. in Trevecker [Trevecca] and 40 ac. in 3 farl. divided:
Sampson Tripper, a moiety; Robert Francis, the other moiety. Heriot as above. Fine £2 17s 6d. Rent 5s 6d.

Another mess. there and 38 ac. in 3 farl. divided:
James Marke gent., a moiety; Thomas Carew, a quarter; Thomas Mounce gent., a quarter. Heriot as above. Fine £2 12s 6d. Rent 5s 4d.

Thomas Mounce gent. in his own right, mess. in Halbathicke [Halbathick] and 22 ac. in 1 farl. No heriot. Fine £2 6s 8d. Rent 7s.

A mess. and 16 ac. in 1 farl. there divided:
John Hancocke sn., a quarter; John Hancocke jn., a quarter; Jane Langford wid., an eighth; Francis Victor gent., in right of his w., an eighth; Robert Hicks, a quarter. Heriot as above. Fine £1 12s 4d. Rent 8s.

'There is 15 acres of land moore called Halbathicke Moore divided by surrender':
Thomas Mounce gent., a quarter; Jane Langford wid., a quarter; James Marker, a quarter; Sampson Tipper, a quarter. Heriot as above. Fine 8s. Rent 1s 3d.

There are 3 ac. 'in one peece of land called Helland divided by surrender':
Bernard Bennicke, all except an eighth; John Mawre, two-thirds of an eighth; Richard Mawre, a third of an eighth. Heriot as above. Fine 7s 8d. Rent 1s 8d.

Mess. called Culverland and 32 ac. in ½ ac. C. divided:
Margery Cole wid., two-thirds; John Cole, a third. Heriot as above. Fine £2 1s. Rent 5s 4d.

Mess. called Poldew [*id.* in Liskeard] and 34 ac. in ½ ac. C. divided:
William Byland sn., a moiety; William Byland jn., a moiety. Heriot as above. Fine 12s. Rent 4s. 4d.

Edward Grosse gent., in his own right, mess. in Treburgie [Treworgey?] and 17 ac. in ½ ac. C. Heriot as above. Fine £1 10s. Rent 4s 4d.

id., mess and 22 ac. there in ½ ac. C. No heriot. Fine £1 11s. Rent 4s 1d.

Lionel Boddy by surr., mess. there and 24 ac. in ½ ac. C. Heriot as above. Fine £1 10s. Rent 3s.

Richard Parkin by surr., pasture of Connigswoode. Heriot as above. Fine 4s Rent 4s.

Edward Vowell esq. in right of his w., pasture of Highwoode with le Blicke. Heriot as above. Fine nil. Rent 2s 3d.

Mess. in Loodowne and 80 ac. divided:
Sampson Lucas, quarter of a moiety; Thomas Lucas, half of a moiety; *id.*, quarter of a moiety; Susanna Trenaman, half of a moiety; William Byland and William B. jn., half of a moiety. Heriot as above. Fine £1. Rent 17s.

19 ac. of wastê there 'by admensuracion' divided into 2 equal parts:
John Tipper, a moiety; John Cole de Culverland, a moiety. Heriot as above. Fine 3s. Rent 4s.

John Bickton in right of his w., mess. in Caduscott [*id.* in St Pinnock] and 27 ac. in ½ ac. C. Heriot as above. Fine £1 12s 7d. Rent 6s 4d.

id. as above, mess. there and 34 ac. in ½ ac. C. Fine £1 1s 8d. Rent 6s 4d.

Beniamin Steede, 15 ac. in Trayland. Heriot as above. Fine 4s 4d. Rent 2s. 6d.

Edward Vowell esq. in right of his w., a corn mill near High Woode. Heriot as above. Fine 6s 8d. Rent 5s.

William Beyle in his own right, mess. in Loodowne and 20 ac. 'of parte of [3] messuages' and 100 ac. of waste. Heriot as above. Fine 3s 4d. Rent 4s 2½d.

35 ac. of waste 'by admesurement' in Colwindowne divided into 2 equal parts by surr.:
John Grills kt in right of his w., a moiety; Anthony Buckler sn. and Anthony B. jn., the other moiety. Heriot as above. Fine 6s. Rent 2s 4d.

35 ac. of waste 'by admeasurement' divided by surr.:
Thomas Cole, a moiety; John Prine, a quarter; Dorcas Vyler, a quarter. Heriot as above. Fine 6s. Rent 2s 4d.

Nicholas Grosse gent., by surr., 2 water mills in Doble boys. No heriot. Fine nil. Rent 10s.

35 ac. of waste 'by admesurement' in Colwin Downe divided:
John Browne sn., a tenth of a moiety; John Browne jn., a tenth of a moiety; Richard Robins, rest of the moiety; Willmot Robins wid.,[6] the other moiety. Heriot as above. Fine 6s. Rent 2s 4d.

'These tennantes hereafter named clame to hold by the same tenure as the convencionary but are not (by some of them) acknowledged to be customary'.

Philip Trenaman claims to hold in free conventionary ½ rood of land C., containing 7 ac. 3 roods 9¼ perches in Liskeard Borough, heretofore Robert Focke's' in whose tyme it fell into the Lord's hand by escheate', now in P.T.'s hand by surr. Heriot, as above. Fine £3 6s 8d. Rent 3s 4d.

Richard Pawlin, as above, a part of a ten. in Liskeard which fell into the Lord's hand by escheat after the d. of Richard Bray Basterd who died without heir; now occupied by said R.P. No fine. Rent 2s.

John Harris esq., at the will of the Lord: 'the herbage as well within as without the Castle of Liskerd with all comodities belonginge to the said castle (except the tenements of the said Mannor). And he is to suffer the tennants of the said Mannor to keepe cortes there and alsoe to make up shooteing butts that the children of the said tennants may shoote there as long and when they please without impeachement.' No fine. Rent 4d.

id., the royalties of the manor that are not customary. Fine 6d. Rent 1s.

'There is a piece of waste called Blicke alias Kildew which lyeth nigh the land late in the tenure of Nicholas Kempe on the south and is bounded with the land late Nicholas Hargotts on the west and with the land of Thomas Jane on the north, which said parcell was of late the said Thomas Janes but is now in the Lords hand.' No fine. Rent 6d.

Two other ten. with a garden; 'the one of them lieth in a streete called Prick Streate heretofore in the occupation of John Beareman which happened into the hands of the late Queene Elizabeth by escheate; the other fell into the hands of the said Queene by the death of Nicholas Morris Basterd for which there was paid to the Lord'. Fine 1s. Rent 6d.

'Where these tenements lye or in whose occupacon they are in wee cannot finde out. But the Reeve is to make good the rent unto the Lord of all the tennants of the Mannor.'

[6] 'Widow' omitted from DCO text.

Total assessionable rents £30 12s 0½d.
Total of fines to be paid in six years [i.e. after each Assessions Court],
£158 13s 11d.

[A Rental of free and conventionary tenants occupies memb. 38–47].

[BOUNDS]
'This Mannor lyeth dispersed and severed into divers partes and places, other Mannors and lands intervening betweene the tenements thereof, by reason whereof wee cannot sett out the distinct lymitts and boundes of the same. But if there happen any encroachement it is usually presented by the respective tennants that are iniured at the next law courtes which are held for the said Mannor by which meanes the same is rectified.'

THE CUSTOMS OF THE SAID MANOR
Tenants are to do their suit and service to the Lord's courts every three weeks.
Customary tenants hold in free conventionary for ever. They are to execute the office of reeve, beadle and tithingman whenever they shall be thereunto elected.
They are 'to take theire land every seventh year' and to pay their fine and new knowledge money over the succeeding years.
Widows have the right to continue to hold their late husband's tenement during their widowhood. The right of primogeniture is maintained.
Customary tenants owe a best beast as a heriot. It is to be seized by the Reeve and to 'be appraised at the next court by two tennants on oath, the which apprizement the said reeve is to pay with other his payments at the next auditt. The lord not being to have the best beast in kinde nor any more than one best beast onely for a herriott althoe such tennant die possessed of divers tenements.
None of the said customary tennants can forfeite or losse his customary estate for any thing done by him but for want of claime which in three sessions (except a feme covert or a person beyond the seas in captivitie) the person so neglecting may be debarred for ever.'
Heriots, amercements, new knowledge money and other perquisites amount on average to £13.

AN ABSTRACT OF THE PRESENT RENTS AND FUTURE IMPROVEMENTS

Rents of assize and perquisites of court	£16 8s 5d
Rents of assessionable lands	£30 12s 0½d
Rents by 'fine certeine', on average	£22 13s 5d
Rents of lands held by lease	£25 13s
Total	£95 9s 10½d[7]
Improvement of the lands and woods let by lease after the expiry of the lease	£129 18s 6d.

'This is an exact survey . . . [sd].'

[7] The last part of this abstract is missing from the DCO text.

24 BOROUGH OF LOSTWITHIEL

DCO S/4; PRO E 317 (C)/26. The borough received its first charter in the late twelfth century from William de Cardinham. His rights over the borough, together with his estates in the neighbourhood of Lostwithiel, were acquired by Richard, Earl of Cornwall, and ultimately passed to the Duchy in 1337. The charter of James I referred to in the text was the last of several granted by the King or Duke.

'A Survey of the borrough of Lostwithiell . . . Retorned 20 February 1649/50.

There is in the said borroughe one old ruined house which was heretofore the Dukes Pallace,[1] with a large hall wherein was used to be kept the Assizes and Sessions for the whole county but now there is onely the walles thereof standing, the scite of which house conteynes by estimaton one acre of land and is reckoned to be worth now to be sould in ready money: £6 13s 4d.

There is alsoe within the said borroughe one Water Mill held by Walter Kendall gent. by vertue of an assignment from Stephen Kendall his father beareing date [18 Aug. 1632], whoe held it by deede indented under the hand and seal of Thomas Caldwell esq. dated [13 Nov. 1629], who had it assigned unto him by like deede from Sir John Walter knight, Sir James Fullerton knight, and Sir Thomas Trevor knight, dated [14 March 1629], whoe had it graunted unto them in trust by the late King by letters pattents dated at Westminster 14 June 1628; to hold for and dureing the terme of thirty and one yeares from the feast of Lady Day before the date of the said letters patente; paying the yearely rent of some of forty shillings to the Receaver of the premisses for the tyme being at the two most usuall feasts of the yeare by even and equall portions, which said mills [sic] is worth at an improved value beside the present rent, p.a.   £5
[Margin] Redd' 40s.

FREE TENNANTES OF THE SAID BORROUGH

John Lord Roberts holdeth freely to him and his heires for ever forty two burgadges and one third parte of a burgadge for which hee paieth p.a.'
     21s 1½d.

Francis Buller esq., 5½ burgages, 17s 4d;   Jonathan Rashley esq., 4 burgages, three-fourths and a twelfth part of a burgage, 2s;   John Arundell esq., 4 burgages, 2s;   Thomas Wood esq., 3 burgages, 21s 6d;   Mr Luxton, 47½ burgages, 23s 9d;   Arthur Harris, 9 burgages, 4s 6d;   Henry Vincent gent., 2 burgages, 1s 1d;   Walter Kendall gent., 20 burgages, 10s;   Joan Couch wid., 2 burgages, 1s;   Thomas Bullock gent., 26 burgages and a third, 13s 1½d;   Thomas Lower esq., 18 burgages, 9s;   Peter Jenkin esq., 10 burgages, 5s;   Walter Kendall gent., 1 burgage, 6d;   Elizabeth Taprell wid., 2 burgages and a half, 1s 3d;   Mr Hullare, 12 burgages, 6s;   Walter Porth, 5 burgages, 2s 6d;   Trevenard Kestle, 2 burgages, 1s;   Francis Scobell, 1½ burgages, 9d;   Philip Wallis gent., ½ burgages, 3d;   George Courtney, 5 burgages, 2s 6d;   Joan **Snelling, 8 burgages,** 4s; Dorothy Barent, 7 **burgages,** 3s 6d; Mr Trethues, 2 burgages, 1s;   Peter Cosins, 1 burgage and a sixth,

[1] See *The Archaeological Journal*, vol. 136 (1979), 203–17.

8d²; George Hodge, 1 burgage, 6d; Robert Moore, ½ burgage,
3d; Nicholas Goodman, ½ burgage and one sixth, 4d.

'The towne paieth for the Torvis [turf], p.a.'	1s 0d
'The towne paieth more for certeine lands p.a.'	13s 1d
Total rents	£8 10s 11½d.

'BOUNDES OF THE SAID BORROUGH

The said borrough of Lostwithiell is bounded on the east with Newbridge,
on the west with Peline [Pelyn in Lanlivery], being the lands of Walter
Kendall esq., on the north with Restormell parke, on the south with Will
Pointe³ ioyninge with the lands of John Skory gent.

Md. the said borrough was made a towne corporate by charter graunted
under the greate seal of England by the late King James dated [21 Sept.
1608], by which the said borrough is to be governed by a Maior and seven
burgesses or aldermen, and alsoe power is given them to elect and choose
two burgesses to sitt every session of Parlyament.

There is to be paid the one halfe of the perquisites of courte ariseing within
the said borrough unto the Lord thereof which will amount unto com.
annis'   20s.

AN ABSTRACT OF THE PRESENT RENTS, FUTURE IMPROVEMENTS
AND OTHER PROFITS OF THE SAID BORROUGH

Rents of assize and perquisites of court		£9 10s 11½d
Rents by lease		£2 0s 0d
	Total	£11 10s 11½d

'The scite of the Palace with the hall valued to be worth in ready money to be paid by the purchaser'.	£6 13s 4d
Improved value of the mill	£5 0s 0d.

'This is an exact survey . . .'

25 MANOR OF MORESK

DCO S/5; PRO E 317 (C)/27. The manor made up the southern part of the parish of St
Clements and included the eastern suburbs of the borough of Truro. It was part of the
ancient demesne of the Duchy.

'A Survey of the Mannor of Moreske . . . Returned 10 May 1650.

There are within the Mannor . . . certeine woodes knowen by the name of
Morreske woodes conteyning by estimacon 46 ac. and are worth com.
an.'   £6 8s.

'The woods groweing thereon and being about 20 yeares groweth and at the
present disposall of the Lord, are valued to be worth ultra reprises' £225

'The timber trees and sapplins alsoe groweing in the said woodes about the
Cockrodes of John Polewheele esq. being in number 580, are valued to be
worth one with the other 4s. per tree . . . in toto £116.

---

² Should be 7d.
³ The name has been lost; possibly Shirehall Moor.

Md. that the said Polewheele claimeth the herbage and weedeings of the said woodes, as alsoe the royalty of takeing birds in the said woodes, with all manner of bootes by vertue of a graunt from Matilde Countesse of Cornewall under the rent hereafter mentioned.

'FREE-TENNANTS OF THE SAID MANNOR

Henry Vincent gent., sonne and heire to Henry Vincent gent., holdeth freely to him and his heires for ever in soccage halfe an acre of land Cornish in Tresimple [Tresemple] within the parish of Clements, conteyninge by estimacon threescore acres of land English,

	Rent	Aide money p.a.
for which he payeth per annum'	1s 0d	3d
John Cooke esq. s. and h. of John C. esq., 'one course of water that runneth to his Corne Mill at Truro'	1s 0d	nil
John Gregor gent. s. and h. of Francis G. gent., ½ ac. C. in Tresimple being 25 ac. E.	1s 0d	6d
Henry Vincent [as above], 1 ac. C. in Tresimple, being 50 ac. E.	2s 6d	1s 0d
Nicholas Cossen gent., ⅓ ac. C. in Nansogge	8d	4d
James Launce gent., s. and h. of John L. ⅔ of ½ ac. C. in Truroevighan, John Parnall, the other third	2s 0d	1s 0d
Heirs of Walter Angollan, 2½ ac. C. in Trenanswithicke [Tresithick ?] in the parish of Eremise [St Erme], being 100 ac. E.	1lb pepper	
James Launce gent. by d. of John Launce gent., moiety of 2 corn mills called Trurovighan [Truro Vean] Mills, heretofore Bennett Browne's and Richard Holland's	6s 0d	
id. [as above], moiety of 2 fulling mills there		2d and 2 capons
id. [as above], moiety of 2 corn mills in Trurovighan with mulcture of the moiety of the tenants of the Manor of Moresk	66s 8d	
Thomas Polewheele, two-thirds of 2 ac. C. in Treworthgan [Treworgan] 'with the liberty of takeing birds in the woodes of Morreske'	5s 0d	1s 0d
id., 2 ac. C. in Polewheele [Polwhele] and Tregantilian	6d	
John Cooke esq. s. and h. of John C. esq., 1 ac. C. in Nansmere [Nancemere in St Clements], being 40 ac. E.	2s 8d	
Grace Pendarves wid., 2 pieces of land called Pound Parke, of 6 ac.	4d	
Hugh Trevanion esq., ⅓ of 2 ac. C. called Penarth [Panarth near Truro] lying neare the streete called Clements streete'	2s 0½d	
id., 1 ac. C. 'lying neare the foresaid streete'	10d	
id., ½ ac. C. there	6d	

	Rent	Aide money p.a.
id., 2 ac. C. in Tregollas [Tregols]	3s 0d	1s 0d
Richard Porter esq. by d. of Richard Porter esq., moiety of 1 ac. C. in Trewethenicke [Trennick in St Clements]; Michael Avery in right of Mary his w. the other third part of the said moiety [sic]	4s 6d	
id., [as above] moiety of 1 ac. C. in Parke; Richard Harris gent., the other moiety	2s 6d	2s 8d
id., [as above] moiety of ½ ac. C. called Nans [Nance Farm in St Clements]; John Chattey, s. and h. of John C. gent., the other moiety	1s 4d	
Charles Trevanion Kt, by d. of Charles T. his f., 1½ ac. C. in Tirris	3s 0d	
William Earl of Salisbury, ½ ac. C. in Morreske called Lambedow alias Lambessow [Lambessow in St Clements], heretofore the Prior of St Michaels [St Michael's Mount]	3s 9½d	
John Cooke esq., s. and h. of John C. esq., 1 ac. E. in Nansmere	1d	
Hugh Trevanion, 1 farl. in Pennarth	8½d	
Richard Porter [as above], moiety of 1 ac. C. in Tresimple; Richard Harris gent., the other moiety	2s 6d	1s 0d
Nicholas Cossen gent., 2 parts of 1 ac. C. in Nansogge	1s 4d	8d
Nicholas Boscawen esq. s. and h. of High B., 1 ac. C. Trewethenicke	2s 6d	1s 0d
Heirs of Anthony Maypowder esq. by d. of Narcissus Maypowder, a mill in Reskaddon alias Tregasowe [Tregassow in St Erme]	6d	
Heirs of the Earl of Oxford, another mill in Tregaveran alias Tregosa [Tregassow in St Erme ?]	6d	
Total of rents of assize and aide money		£6 10s 3½d.

'CONVENTIONARY TENNANTS OF INHERITANCE WITHIN THE SAID MANNOR

James Launce gent. by the death of John Launce gent. in his own proper right holdeth . . . in free Conventionary from seaven yeares to seaven yeares . . . one fouerth parte of all that wast land called Woodland. John Free . . . one moiety, and John Hill in his own proper right . . . the other fouerth parte.' No fine.
Rent 1s 8d.

Susan Painter wid., by the d. of William P. gent., a mess. in Pengarth [Penarth?] and 47 ac. and the moiety of 30 ac. in Cosarth heretofore John Alsull. Fine 1s.
12s 6d.

John Polewheele esq. by surr. of Thomas P. his f., a mess. in Tregorianwartha [Tregurra?] and 12 ac. No fine.
7s 2d

John Chattey gent., by surr. of John C. his f. a mess. in Nans and 18 ac. Fine 13s 4d.
9s 0d

Mary Angollan wid., by surr. of Walter Angollan in her own right,
mess. in Polucan alias Poleskan [Polisken in St Erme] 'with
certeine land thereto belonginge'. Fine 13s 4d   4s 0d

John Barrett, by surr. of John Barrett sen. in his own right, a mess.
and 18 ac. E. in Treworhanvighan [Truro Vean] Fine 14s.   12s 0d

John Hill in his own right, moiety of a messuage and 18 ac. in
Bodrian Jane [Bodrean in St Clements] Jane and Walter Hill,
by surr. of John Hill, the other moiety. No fine.   9s 9d

id. [as above], moiety of a mess. in Bodrian Jane [sic] and 18 ac.;
Walter Hill, by surr. of John Hill, the other moiety. No fine.   8s 0d

id. [as above], moiety of 9 ac. there; Walter Hill [as above], the
other moiety. No fine.   1s 6d

John Polewheele esq., by surr. of Thomas Polewheele, mess. and
lands in Hendrawena [Hendrewena]. No fine.   6s 8d

id. [as above], mess. and 16 ac. in Hendrewena. No fine.   6s 8d

id. [as above], mess. and 16 ac. there. No fine.   6s 8d

Margarett Catcher wid. by d. of William C. gent. her hbd, mess.
and 20 ac. in Moreske. Fine 3s 4d.   11s 0d

William Penrose, by surr. of William P. his f., moiety of a mess.
and 16 ac. in Moreske; Mary Saundry sp., by marriage of Clare
Saundry, the other moiety. No fine.   8s 0d

John Lord Roberts, by d. of Richard Lord Roberts his f.,
a mess. 'and lands thereto belonginge in Moreske'. No fine.   10s 0d

Richard Harris gent. by surr. of Phillip Harris Clerke, a mess.
and 18 ac. in Moreske. No fine.   10s 0d

Margaret Catcher wid. [as above], a mess. there with 'certeine
land belonginge conteyning 20 ac.' No fine.   8s 0d

John Chattey gent. by surr. of John C. gent. his f., piece of land
in Moreske of 20 ac. No fine.   20s 0d

id. [as above], mess. and 20 ac. there. No fine.   14s 0d

id. [as above], Henry Vincent gent. by surr. of Richard Launce;
Honor Gregor wid. by d. of Francis Gregor, and Richard Harris
by surr. of Richard Launce, a piece of land in Morreske of
16 ac. No. fine.   9s 0d

James Launce gent. by marr. of Isabell his m., mess. and 9 ac. in
Tregorawolas [Lower Tregurra in St Clements] lately Stephen
Polewheele. Fine 4s 8d.   6s 0¼d

id. [as above], mess. and 9 ac. there. No fine.   4s 0¼d

id. [as above], mess. and 9 ac. in Tregoravighan [Higher Tregurra].
No fine.   6s 0¼d

John Greenefield, quarter of 3 mess. and 30 ac. in Penhilleck
vighan [Penhellick in St Clements]; John Lord Roberts [as
above], a moiety; John Greenefield, a close called the greate
Close, being the other quarter. Fine 3s 4d.   13s 4d

John Lord Roberts [as above], moiety of a mess. in Chicoye
[Chycoose] and 18 ac. in King Meade; William Tregoninge by
surr. of William T. his f., the other moiety. No fine.   4s 0d

John Lord Roberts [as above], 6 ac. in Fentenwinecke [Higher
Coldrose]. No fine.   1s 8d

id. [as above], 2 ac. in Fentenwinecke. No fine.   1s 0d

James Launce [as above], certain parcels in Nansentres
[Vineyard in Truro] and 16 ac. of waste. Fine 26s 8d.   25s 0d

John Free gent., mess. in Bodrean Tonkin [Tonkyn] and 16 ac. of
waste in Fentengollen and 16 ac. of waste in Gonnenglostennen
[Glasteinan in Truro]. No fine.   17s 0d

James Launce gent. [as above], mess. and 36 ac. in Enis [Enys].
No fine.   16s 0d

John Lord Roberts [as above], one ninth of 93 ac. 'in a Parke
called Coisparke' [Coyse Park, nr Malpas]; Richard Harris by
surr. of Phillip Harris cler., 5 parts in 9 parts divided; the same
Richard Harris by surr. of William Thomas and Mary his w.,
moiety of a ninth; Richard Porter esq. by d. of Richard Porter
esq., the other moiety of the same ninth; Richard Harris by surr.
of Phillips H., a ninth; Mary Saundry sp., moiety of another
ninth; William Penrose his f. [sic], the residue. Fine 12s 0d.   40s 0d

Mary Angollan wid. by surr. of Walter Angollan, a mess. and 20
ac. in Nanyley [Laniley in St Clements]. No fine   9d

id. [as above], mess. and 20 ac. there. No fine.   9d

John Polewheele esq. by surr. of Thomas P. his f., 32 ac. in
Kinlyne. No fine.   1s 0d

id. [as above], 8 ac. in Lostingarth. No fine.   4d

id. [as above], piece of land called Coresawsin [Coresawsin alias
Gwellond] 'nigh Langarth of 6 ac. No fine.   4d

id. [as above], mess. and 16 ac. in Carluricke [Calenick]. Fine 14s. 12s 0d

id. [as above], 6 ac. there. Fine 1s.   1s10d

id. [as above], 19 ac. there. No fine.   7s 6d

id. [as above], 3 ac. there. No fine.   6d

Mary Saundry sp. by marr. of Clare Saundry wid. her m., mess.
and 19 ac. in Penkalveigh [Pencalenick?]. No fine.   5s 0d

id., granted by the Commissioners at the last Assession 'the liberty
of digging slate within the said tenement until the next Assession
onely'. No fine.   2s 0d

John Polewheele esq. [as above], mess. and 15 ac. in Gwellond
[*id.*]. No fine.   7s 6d

Hugh Penhallowe gent. by surr. of John Free gent., mess and
16 ac. in Bodrian Pella. No fine.   3s 4d

id. [as above], mess. and 16 ac. there. No fine.   5s 3d

id. [as above], mess. and 16 ac. there. Fine 2s.   6s 0d

Richard Prideaux kt by d. of Zenobia Prideaux wid., 1 ac. in
Killigorden [Killagorden in St Clements] 'whereon to build a
bloweing house'. No fine.   1s 8d

John Polewheele [as above], 'a peece of land called Woodeland'.
No fine.   1s 8d

John Chattey [as above], mess. and 16 ac. in Penfentyniowe.
Fine 15s.   11s 0d

Mary Saundrie sp. and William Penrose gent., 'one Stone Quarry
called the Quarry of Morreske alias Lees Denis'. No fine.   10s 0d

Honor Gregore wid. by d. of Francis Gregor gent., moiety of a
piece of land in Killigarden, lately Laurence Bray; John

Stephens, by surr. of George Cocke and Agnes his w., other
    moiety. No fine.   4s 0d
John Chattey [as above], piece of land in Killigarden, lately
    Lawrence Bray. No fine.   1s 6d
John Parrett jn. by surr. of John P. his f., mess. and 18 ac. in
    Treworthgan [Treworgan in St Erme]. No fine.   12s 0d
Henry Vincent gent. by surr. of Roger Robins, quarter of a mess.
    and 20 ac. in Penhillecke Muer (except a house, garden and
    barn adjoining) and a quarter 'of that parcell called the
    Towneplaces there'; John Robins by surr. of·John Cocke and
    Agnes his w., the said house, garden and barn; John Chittey,
    moiety of the Towneplaces; John Stephens, residue. Fine 3s.   12s 0d
John Parrett jn. [as above], piece of land in Penfentyniowe alias
    Pennenythrow. No fine.   3s 4d
John Polewheele esq. [as above], mess. and 21 ac. in
    Tregoriawartha. Fine 6d.   19s 0d
Susan Paynter wid. by d. of William Paynter gent. her hbd. mess.
    and 46 ac. in Pennarth Coisarth and a moiety of 30 ac. of waste.
    Fine 1s 0d.   12s 0d
William Allen and Johan his w. by d. of Petornell Harrie, quarter
    of a fulling mill; Mary Saundry sp., residue. No fine.   3s 4d
Thomas Burges gent., garden lying in the Borough of Truro 'in
    a streete called Trurovian'. No fine.   1s 0d
id., a fulling mill 'in Trenanswithicke neare Truro [Trennick].
    No fine.   2d
James Launce gent. by marr. of Isabell Launce his m., 'Two Mills
    under one roofe called Tregartha Mills'. No fine.   6s 0d
John Polewheele esq. by grant of the Commissioners of the last
    Assession for 7 years only, royalty of fishing, fowling, hunting,
    hawking and taking of little birds in the Manor of Moresk.
    Fine 6d.   1s 0d

'BOUNDS OF THE SAID MANNOR

This Mannor cannot be distinctly bounded for that it lyeth dispersed into
divers partes as alsoe because that the lands of other lords doth intervene
and sever the lands of the said Mannor. But if it happen that any incroach-
ments be made upon any parte of the lands belonginge to the said Mannor
the same is usually presented at the Law Courtes held there, by which
meanes all the lands thereof are always kept unaltered.

OFFICERS WITHIN THE SAID MANNOR

There is and allwayes hath bene chosen by the lord of the said Mannor a
Steward whoe is to kepe the Lords courtes of the said Mannor, which are a
Courte Barron every three weekes and a Courte Leete twice a yeare, in
which anything betweene the tennants . . . is determinable except felony
and treason.
Att one of the law courtes kept at Michaeltide . . . is yearely presented by
the homage a fitt person of the customary tennants to be Reeve whoe is to
execute that on oathe, and is to collect the Lord rents and to be accountable

for the same. Alsoe to choose and nominate one of the said tennants to be tithingman for the said Mannor.

The said Reeve is alsoe to seize and collect all such wayfes, estrayes, felons goods, fines, amerciaments, relieffes, herriotts and other perquisites and casualties which heppen dureing his yeare, and which may amount unto com. an.

£3 4s.

Customes of the said Mannor

The free tennants of this Mannor are to doe suite and service twice in the yeare to the Lords courtes (vizt) at two Courtes Leetes and alsoe when any one of them die theire heires are to give a relieffe to the Lord (vizt) twelve shillings sixe pence for every acre of land and soe proporcionably accordinge to the custome of the countrey.

The customary tennants are to doe suite and service to the Lords courtes from three weekes to three weekes, and when any of them die the Lord is to have his best beast in the name of a herriott or the worth of it in money as it shalbe apprised by two men sworne for that purpose. Alsoe his land is to descend to his wife (if he have any) whoe is to enioy it dureinge her widowhood, but upon her marriage or death it descends to the next heire be it male or female, according to the custom of the Mannor.

There ought to be kept every seventh yeare an Assessions . . . for the said Mannor at which all the tennants are bound to be, and there, according to theire custome, to claime or new take theire severall holdings, not that theire former estates doe then determine (it being held to them and theire heires for ever from seven yeares to seaven yeares) but because thereby divers comodities doe accrue to the Lord as:

1.   Thereby the way of payinge the Lords rents and fines are duely kept and observed, which are paid as followeth (vizt) the whole rent and a sixth parte of the fine is paid yearely for the first sixe yeares after every Assessions yeare and on the seventh yeare the rent onely.

2.   Thereby the Lord shall alsoe come to the knowledge of his present Tennants, there being divers surrenders made within the space of seven yeares, the customary tennants haveinge power to sell or surrender any parte (or the whole) of theire respective tenements to whom they please.

3.   For that, by such surrenders there ariseth a new rent to the Lord, which is double the rent and fine of such tenement or parte of tenement soe surrendered; which rent is called newknowledge money, and amounteth unto com. an. 14s.

The tennants of this Mannor pay to the Lord a certeine rent called oldknowledge money, which amounteth unto com. an. 7s.'

[*Continued on next page*]

AN ABSTRACT OF THE PRESENT RENT AND OTHER
PROFITS OF THE SAID MANOR

Rents of assize and perquisites of court	£9 14s 3½d
Rent of conventionary tennants	£22 19s 4d
Fines paid by conventionary tennants within six years of every	
Assession, on average	18s 3¼d
	and a seventh of 5 farthings
Old knowledge money, on average	7s 0d
New knowledge money, on average	14s 0d
Woods value at	£6 8s 0d
Total	£41 0s 10¾d
	and a seventh of five farthings
Timber trees, saplins and underwoods at the Lord's disposal	
valued at	£341

'This is an Exact Survey . . .'

26　MANOR OF NORTH HILL

DCO S/4; PRO E 317 (C)/28. The manor lay in the Parish of North Hill. It was formerly part of the lands of Henry Courtenay, Marquis of Exeter, and was annexed to the Duchy in 1540.

'A Survey of the Mannor of Northhill alias Northpill . . . retorned [5 Dec. 1649].

This Mannor lyeth in the parish of Northhill and consisteth of free-holders and coppyholders. The freeholders hold in free soccage and pay yeerely to the Lord a quitt rent and upon every death or alienacon a relieffe according to the custome of the countery . . . They alsoe owe suite and service to the Lords courtes when they shalbe thereunto called.

The coppyholders hold by coppy of courte rolle and owe suite to the Lords courte ut supra. Alsoe the tenement which is now in the possession of the relict of John Vincent is to execute the office of reeve, whoe is to collect and pay the lords rent.

FREEHOLDERS OF THE SAID MANNOR

John Vincent jn. gent. holdeth freely to him and his heires for ever one messuage with the appurtenances in North Hill, late Henry Chivertons and John Reeds, for which he payeth the Lord p.a. one pound of cumin, et valet 8d.'

James Bond, the same. Rent, a pound of cumin worth 8d;　John Pithin, the same, rent 3s;　John Vincent sen., half a tenement, 1s 3d;　John Luskey, half a ten., 1s 3d;　Heirs of George Kekewick, 3 ten., 1s;　John Spoore, ten. called Bondswall, lately the heirs of John Spedridge, 1s 5d;　Henry Hender and occupiers of the land of Mr Willis, for pasture of Kitchcraft, tenants of the manor of Landreyne, 1s 6d.

Total　　　　9s 5d, and 2 pounds of cumin.

'COPPYHOLDERS OF THE SAID MANNOR

Henry Spoore gent., Thomas S. and George S. sonnes of Richard Spoore esq. deceased hold by coppy of courte rolle beareing date the 28 August 1612 one tenement or close of land with the appurtenances called Newhams conteyning by estimacon 32 acres for and dureing the lives of the said Henry S., Thomas S. and George S. and the longest liver of them successively, paying therefore to the Lord the yeerely rent or some of 5s., and it is worth at an improved value (besides the present rent) p.a. £10 15s.

Henry S. is onely liveing and is aged 50 yeeres. [In margin] Fine at the will of the Lord. Rent 5s.'

John Vincent (dec.) and George V. (53) and Thomas V. (50) his bros; 2 Oct. 1617, mess. and 20 ac. Term: lives. Rent 11s. Fine at the Lord's will. Imp. val. £8 2s.

AN ABSTRACT OF THE PRESENT RENTS AND FUTURE IMPROVEMENTS

Rents of assize and perquisites of court   12s 9d and 2 pounds of cumin.
Rents of copyhold tenants   16s 0d
                        Total   £1 8s 9d and 2 pounds of cumin.
Improved value of the Manor p.a.   £19 13s 0d.

27   MANOR OF PENKNIGHT

DCO S/5; PRO E 317 (C)/29. The manor lay in the parish of Lanlivery. The borough of Penknight was formerly part of the manor, but was granted a charter by the Cardinhams in the thirteenth century. The borough was subsequently merged with the neighbouring borough of Lostwithiel. This was an ancient manor of the Duchy.

'A Survey of the Mannor of Penkneth . . . Retorned 22 February 1649/50.

This mannor was heretofore joined with the borrough of Lostwithiell by writeing made by Edward the Third, and had like priveledges graunted to them as the said borrough had till by King James the borrough of Lost-withiell aforesaid was made a corporation.

There is one coppice wood within the said mannor the herbage whereof the conventionary tennants claime to hold by custome, the woodes and under-woodes whereof are at the Lords disposall, which said woode conteynes by estimacon [blank] acres and is worth p.a.' 12s.

'The wood now groweing thereon and at the present disposall of the Lord, being of three yeares groweth, is now worth to be sould' £1 5s.

There are alsoe groweing in the said wood one hundred and thirty sapplins worth in ready money' £3 10s.

FREE-HOLDERS

'John Lord Roberts holdeth freely to him and his heires for ever one tenement in Polcan [in Lanlivery] for which he paieth' 1s 3d.

Walter Kendall esq., part of Polcan and Penlyne [Pelyn in Lanlivery], 2s 1d; Jonathan Rashleigh esq., ten. called Scracies [Scratious in Lanlivery], 4s 0½d; Burgesses of Lostwithiel, land called Poldew [in

Lanlivery], 4s 1d; Philip Wallis gent., a piece of ground called Newland, 1s 7d; Thomas Bullocke gent., mess. and piece of land near Newland, 2s 7d; John Hellman, ten. in Penhale [in Lanlivery], 7d.

'CONVENTIONARY TENNANTES OF INHERITANCE

	Rent	Stablish money
William Helman holdeth in free conventionary two tenures in Penhale for which he paieth'	15s 8d	2d
Elizabeth Tom, 2 other tenures in Polan Gascon [in margin: Polcan Gascon]	12s 8d	2d
Philip Wallis gent., a tenure in Penkneth	17s 0d	2d
id., a tenure in Penkneth Carhallocke	3s 0d	—
Emlyne Kendall, mess. or ten. in Tarrs	8s 8d	2d
id., 2 mills called Bladiford alias Redford Mill, and Jagouse Mill [in margin: Redford Bridge]	20s 0d	nil

'BOUNDES OF THE MANNOR

The said mannor is bounded on the southward with the lands of Walter Kendall esq.; on the north and west with the lands of John Lord Roberts, and on the east with the borrough of Lostwithiell.'

CUSTOMS OF THE SAID MANOR

1.   An assession Court held every seven years, a Court Leet twice yearly, and a Court Baron every three weeks.

2.   Customary tenants hold 'from seven yeares to seven yeares', and pay their accustomed rents, duties and services.

3.   The widow of a customary tenant continues to hold the tenement during widowhood, but can surrender the same only to the next heir of her late husband. But 'in case that females be heires it cometh to the eldest of them, and is not devided by copecinary. The use of takeing hath tyme out of mind runn in this mannor.'

4.   A heriot is payable on the death of every 'herriottable' tenant, 'and though he die possessed of more than one tenement yet he paieth but one herrriott'. The heriot is to be seized by the reeve, appraised by men sworn for that purpose, and the apprizement paid to the lord. Heriots, together with perquisites of court amount on average to 6s 8d.

5.   No tenant may let his tenement for more than seven yeares, and must be in possession at the next Assession.

6.   Customary tenants who have no freehold elsewhere may not 'be retorned in juries at the Assize or Sessions nor be called either without or within this mannor before the Clerke of the Markett or Judge of the Admiralty'. The tenants are to be 'free from all pontage, passage, tolsarie and coverage in faires and marketts within the County of Cornewall'.

7.   A reeve to be chosen yearly by the hommage, and to collect rents and gather waifes, estrays, etc.

AN ABSTRACT OF THE PRESENT RENTS, FUTURE IMPROVEMENTS
AND OTHER PROFITS OF THE MANOR OF PENKNETH

Rents of assize and perquisites of court	£1 2s	2½d
Rents of conventionary tenants	£3 17s	0d
Stablish money paid by the conventionary tenants		8d
Value of wood ground now in hand	12s	0d
Total	£5 11s	10½d
Wood and saplin now growing and at the lord's disposal	£5.	

'This is an exact survey . . . [Signed].'

28   MANOR OF PENLYNE

DCO S/5; PRO E 317 (C)/30. The manor formed the northern part of the parish of St Winnow. It was one of the ancient manors of the Duchy. It is noteworthy that the word Penlyne does not appear ever to have been a place-name within the manor.

'A Survey of the Mannor of Penlyne . . . retorned 22 February 1649/50.

There is one wood within the said mannor called by the name of Kings Wood conteyning by estimacon fifteene acres, the herbage whereof is held by Walter Kendall esq. in free conventionary, soe that the Lord hath onely the cutting of the wood which is now about twenty yeares groweth. And the improved value thereof (being set out by lease for yeares) is worth . . . p.a. £3 15s.
The wood now groweing thereon and ready to be fallen is worth in present money £3 15s.

FREEHOLDERS

Richard Simons gent. holdeth freely to him and his heires for ever one messuage and one acre of land Cornish in Possemaken [Bosmaugan in St Winnow] for which he paieth to the Lord p.a. 3d.
John Lord Roberts, 7ac. C. in Polscoth [Polscoe in St Winnow], 1s 9d; Warwicke Lord Mohun, 1ac. C. in Polscoth [Polscoe], 4s; Thomas Lower, 1 ac. C. in Polscoth, 7s 3d; *id.*, 1 farl. in Bridgend [in Lostwithiel], 1 pound of pepper; John Lord Roberts, 4 ac. of land which 'were exchanged for a certeine mill, millpoole and close lying in the borrough of Penkneth', 3s.

'CONVENTIONARY TENNANTS OF INHERITANCE

John Bedford. holdeth in free conventionary one water mill in Polscoth for which he paieth' p.a.   8s 6d.
John Harris, in right of his w., ten. in Polscoth, 7s 4d; *id.*, another ten. in Polscoth, 5s 9d; John Moone, in right of his w., ten. in Polscoth, 8s 3d; John Harris, in right of his w., another ten. in Polscoth, 5s; Edward Reede, mess. or ten. called Poolebargaine [Polmaugan in St Winnow], 6s 9d; Hugh Rowe, in right of his w., mess. or ten. in Penlyne, 7s 3d; William Couch, piece of land called Lowersland, 2d; Warwicke Lord Mohun, 2 closes called Skracies, 8s 6d; *id.*, certain land,

13s 4d;   John Taprell, a piece of land, 5s;   William Couch, a close, 4s;   Thomas Snelling, a close by Harts, 4s;   Walter Kendall gent., herbage of Kings Wood, 6d.
All the tenants hold certain commons paying, 3s.

'There is one peece of ground within the said mannor called Peakes Meadow conteyning about three yards of land which hath beene tyme out of mynde held in free conventionary by the tennants thereof, and for which the tennant paid a yeerely rent and was to execute the office of reeve, beedle and tithingman within the mannor when he shold be thereunto chosen. But about foure yeares since (as we are informed on oathe) one Edward Hearle hath made an entry into it and doth still keep the possession thereof under pretense that it belonged to him as being a parte of the impropriation of St Winnow of which he hath the tithe. The said peece of meadow ground is worth [p.a. 10s]. The present rent usually paid for the same is . . .'   6d.

Customary tenants are not liable for jury duty and are exempt from pontage, etc.
Free tenants pay a relief at the customary rate on death or alienation.
Conventionary tenants pay a best beast as a heriot at death. Heriots with perquisites amount p.a. to 33s 4d.
A reeve is chosen annually to collect rents and gather waifs, estrays, etc., and to be accountable for the same.

'Boundes of the said Mannor

The said mannor is bounded on the east with the lands of Warwicke Lord Mohune, on the north by the lands of Mr Glyne, on the west with the land of John Lord Roberts, and on the south with the lands of Thomas Lower esq.'

Customs of the said Manor

An Assession Court held every seven years, two Courts Leet annually and a Court Baron every three weeks.
The tenants hold from seven years to seven years according to the custom of the manor.
The widow of a customary tenant is to enjoy his tenement during her widowhood, but not to surrender it except to the next heir. If heirs are female the eldest is to inherit. The tenement is not to be divided.
No tenant may let his tenement for more than seven years, and should be in possession of it at the time of the Assession.

An Abstract of the present Rents and other Profits of the Manor of Penlyne

Rents of assize and perquisites of court	£2 9s 7d
	and a pound of pepper
Rents of conventionary tenants	£4 7s 10d
Value of woods 'after the wood is of'	£3 15s 0d
Total rents	£10 7s 5d[1]
Wood is now growing and at the lord's disposal is worth	£3 15s 0d.

'This is an exact survey . . .'

[1] Should be £10 12s 5d.

29 MANOR OF PENMAYNE

DCO S/5; PRO E 317 (C)/31. The manor lay in the western part of the parish of St Minver, known as St Minver Lowlands.[1] It was an ancient manor of the Duchy.

'A Survey of the Mannor of Penmayne alias Polmayne . . . retorned [7 June 1650].

FREE-TENNANTS OF THE SAID MANNOR

The Heires of Charles Roscarrocke hold freely to them and theire heires for ever in soccage certeine lands in Porthquin [Port Quin in St Endellion] for which they pay' p.a.   8½d.
Dennis Rolles esq., land in Trewarthan [Trevathan in St Endellion], 2s 1½d;   Heirs of John Nicoll esq., land in Higher Polaworgan, 3s 6½d;   John Trehane gent., land in Trewortheren [Trewethern in St Kew], 5½d;   Heirs of Carie, land there, 3d;   Heirs of Trefrie cum aliis, land in Trewothoren, 5½d;   Heirs of Escott, land in Trecreege, 6s;   Heirs of Douglas, land in Treswarrowe [Treswarrow in St Endellion], 2s 6d;   John Rowe esq., land in Trewarthan, 2s 1½d.

Total   18s 2d.

'COPPIEHOLDERS OF INHERITANCE

William Rownsevall gent. holdeth to him and his heires and assignes for ever in free convenconary from seven yeares to seven yeares according to the custome of the Mannor one messuage or tenement there with appurtenances for which he paieth p.a.:

	Fine	Rent
	14s 3d	15s
Maud Bilkey wid., mess. or ten.	6s 6d	4s
Humphrie Grey, mess. or ten.	9s	7s
id., part of ten.	6d	10d
William Burke, part of the same ten.	3s	3s
John Stephen, part of the same ten.	1s	4d
Phillip Gladdon, part of the same ten.	6d	2d
John Harris and Julian Harris wid., mess. or ten.	18s 6d	10s 8d
Richard Rowe, part of a ten.	6d	2d
John Stephen jn., part of the same ten.	1s	4d
Samuell Sarre, part of the same ten.	2s	8d
Thomas Sparnak, part of ten.	2s	2s 4d
Phillip Gliddon, part of ten.	6d	2d
William Rownsevall gent., part of ten.	2s	6s 8d
Richard Thomas, part of ten.	3s	2s 6d
Humphrey Lander, part of ten.	6d	2d
William Burte, part of ten.	3s	2s
Constantine Hambley, part of ten.	1s	4d
Edward Harris, part of ten.	1s	4d
William Burte, part of another ten. in Polmeane	1s	4d
Julian and John Kent, part of the same ten.	10s 6d	6s
Richard Thomas, part of the same ten.	12s	4s

[1] See Sir John Maclean, *Parochial and Family History of the Deanery of Trigg Minor*, Vol. III (London, 1879), pp. 44–50.

	Fine	Rent
Elizabeth Lange wid., part of the same ten.	1s	6d
John Gliddon, a ten.	12s	4s
id., moiety of the 'Passage boat over the water to Padstowe'	nil	6s 6d
Digorie Ball, 'the other moiety of the said passage boat'	nil	6s 6d
William Rownsevall, part of a ten. in Polmean	5s	1s 4d
Richard Brabant gent., part of the same ten.	2s	1s
Agas Shole, part of the same ten.	6d	2d
Richard Chevall, part of the same ten.	6d	2d
Richard Thomas, part of the same ten.	1s 6d	3s10d
Edward Harris, part of the same ten.	3s 6d	1s 4d
Constantine Hambley, part of the same ten.	3s 6d	1s 4d
John Hockin, in right of Elizabeth his w., part of the same ten.	nil	3s 1d
John Grey, part of the same ten.	6d	8d

'The reeve of the mannor for the time being paieth for the tennants of the said mannor for spires [rushes], conies [rabbits], chapell, bedleship and aide money' p.a.   31s 4d

Total conventionary rents   £6 9s 1d

Fines on average p.a.   17s 7¼d
and 1/7 of a farthing.

'BOUNDES OF THE MANNOR OF POLMAYNE

The said mannor is bounded on the east, south east and north east with the lands of John Rowe esq., Charles Roscarrock esq. and Lady Jane Carew; on the south with the lands of the Lord Mohun, on the west with the sea, and on the north with the lake called Bie Lake [Brea brook] and Trewint Bridge.'

CUSTOMS OF THE SAID MANOR

Assession courts are to be held every seven years; a court leet twice yearly and a court baron every three weeks. The reeve is to be chosen at one of the courts leet.

Free tenants pay a relief on every death or alienation. Customary tenants pay 13s 4d in lieu of a heriot. Reliefs, heriots, waifs, strays, etc. amount on average to 30s p.a.

The widow of a customary tenant to hold the tenement during widowhood.

'Customary tenants pay on the surrender of a tenement or part thereof 'double the rent and fine . . . which is called New Knowledge money, to be paid within three years after the assessions year held after such surrender', amounting on average to 6s 8d.

ABSTRACT

Rents of assize and perquisites	£2 8s 2d
Rents of customary tenants	£6 9s 1d
Fines paid by customary tenants, on average	17s 7¼d
	and 1/7 of a farthing
New knowledge money, on average	6s 8d
Total	£10 1s 6¼d
	and 1/7 of a farthing

'This is an exact survey . . . [Sd].'

30   MANOR OF PORTHEA

DCO S/4; PRO E 317 (C)/32. The manor lay in part in the borough and parish of St Ives and in part in Manaccan and St Anthony in Meneage parishes, in the Lizard Peninsula. 'Porthea' is an early form of the name St Ives. The lands formerly belonged to Tywardreath Priory and were attached to the Duchy in 1540.

'A Survey of the Mannor of Porthea Prior . . . retorned [2 April 1950].

FREE TENNANTES OF THE SAID MANNOR

John Lord Roberts holdeth freely to him and his heirs for ever in soccage certeine lands in Tregenna [Tregenna in St Ives] for which he paieth p.a. 10s.
Heirs of Porter, lands in Tregenna, 2s 8d;   Sir Charles Trevannion, lands in Bussulsacke alias Keswellack, 2s;   John Hele esq., lands and ten. in St Ives, Penwella and Carwellan, 15s 8d;   *id.*, ten. in St Ives, lately Beare's heirs, 1s;   *id.*, ten. in St Ives, sometime Trewinard's, 6d;   *id.*, ten. in St Ives, sometime George Paine's, 9d;   Thomas Trevuwith, lands in Trevuwith [Trenoweth], Penvegell [Penbeagle in St Ives], Penellow and 4 ten. with 2 mills in Porthea, £4;   Heirs of John Geyrveys, lands in Eglosmere, 1s;   Richard Veale, lands in Eglosmere, 6d;   Alice Phillipps, lands in Eglosmere, 6d;   Thomas Trevuwith, ten. in St Ives, 3d;   James Praed esq., tenements in St Ives, 4s 2d;   *id.*, lands in Hendra [*id.* in St Ives], 1s;   John Lord Roberts, heirs of Nanspean, heirs of Chinowth and heirs of Murth, lands in Carnebelenowe and Chingwele, 6s;   William Keigwin gent., lands in Bussevale [Bussow in St Ives and Towednack], 1s;   Jane Williams, lands in Buscombe [probably near Bussow], 8s;   William Harris esq. and heirs of William Noye, lands in Arthea alias Trereva, 2s 6d;   Willmott Williams and Humphrey Thomas, tenements in St Ives, 1s 6d;   Thomas Stephens, tenements in St Ives, 1s 6d;   John Stephens, tenements in St Ives, 1s 6d;   Thomas Stephens, tenements in St Ives, 9d;   Vernon Browne, tenements in St Ives, 6d;   Pentecost Sist, tenements in St Ives, 6s;   Stephen Tremenheire, tenements in St Ives, 1s 6d;   John Goodall, tenements in St Ives, 2s;   William Pendarves esq., lands in Rescadden [Roscadden in St Anthony in Meneage], 4s;   Heirs of Murth: a grist mill in Manucca [Manaccan], 2s.

Total rents of assize   £7 16s 7d.

LEASEHOLDERS OF THE SAID MANNOR

Sir John Walter, Sir James Fullerton and Sir Thomas Trevor, by L.P. of 14 June 1628, ten. in St Ives, for 31 years. Rent 10s. Imp. val. £5. Lease assigned 17 March 1629 to Thomas Caldwell, who by indenture of 13 Nov. 1629 assigned it to Andrew Phillips of St Ives. A.P. is now dead, leaving the premises to Edward Westcott, his son-in-law who now has possession.

Thomas Sentawbyns, by L.P. of 27 Oct. 1626, mess. and ten. called Skybugo [Skyburrio in Mawgan in Meneage], Daniffe alias Danesse [Dennis] and Milman in the parish of St Anthony in Meneage, in all 24 ac. for 31 years. Rent 22s 4d. Imp. val. £24. Excepted, all great trees, woods, etc. Lease assigned 24 March 1626, a third to Thomas Jenkins dec., whose w. Susan J. now occupies the premises, a third to Edward Moth of Talland, and the other third to Augustine Tresprison.

Md. Parts of two of the tenements, those of Jenkins and Moth, containing about 8 ac. were 'fortified and garrisoned by the late King and is now soe continued by the Parlyament which forte is called the Little Dennis[1] and valued to be worthe before the same was converted to that use three pounds p.a. soe that the same being reprised to the purchaser the foresaid tenements are worth at an improved value besides the rent and reprisall as aforesaid p.a. £21.'

BOUNDS

'The mannor cannot be bounded for that there is one parte thereof lying in St Ives and the other parte in St Anthonys neare Helford Haven being about fifteene miles distant the one from the other.

There hath beene usually kept like courts for the said Mannor at the same time as there are courtes kept for the Mannor of Porthea belonginge to the Marquesse of Winchester, at one of which the tennants thereof are accustomed to bring in their rente and pay it to the Steward or Bayliffe.'

ABSTRACT

Rents of assize and perquisites		£7	16s 7d
Rents of Leasehold tenants		£1	12s 4d
	Total	£9	8s 11d
Improved valued of leasehold lands		£26	0s 0d.

'This is an exact survey . . .'

31   MANOR OF PORTLOOE

DCO S/4; PRO E 317 (C)/33. The manor lay in the parish of Talland, a mile from West Looe, which constituted the separate borough of Portpigham (no. 32). It was formerly part of the lands of Henry Courtenay, Marquis of Exeter, and was attached to the Duchy in 1540.

'A Survey of the Mannor of Portlooe . . . retorned [12 Feb. 1649–50].

FREE-HOLDERS OF THE SAID MANNOR

William Martin esq. holdeth freely to him and his heirs for ever in free soccage certeine lands in Kilme North' [Kilminorth in Talland]. Rent 3s 0d.

Sir John Trelawney kt and Francis Buller esq., lands formerly Winslade's, called Penfite [?]	1s 11d
Heirs of Lord Brookes, lands called Froone [?]	5½d
Heirs of Garrell, lands called Corligham	2s 0d
Mr Ketchwich, lands called Buckenvor	2s 0d
Borough of Port Pigham [West Looe], a close called Pound Parke	5s 0d
Total	14s 4½d.

---

[1] The Little Dennis was an Iron Age fortification on a headland to the south of the entrance to the Helford River. It was fortified for the King by Sir Richard Vivian in 1643, and surrendered to the Parliamentary forces in 1646. See Mary Coate, *Cornwall in the Great Civil War and Interregnum 1642–1660*, Oxford, 1933, pp. 121–4, where it is claimed that the land belonged to the Vivians of Trelowarren. It appears from this survey that the lease was in fact held by the St Aubyns of Clowance.

COPYHOLDERS FOR LIVES WITHIN THE SAID MANOR

Henry Francis (70), by copy of 14 Aug. 1612, ten. in Portlooe of 60 ac. for life. Fine at the will of the lord. Rent £2 0s 7d. Imp. val. £38.
Reversion granted 3 June 1619 to Elizabeth (46), w. of H.F. and Robert F. (30) his s., for lives successively. Fine at the Lord's will. 1 ac. of wood on the premises worth £1.

Francis Lobb (72), Anne (dec.) his w., and Thomas L. (42), s. of Roger L., by copy of 8 April 1616, ten. in Higher Portlooe of 35 ac. for lives. Fine, as above. Rent £1 4s 11d. Imp. val. £22 4s.

John Pope sn. (42), John Pope jn. (dec), and Thomas P., s. of Thomas P., by copy of 8 April 1616, ten. called Woodland alias Wayland of 35 ac. for lives. Fine, as above. Rent £1 0s 7d. Imp. val. £16 10s.

Lodomix Fortescue gent. (dec.), Tristram Couch (64), and Hanaball Couch (38) his s., by copy of 8 April 1616, ten. in Lower Portlooe of 76 ac. for lives. Fine, as above. Rent £2. Imp. val. £44 13s 4d.

William Wills (48) sn., Francis (25) and William (23) his sons, by copy of 20 Oct. 1629, ten. in Higher Portlooe of 55 ac. for lives. Fine, as above. Rent £1 8s 10d. Imp. val. £27 4s.

John Cloake (dec.) of East Looe, Henry C. (50), and Thomas C. (dec.) his sons, by copy of 14 Aug. [—] Chas., ten. in Wayland alias Broadcoke of 30 ac. for lives. Fine, as above. Rent £1 4s 10d. Imp. val. £17 13s.

John Vyan (dec.) and John V. (30) his s., by copy of 19 Jan. 1620, ten. in Portlooe of 76 ac., for lives. Fine, as above. Rent £2. Imp. val. £44 13s. Agnes V. wid. of J.V. has possession during her widowhood. 'She is aged [—].'

Elizabeth Foote (dec.) w. of Henry F., Robert Francis (dec.) her s. and Nicholas Foote s. of Henry and Elizabeth F. (37), by copy of 8 April 1616, ten. in Portlooe of 76 ac., for lives. Fine, as above. Rent £2. Imp. val. £44 13s 4d. Fridiswed Francis (57), relict of Robert F. is in possession.

Robert Francis (dec.), Fredisswed (57) his w. and Pascatius (34) their s., by copy of 8 April 1616, 2 corn mills called Portlooe Mills 'with a course of water and suit of mulcture of all the tennants', for lives. Fine, as above. Rent £1 6s 8d. Imp. val. £6.

John Truscott (dec.), Anthony Deacon (dec.) of Talland and Thomas Cornish (54) of Talland, by copy of 29 Sept. 1620, for lives: 'house called the New Hall with the houses thereunto adjoyning late in the tenure of the said Truscott', a close called the Westhay, the West Orchard, herbers and gardens, a close called the Hempe Parke, a close called the Gratna and a little pasture called the Moore Meadow adjoining the same; pasture called the Greate Meadow alias the Above Towne; a close called the Westmagna Parke; a close called the Midle Parke; a close called the South Combe Park; 'the moiety of the Towne Places and Towne Flores all which . . . are the moiety of a tenement in Wayland known by the name of the Tenement Devided and conteynes' 27 ac. Fine, as above. Rent 13s 7½d. Imp. val. £17 8s. Joan Deacon (55) relict of Anthony D. is in possession during her widowhood.

Richard Parker (dec.) and Methusala P. (58) his s., by copy of 29 Sept. 1620: 'one old hall and other roomes to the same adioyning, late in the possession of the aid Richard, one barne and a hey mow, one close called the Meadhay, the Eastgarden or herber, one close called the Well Parke, one other close called Woodland Parke; two other closes called the Combe Woode; a close called the East Magna Parke; one little pasture near the founteine or well there; one close called the North Combe Parke and a moiety of a close called the Menaland; a backe house and the moiety of the Towne Places and Towne Flores, all being the moiety of the tenement of Wayland,' in all 27 ac. Term, for lives. Fine, as above. Rent 13s 7½d. Imp. val. £17 8s. Reversion granted to Nalie Parker (48) w. of Methusala, 16 Sept. 1622.

A RENTAL OF THE MANOR [omitted]

BOUNDS

'The said Mannor of Portlooe is thus bounded: on the east side with the lands belonginge to the Burroughe of Port Pigham alias West Looe; on the south side the sea is the boundes; on the west with the Mannor of Trelawney [Trelawne in Pelynt] being the lands of Sir John Trelawney kt, and on the north with the lands of Mr Marten, one of the free tennants of this Mannor'.

CUSTOMS OF THE SAID MANOR

Two courts baron and two courts leet are held yearly. At one of them a reeve is chosen from among the copyholders. Free tenants pay a relief on every death or alienation. Copyholders, except those who hold mills, pay a heriot. The widow of a copyhold tenant may continue to hold her late husband's tenement during her widowhood.

Tenants who hold the three tenements, formerly the Barton of the Manor 'do pay to the Castle of Domhevell [Dunheved] 12s for which they are to be tolle free in all faires and markets of Cornewall and Devon, but have not of late enioyed that priviledge.'

AN ABSTRACT OF THE PRESENT RENTS AND FUTURE
IMPROVEMENTS OF THE SAID MANOR

Rents of assize and perquisites		£4 7s 8½d
Rents of copyhold tenants		£15 12s 8d
	Total	£20 0s 4½d
Improved value of copyhold land		£296 7s 0d
Woods reserved to the Lord are worth		£1 0s 0d

'This is an exact survey . . . [Sd].'

32 BOROUGH OF PORTPIGHAM

DCO S/4; PRO E 317 (C)/34. Portpigham, literally the 'little port', is an old name for the town of East Looe. It was formerly part of the lands of Henry Courtenay, Marquis of Exeter, and was attached to the Duchy in 1540.

'A Survey of the Borroughe of Portpigham alias Westlooe . . . retorned [12 Feb. 1649/50].

This Borroughe lyeth within the parish of Talland and was formerly part of the Mannor of Portlooe, but by the Earls of Devonshire it was made a borough towne. And afterwards it was made a towne corporate by charter granted unto them by Queene Elizabeth whereby power is given to them to chose one of the burgesses yeerely to be Mayor. And alsoe to choose two burgesses to sitt in Parlyament every session with many other priveledges therein conteyned.
The tennants of the Borough are all of them free tennants soe that there doth accrue to the Lord from the said free tennants the hie rents onely. And on every death or alienacion a relieffe which is double the rent, which is paid to the Lord for such messuage or burgage that is alienated.

FREE TENNANTS

Richard Tregenno holdeth freely to him and his heirs for ever one messuage or burgage for which he payeth a quitt rent   6d.'
Heirs of Wilcocke, Richard Short and Joan Francis, 3 mess.   7s 6d
Richard Buller esq., Sir John Trelawney kt and the heirs of Winslade, 2 mess.   6d
Heirs of Philip Dale, Walter White and John Hicks, 1 mess.   6d
John Sharpe and the heirs of Norton, 2 mess.   1s 4d
John Sharpe and the heirs of Colling, 2 mess,   2s 0d
John Sharpe and the heirs of Roothe, 2 mess.   3d
John Sharpe and Richard Tregane, 2 mess.   3d
John Sharpe, Henry Francis and the heirs of Poanit, 1 mess.   3d
John Hodges and the heirs of Vivian, 2 mess.   6d
Heirs of Edward Whitte, Sir Bernard Greenevile and Thomas Tente, 1 mess.   3½d
Heirs of Little, Thomas Arundell and Joseph Mellow, 2 mess.   1s 0d
John Joseph, Walter Francis, [—] Garrett, Robert Wenn, 4 mess.   2s 0d
Heirs of William Cocke, a ten.   1½d
Heirs of Kendall, Sharpe, John Hodge and Vian, 2 mess.   1s 8d
Heirs of Walter Parker and Mathew Sela, 2 mess.   3d
Heirs of Moone and Walter Pethen, 2 mess. and 3 gardens   2s 0d
The Mayor for the use of the borough, 'a certeine peece of ground called the Mayors ground'   8d
Heirs of Boyne, Thomas Arundell, Stephen George and John Harle, 4 mess.   3s 11d
Sir John Trelawney and Francis House, a mess.   1s 1½d
John Wills, a mess.   6d
Henry Lawry, 2 mess.   11d
John Sharpe and William Gadgecombe, a mess.   6d
Sir Samuel Rolles kt, 2 mess.   4s 3d

George Epps, 2 mess.	6d
Walter FitzWilliam, a mess.	6d
Joseph Mellow, 4 mess.	1s 10½d
Walter FitzWilliam, ¼ mess.	9d
Hugh Trevanion and Thomas Furse, a mess.	1s 0d
Walter Landon and [—] Mungle, 1¼ mess.	10½d
William Dandy, 1¼ mess.	2s 0d
Thomas Francis, 3 mess.	1s 11d
George Epps and Richard Archard, a mess.	1s 10d
Peter Mellow and John Hodge, 2 mess.	9d
Joseph Melow, a mess.	1s 1½d
Margarett Lukes, Edward Murth and William Wills, a mess.	1s 3d
Sir Bernard Greenvile and Thomas Trute, a mess.	3d
Edward White, a mess.	3d
John Hodge, Symon Harris and Walter White, 8 mess.	11d
John Bradcocke, John Grills, Peter Liston and Thomas Trute, 2 mess. and ¾ mess.	2s od
Paid by the Borough 'for one messuage and a halfe called parish Ground'	1s 1d
Denis FitzWilliam and George Richards, a mess.	4d
Thomas Trute, a mess.	4½d
Walter Witte, a mess.	7d
John Sharpe, a mess.	1s 0d
Sir John Trelawney kt, a mess.	1½d
John Garrett, a mess.	6½d
John Hodge, a toft of land	1½d
Heirs of Bradcocke of Lostwithiell, 2 mess.	6d
German Pukey and George Epps, a burgage	6d
'for the Towne Well'	3d
'for a certeine peece of land called Marquesse Parke'	6½d
John Sharpe, a mess.	1s 4d
Richard Peake, 2 mess.	7½d
Thomas Backe and Thomas Trute, 2 mess.	7½d
Thomas Chubb and Digorie Chubb, ½ burgage	3d
John Sharpe, a mess.	3½d
Total	£2 19s 8½d.

'The said Borroughe is bounded on the south, south west and west by the Mannor of Portlooe; on the north by a lake that falleth into Looe River, and on the east by the said River of Looe.

There is a comon belonging to the said Borough conteyning by estimacon thirty six acres where none but the tennants of the Borough that pay six pence rent and upward have right to commonage.'

Rents of assize	£2 19s 8½d
Perquisites of court and 'other casualties which accrue'	5s 0d
Total	£3 4s 8½d

'This is an exact survey . . .'

33 MANOR OF RESTORMEL

DCO S/5; PRO E 317 (C)/35. The manor of Restormel, which included Restormel Castle, lay in the parish of Lanlivery, to the north of the borough of Lostwithiel. It was one of the ancient manors of the Duchy.

'A Survey of the Mannor of Restormell . . . retorned 22 February 1649/50.

The Mannor house is knowen by the name of Restormell Castle, and is scituate and being within the parke of Restormell, which said castle is utterly ruined, nothing but the out walles thereof remayning which are not (where they stand) worth the takeing down. The scite whereof conteynes by estimacon one acre and is now in the present possession of the Lord, and is worth p.a. 6s 8d.

All that farme house comonly knowen by the name of Trinity House,[1] consisting of two halls, one kitchen, one larder, one pastrie and one dayrie house below staires; over the said roomes are eight little chambers for lodging and other necessary uses. Without doores there are three barnes, the first consisting of seven bayes, the second of sixe bayes and the third of three bayes. Alsoe one stable conteyninge five bayes and two maulthouses open to the roofe, which said house and outhouses are in greate decay and out of repaire. The scite consists of one garden, one hop-yard, two orchards, one courteyard and divers other outyards aboute the said house, which with the house and outhouses conteyne by admeasurement eight acres.'

Castle Parke, arable and coppice, 22 ac.; Home Parke, arable, 14 ac.; Barne Parke, arable, 7 ac.; Stone Parke, arable, 14 ac.; North Parke, arable, 10 ac.; Grubbs Close, arable, 9 ac.; Three parcels of marsh ground called White Marshes, 26 ac.; 2 parcels of pasture called West Comon and Grubbs, 32 ac.; East Comon, pasture, 45 ac.; Long Parke, arable, 18 ac.; Code Parke, arable, 9 ac.; Tanners Parke, arable, 8½ ac.; Galhouse Parke, pasture, 5 ac.; South Galhouse Parke, pasture, 6 ac.; Hill Parke, arable, 9½ ac.; Above Home, arable, 4½ ac.; Alder Marsh, marsh, 7 ac.; Alder Meadow, meadow, 8 ac.; Little Meade, meadow, 1 ac.; Church Parke, 'rough, bushie ground', 24 ac.; Greene Parke, arable, 18 ac.; Hill Parke, 'rough, bushie ground', 28 ac.; The Marsh, 'parcell of boggie ground', 7 ac.; Over Marsh, marsh ground, 11 ac.; Greate Wood, furse ground, 54 ac.; the Foxholes, pasture, 48 ac.; Higher Purloyne heeys, pasture, 16 ac.; Lower Purleyne heyes, pasture, 20 ac.; Higher Meesball, pasture, 13 ac.; Lower Meesball, pasture, 9 ac.; Little Wood, coppice ground, 15 ac.; Littlewood close, pasture, 13½ ac.; Mow Parke, pasture, 13½ ac.

'All which . . . belong to the said house called Trinity house and doe conteyne in the whole [549½ ac.] . . . being heretofore a parke but hath beene long since disparked, and is comonly knowen by the name of the Disparked Parke of Restormell.'
The premises were let by L.P of 11 May 1627, with 3 ac. of wood to Mr John

---

[1] Trinity House, on the site of a medieval hermitage, lay at the foot of the castle hill, beside the River Fowey. A late eighteenth century house now occupies the site.

Samuel, for 99 years on the lives of Mary (60) his w. and William (dec.) and John (dec.) their sons. Heriot 53s 4d. Rent £28 7s. Imp. val. £228 13s 6d. Exceptions: the castle, great trees, woods, underwoods, marriages, reliefs and other royalties belonging to the castle. Provisions and conditions, as previously; to plant 8 trees yearly.

Coppice wood not granted is worth £15. 'The pollards, dottards and saplins' reserved number 700 and are worth £40.

Andrew Trewill has possession by assignment of John Samuell, Mary his w., William s. and h. of John and Anne his w., with Christopher Ough gent. and others, dated 23 June 1638.

The Park is bounded 'on the south side with certeine lands belonginge to the Borough of Lostwithiell, on the east with the lands of the Lord Roberts and the Lord Mohone; on the west by the Manor of Restormell and the highway that leadeth from Lostwithiell to Bodman.'

'Growing in the Lord's wood called Coppice Wood . . . certeine thinne wood of thirty yeares groweth worth' £12.

Freeholders

'John Lord Roberts holdeth freely to him and his heires . . . two peeces of land neare the parke of Restormell conteyning about' [1½ ac.].   Rent 6d.

'Conventionary tennants of Inheritance

	Rent	Fine	Old Recognition Money[2]
Thomas Bullocke holdeth in free conventionary one tenement in Barneyate [Barngate in Lanlivery] for which he paieth' p.a.	8s 8d	1s 0d	8d
Thomas Collinar, ten. in Polding Towne [Puddingtown] and Loggett Walls	12s 8d	6d	8d
Stephen Collinar, ten. in Polding Towne and Loggett Walls	5s 8d	6d	8d
Elizabeth Bullocke, the same	6s 0d	nil	nil
Robert Cully, the same	1d	nil	nil
Ellizabeth Bullocke, 2 ten. in Connistowne	14s 0d	12s 0d	6d
Emlyn Atchins, 2 ten. in Combe	14s 8d	nil	8d
John Elcocke, 2 tenures in Woodland	14s 2d	6d	4d
id. and Simon Diar, 2 tenures in Woodland	14s 2d	6d	4d
Emlyn Atkins, 2 tenures in Woodland	7s 7d	nil	8d
id., a mill called Langford Mill	10s 2d	nil	nil
Abraham Foote, a tenure in Connistowne	6d	nil	nil
John Lord Roberts, 2 pieces of 'moorish land' on the north side of Lostwithiel	1s 0d	nil	nil
Walter Kendall esq., the royalty of hawking and hunting within the manor	2s 0d	nil	nil

[2] Old recognition money was payable on all assessionable manors, but generally varied with the rent. Restormel was exceptional in having a fixed payment.

'BOUNDES OF THE MANNOR

The said Mannor of Restormell is bounded on the north with the lands of the Lord Roberts, and on the east with the Parke of Restormell unto the river of Fowey, and with the river of Foy on the south-east and south, and by the way that leadeth from Bodman to Lostwithiell unto the wall of Restormell Parke on the south-west and west side.'

CUSTOMS OF THE SAID MANOR

These are identical with the customs of the customs of the manor of Penkneth, though listed in a different order.

AN ABSTRACT OF THE PRESENT RENTS AND FUTURE IMPROVEMENTS

Rents of assize and perquisites		7s 2d
Rents of conventionary tenants		£5 11s 4d
Fines and old knowledge money		1s 2½d
Value of the castle and site		6s 8d
Rent of leasehold tenants		£28 7s
	Total	£34 12s 4½d
Improved value of the land in lease		£228 13s 6d
Value of coppice wood		£27
Pollards, dottards and saplings		£40

'This is an exact survey . . .'

34 MANOR OF RIALTON AND RETERTH

PRO E 317 (C)/36. This joint manor lay scattered in the parishes of Colan, St Columb Minor, Crantock, St Enoder and St Columb Major. The manor house of Rialton, of which a good deal remains, lay in Colan; that of Reterth in St Columb Major. Both manors had belonged to Bodmin Priory. After the Dissolution they remained the property of the Crown, but were leased to the Munday family. Title was later transferred to Queen Henrietta Maria as part of a settlement made in her favour.

'A Survey of the Mannor of Rialton and Reterth . . . parcell of the possessions and joynture made by the late King Charles unto Henrietta Maria the late Queene, but now settled on Trustees for the use of the Commonwealth. Held as of the Mannor of East Greenewich in free and common soccage by fealty onely . . . retorned [31 July 1650].

MANOR OR MANSION HOUSE KNOWN [AS] RIALTIN HOUSE [RIALTON BARTON, IN COLAN PARISH]

The said house consisteth of one faire Hall with a roome adioyning to the said Hall for servants to dine in, on kitchen, one larder, one brewhouse with a roome for the cooleing of worte, one dairy house (with a lodgeing chamber for servants over it) and one buttery; these below staires. Over the said lower rooms there is one faire dyning roome with divers others rooms thereto adioyning, viz. the kitchen chamber, the Crosse Chamber, the Priors Chamber, the Chaple Chamber, the Inner Chamber, the Maids Chamber, and a chamber at the head of the staires, all which are in reasonable good repair, the said house being built of stone, and the windowes barred with iron barres. The outhouses belonginge to the said house are as followeth viz. one water corne mill, two stables, each of them consisting of three bayes of buildinge, one waynehouse, one cartehouse, two barnes consisting of eight bayes of building and one oxehouse thereto adjoyninge.

The scite of the said House consisteth of one square close in the midest whereof there is a well of fresh water; on the west side of the said house there is one other courte, two gardens, two orchards and divers parcells of wast land neare unto the said houses and two groves of trees neare adjoyning. All which scite conteyneth in the whole six acres of land.

DEMEASNES LAND BELONGING [TO] THE SAID HOUSE

All that parcell of arrable ground knowen by the name of the Highe Hill Close conteyninge 3½ ac.,'
Lower Hill Close, pasture, 3½ ac.; Quarry Close, arable, 8 ac.; The Moore, moorish ground, 3 ac.; Calves Hill, pasture, 1½ ac.; Mill Hill, arable, 6½ ac.; Tanner Close, pasture, 13½ ac.; Mill Moore, moorish ground, 6½ ac.; Upper Barne Close, arable, 5½ ac.; Nether Barne Close, arable, 6 ac.; Upper West Close, arable, 16 ac.; Upper East Close, pasture, 18 ac.; Southdowne, arable, 10 ac.; Northdowne, arable, 11 ac.; Minors Hill, pasture, 3 ac.; Carnes Hill, 2 parcels of arable, 7 ac.; Sleighmans, pasture, 3 ac.; Sleighmans Lower Hill, pasture, 3¾ ac.; Robert Mondaies Close, arable, 3 ac.; Carnes Middle Hill, arable, 3 ac.; Foxes Hill, pasture, 3¾ ac.; Carnes Nether Hill, arable, 3 ac.; Rawlings Hill, arable, 3 ac.; Penventon Close, pasture, 14 ac.; Parke Farme, pasture, 11 ac.; Pond Close, pasture, 10 ac.; Home Downe, meadow, 5¼ ac.; Horse Close, pasture, 3¾ ac.; Normunday, pasture, 19¾ ac.; Sterlings Close, pasture, 10 ac; Calver Close, pasture, 13 ac.; Southmoore Close, moorish ground, 5 ac.

In all 244½ ac.; with house, mill and site valued at £203 19s p.a.
Trees valued at £80.

'FREE-TENNANTS OF THE SAID MANNOR

James Day holdeth in free soccage to him and his heires for ever one acre of land Cornish in Penhalewin [Penhale in St Enoder] for which he paieth p.a.　10s.'
Sir John Arundell kt, Nicholas Burlace, John Lord Roberts, Sir Samuell Cuswarth, Thomas Lower and William Kente, 4 ac. C. in Bossoughan [Bosoughan in Colan]　16s 5d
Sir Samuel Cusworth kt, 3 ac. C. in Cutforth, [including] for suit of court, 1s 1d,　4s 7d
id., 2 ac. C. in Carveire [?]　5s 10d
[—] Beauchampe, 1½ ac. in Mellionecke [Mellionnec in Colan]　2s 9d
John Lord Roberts and Colan Blurte, 2 ac. C. 'Being the Mannor of Colan'　1s 1½d
Heirs of John Watts, ½ ac. C. in Gustavean [Gusti Vean in Colan]　1s 8d
John Penrose, lands in Burthy [*id.* in St Enodor]　4s 1d
Thomas Vivian and Sir Samuell Cuswarth, 3 ac. C. in Retyne [Retyn in St Columb Major]　7d
Richard Carter, lands in Tresannoe [Tresawna in St Columb Major] 7d

Francis Gully, Samuell Cusworth, John Richard and [—] Flamancke, 2½ ac. C. in Treverricke   7s 4d

Sir John Arundell, 3 ac. C. in Porth Veire [Porth Veor in St Columb Minor]   15s 7d

Sir Samuel Cusworth kt, 3 ac. C. in Trelawgan   3s 0d

id., 1½ ac. C. in Tregennoe [Tregenna in St Mawgan]   9s 6d

id., 1 ac. C. in Raskeis [? Rosecliston in Crantock]   10s 0d

John Arundell, John Symons and Sir John Arundell, 1 ac. C. in Menewalls [? Menewink in Lanivet]   2s 1d

[—] Trefusis and [—] Lanion, 1 ac. C. in Chappell [Chapel in St Columb Minor]   1s 1½d

Thomas Ben Warne (sic), 1 ac. C. in Trereglos [Treviglas in St Columb Minor]   2s 9d

John Arundell, 9 ac. C. in Trerice [in Newlyn East], Lygena [Legonna in Crantock], Trewerii alias Trewely [Trevilley in Crantock] and elsewhere   26s 1¾d

id., 1½ ac. C. in Tresullian [Tresillian in Newlyn East]   3s 0d

[—] Wollombe, lands in Polgreene [Polgreen in Mawgan or Crantock]   6s 10d

Thomas Wills, 2½ ac. C. in Trewarthen [Trevarthian in Newlyn East]   6s 10d

John Vivian, 3 ac. C. in Trenoweth [*id.* in St Columb Major]   5s 0d

id., 2 ac. C. in Gluvian [*id.* in St Columb Major or Mawgan]   3s 5d

Sir John Arundell, 3 ac. C. in Truenhelicke   3s 1d

William Williams, Sir John Arundell and John Sentawbin, 1½ ac. C. in Tregantullian [Tregatillian in St Columb Major]   6s 0d

John Tippett, John Day and Henry Bligh, 1½ ac. C. in Tresoderne [Tresaddern in St Columb Major]   1s 5d

Thomas Lowre, lands in Ruthvasse [Ruthvoes in St Columb Major] 5s 0d

Rosoclear Arscott, 2 ac. C. in Gluvian [*id.* in St Columb Major]   22s 1d

[—] Flamancke and Sir John Arundell: 1½ ac. C. in Gluvian   4s 6d

John Vivian and [—] Rawlinge, 1 ac. C. in Trembleth   1s 4d

Christopher Arnold, Humphrey Noy, John Rouse, John Munday and [—] Rosogan: 2 ac. C. in Tolcarnevarcas [Higher Tolcarne in St Mawgan]   5s 2d

Richard Serly, 1 ac. C. in Treliner [Treliver in St Columb Major] 1s 2½d

R. Serley, Gilbert Bemfrey and John Lord Roberts, 3 ac. C. in Dymelsa (Demelza in St Wenn)   6s 9d

R. Serley and Henry Rolle, 2½ ac. C. in Treganetha   4s 6d

William Keate and John Garroe, 3 ac. C. and 3 farl. in Pentire Morgan [Pentire in Crantock]   10s 0d

William Chynowth, 1 ac. C. in Trenisacke [Trenissick in Cubert] 1s 9d

John Lord Roberts, [—] Bullocke and John Littleton, 1 ac. C. in Tredenicke [Tredinnick in Newlyn East]   6s 10d

Stephen Gilly, John Gully and Richard Courtney, 3 ac. C. in Tredenicke   7s

Sir John Arundell, [—] Bullocke, [—] Wendon, Nicholas Roseveare and Philip Spry, 3 farl. in Bokedricke [Bokiddick in Lanivet]   7s 7d

Sir John Arundell, 3 ac. C. in Bedwonecke [Bodwannick in Lanivet]   3s 7d

George Collins and John Lord Roberts, 2 ac. C. in Rosewerrecke [Rose-
warrick in Lanivet]   2s 10d
John Fenton and Francis Courtney, 1½ ac. C. in Trebell [? Trebelzue in
St Columb Minor]   2s 9d
Francis Buller, John Hodge, Thomas Crossman, Gilbert Edy and [—]
Bullocke, 1 ac. C. and 1 farl. in Cadwin   6s 2d
Richard Courtney and Anthony Nicoll, 3 ac. in Lanevett [Lanivet] and
Lamorecke [Lamorick in Lanivet]   3s 9d
William Chynoweth, 1 ac. C. in Trecoliecke   2s 4d
John Killow and John Crestle, 1 ac. C. in Tremabin [Tremabyn in Lanivet]
                                                                            3s 7d
Philip Sprey, ½ ac. C. in Tregwellin   1s 9d
Mrs Blight, ½ ac. C. in Bodmyn Camiland [Bodmin Kirland]   4d
Heirs of Mohun, 4 ac. C. in Branjon [Bejowan in St Columb Minor]   8s
                                          Total   £14 19s 3¼d.

'TENEMENTS . . . LETT BY LEASE TO UNDERTENNANTS'

Trewallicke [Trewollack in St Columb Minor]:
> Crosse Close, pasture, 10 ac.;   Bee Close, pasture, 14 ac.;
> Poolegreene, arable, 6 ac.;   the Little Meadow, meadow, 1¾ ac.;   the
> Furse Close, arable, 6½ ac.;   Quarry Close, pasture, 10 ac.;   Three
> Corner Close, arable, 9¼ ac.;   Barne Parke, arable, 9¼ ac.;   Well
> Parke, arable, 5 ac.;   The Moore, moorish ground, 2 ac.

All at present occupied by John Monday, 'whoe holdeth the same as a
legacie left unto him by his father [—] Munday'; in all 76½ ac., 'which with
the house is valued to be worth' p.a. £62.

Trethellin [in Crantock] undertenant George Vivian:
> Little Meade, meadow, 1¼ ac.;   Lower Close, pasture, 3¾
> ac.;   Midle Close, pasture, 4¾ ac.;   Thistle Close, arable, 7¼
> ac.;   Lane Close, 'land' [arable?], 6¼ ac.;   Lurre Close, 'land', 8 ac.

In all 31¼ ac. Worth with house £33.

Trethellin, undertenant Richard Stephens:
> Little Meadow, meadow, 1¼ ac.;   East Close, pasture, 4 ac.;   Out-
> ward Close, pasture, 5 ac.;   Upper Close, arable, 4½ ac.;   the other
> Upper Close, arable, 7 ac.;   Greene Close, arable, 7 ac.;   Mowhay
> Meade, meadow, 4 ac.

In all 32¾ ac. Worth with the house and common 'for the depastureing of
one hundred sheepe' £34.

Tretheris [Tretherras in St Columb Minor] , undertenant John Monday:
> Inner Borroughe Close, pasture, 17 ac.;   Popleton Close, pasture, 10
> ac.;   Ponsa Close, pasture, 9 ac.;   Meryfield, arable, 21 ac.;   Parke
> below the Meadow, meadow, 2½ ac.;   Cleesses, arable, 12
> ac.;   P[ea]cooke, pasture, 11½ ac.

In all 83 ac. J.M. has possession by virtue of a legacy from [—] Monday.
Worth with the homestead £82 5s.

Gustavean [Gusti Vean in Colan], undertenant Robert Kent:
> Little Meadow, meadow 1 ac.;   Lower Meadow, meadow, 1 ac.;

Church Close, pasture, 5 ac.; Coosse Close, pasture, 7½ ac.; Well Close, pasture, 5¾ ac.; Higher Gustaver, arable, 4½ ac.; Lower Gustaver, arable, 5¾ ac.; The Moore, 2 parcels of moorish ground, 4 ac.
In all 34 ac.[1] Worth 'with the house thereto belonging' £18 11s.

Gustavean, undertenant Henry Cooke:
Parken Shatway, pasture, ¾ ac.; Parkenoke, pasture, 1¼ ac.; the comon fields, arable, 8 ac.; Pease Close, arable, 4 ac.; Higher Close, arable, 3 ac.; Church Close, pasture, 3 ac.; Gustaver Close, arable, 5 ac.; Lower Watering Place, meadow, 1 ac.; The Moore, moorish land, 5 ac.;
In all 28 ac. Worth £19.

Md. Robert Kent has 15 ac. in the last 2 ten. which he holds in soccage, 'so that the lease land of the first tenement (parte of the said fifteene acres being deducted thereout) cometh but to [22½ acres] and the rest being taken from the second tenement the lease land is but twenty eight acres according to which deduction wee have sett down the value of the lands in lease onely.'

Gustavean, undertenant Haniball Carne:
Above Towne, meadow, 3¼ ac.; The Moore, moorish ground, 4 ac.; Meadow Undertowne, meadow, 2 ac.; Sparkes Meadow, meadow, 1½ ac.; Upper Penhale, arable, 1½ ac.; Middle Penhale, arable, 1 ac.; Lower Penhale, pasture, 1¼ ac.; Crosse Close, pasture, 5 ac.; Church Close, pasture, 2½ ac.; Long Close, arable, 4 ac.; Middle Close, arable, 1½ ac.; The Above Towne, pasture, 3 ac.; Goldsmith Close, arable, 1¼ ac.; Corner Close, arable, 1¼ ac.; Behind House, pasture, 4½ ac.; The Moores, 3 parcels of moorish ground, 9 ac.
In all 46½ ac. Worth £36 7s.

Gustavean, undertenant John Minor:
The Meadow, meadow, 1 ac.; Quarry, pasture, 1¼ ac.; Church Close, arable, 1¼ ac.; Little Church Close, arable, 1 ac. and 20 perches; The Meadow, meadow, 1 ac. and 20 perches; The Moore, moorish ground, 1¾ ac.; Greate Moore, moorish ground, 3 ac.
In all 10½ ac. Worth £6 15s.

Gustavean ten. or cott. with ½ ac. Valued at 15s.

Gustavean, occupant Robert Munday:
Yoman Close, pasture, 3 ac.; Upper Downe Parke, arable, 1¼ ac.; Lower Downe Parke, pasture, 1¼ ac.; Upper Field, arable, 3 ac.; Lower Field, arable, 1 ac.; The Moores, 2 parcels of moorish ground, 2½ ac.
In all 12 ac. Worth. £8 5s.

Gustavean, occupant William Sleaman:
Church Close, pasture, 3½ ac.; The Moore Close, moorish ground, 3 ac.; Cocke Close, arable, 3 ac.; Poolelocke, arable, 1½ ac.
In all 12 ac. Worth £9.

[1] In the margin 22½ acres. The discrepancy is explained below.

Gustavean, occupant Roger Box:
>Church Closes, 2 pieces of pasture, 3 ac.;   The Meadow, meadow, 1 ac.;   Moore Close, moorish ground, 2 ac.

In all 6 ac. Worth £4.

Gustavean, occupant Thomas Symons:
>Lower Polmoth, pasture, 3 ac.;   Higher Polmoth, arable, 2 ac.; The Moore, moorish ground, 3 ac.;   Church Close, pasture, 1 ac.

In all 9 ac. Worth £6.

Md. 'Two closes of common belong to the tenants of Gustavean who 'doe sometimes enclose and eare up theire respective partes'.
The closes are worth £1.

Trevenson, occupant Christian Gome:
>Oven Close, arable, 2¼ ac.;   Well Close, pasture, 1½ ac.;   The Moore, moorish ground, 1½ ac.;   Calves Close, arable, 1¼ ac.;   The Moores, 3 parcels of ground, 3 ac.

In all 9½ ac. Worth £8.

Trevenson, occupant Robert Carne:
>The Large, pasture, 8 ac.;   Upper Close, arable, 3¼ ac.;   Middle Close, arable, 5 ac.;   The Meadow, meadow, 2¼ ac.;   Church Close, pasture, 6¼ ac.;   Nenthome, arable, 8¼ ac.;   'Meadow ground soe called', 2 ac.;   'Moore ground soe called', 4 ac.

In all 40 ac. [should be 39 ac.]. Worth £35.

Trevenson, occupant John Munday:
>Lower Trevenson, pasture, 15 ac.;   Higher Trevenson, arable, 18½ ac.

In all 33½ ac. Worth £30.

Penrose [in St Columb Minor], occupant Ambrose Munday:
>South Abovetowne, pasture, 14½ ac.;   Abovetowne, pasture, 14½ ac.;   Church Close, pasture, 10 ac.;   Church Hill, arable, 10½ ac.;   Foxholes, arable, 4¾ ac.;   Beefe Close, pasture, 4½ ac.;   The Moores, moorish ground, 2 ac.;   The Meadow under Church Close, meadow, 4¾ ac.;   West Close, pasture, 17¾ ac.;   The Meadow under West Close, meadow, 4 ac.

In all 87½ ac. Worth £63 10s.

Porthe [St Columb Porth in St Columb Minor], occupant William Munday:
>Mowhey, pasture, 5¾ ac.;   Porth Closes, 2 parcels of ground, 10½ ac.;   The Meadowes above Towne, 2 parcels of meadow, 3 ac.;   Greate Meadow, meadow, 3¾ ac.;   Close above Towne, arable, 3 ac.;   Close next above Towne, arable, 2½ ac.;   2 parcels 'of moore ground soe called', 1½ ac.;   Little Meadowes, 2 parcels of meadow, 2½ ac.;   Crosse Close, arable, 10½ ac.;   Greate Close, arable, 13¼ ac.;   Church Close, pasture, 5½ ac.

Total 61½ ac. W. M. claims to hold a third of the ten. in free soccage, so that only 41 ac. count as leasehold. Value £27.

Treworrecke 'in Parochia de Enoder' [Trevorrick in St Enoder], occupant
Richard Cobb:

East Close, pasture, 3 ac.; West Close before the Doore, arable,
3½ ac.; Little Close, arable, 2 ac.; Lower Downe, pasture, 6¼
ac.; Little Rocke Close, arable, 2 ac.; Lower Close, pasture, 6
ac.; Close below house, arable, 3¾ ac.; Rocke Closes, 2 parcels of
arable, 8 ac.; Higher Downe, arable, 13 ac.; The Moore, moorish
ground, 1½ ac.
In all 49 ac. Worth £21.

Longwithes in the 'Parish of Little Collan', occupant Julian Andrewes: 53
ac. divided into 4 separate parcels. Worth £24 10s.

Trevasicke [Trewassick in Colan], occupant Nicholas Munday:

Three Corner Close, pasture, 13½ ac.; East Close, arable, 13½ ac.;
The Moore, moorish ground, 2 ac.; The Mill Leate, meadow, 1½ ac.
'All those parcells of meadow, arrable and pasture ground devided into sixe
severall closes conteyning' 28 ac.
In all: 58½ [58 in margin] ac. Worth £48.

'THE MANNOR OF RETERTH [IN ST COLUMB MAJOR]

The Mannor or Mansion House knowen by the name of Reterth

The said house is very much out of repaire and is held by John Munday
with the lands thereto belonging by vertue of his fathers will for and dureing
the full terme graunted by the lease made of the said Mannor, which lands
are as followeth':

Meadow under Towne, meadow, 6½ ac.; Church Moore Close,
moorish ground, 6½ ac.; Church Close, pasture, 4¾ ac.; Church
Meade, meadow, 1½ ac.; Meadowes above Home, 2 parcels of
meadow, 3 ac.; Meadowes above Home, 2 meadows, 4 ac.; East
Meadow, meadow, 5 ac.; Close under House, pasture, 3¾ ac.; Mill
Moore, moor ground, 5 ac.; The Trages, 4 parcels of arable, 31
ac.; Midle North Closes, 2 parcels of arable, 7 ac.; Moore Ground
under the Midle Close, 2 ac.; Meadow under the Moore, meadow, 2
ac.; East Grounds above the Way, 3 parcels of arable, 16 ac.; East
Close behind the Way, pasture, 4½ ac.; Midle East Close, pasture,
4¼ ac.; East Close, pasture, 2½ ac.; Easter East Close, arable, 3
ac.; East Close beyond the Way, 2 parcels of pasture, 6 ac.; Close
next Northfield, arable, 2½ ac.; Well Close, pasture, 5¾
ac.; Outermost North Close, arable, 9½ ac.
In all 136¼ ac. Worth £82.

FREE TENANTS

Sir John Arundell and Richard Carter, 1 farl. in Lanhinsith	9s 4d
Peter Jenkins and Beele Fursdon, lands in Lisnoweth	6s 10d
Sir John Arundle, 1 farl. in Crostoe	2s 6d
Peter Jenkins, lands in Dennis Cockers [Dennis in St Columb Major]	2s
Peter Jenkins [—] Coswarth, Thomas Lower and Richard Carter, 2 ac. C. in Trewolas	5s 1d
Heirs of Noskawen, ½ ac. C. in Tresoderne [Tresaddern in St Columb Major]	1s 1½d
Total	£1 6s 10½d.

LEASEHOLD TENEMENTS LET OUT TO UNDERTENANTS

Lisnoweth 'devided into five severall closes of meadow, arrable and pasture' in all 25½ ac. Occupant William Keate. Worth £18 16s.

Tregatilian [Tregatillian in St Columb Major], occupant Mr Carter:
    Lower Moore, moorish ground, 2½ ac.; Furse Close, arable, 2 ac.; The Above Furse Close, arable, 3½ ac.; The Way Close, pasture, 5½ ac.; Wills Moore, moor ground, 1¾ ac.; Higher Hill Close, arable, 5 ac.; Lower Hill Close, arable, 2½ ac.
In all 27½ ac. Worth £22.

Trewethicke [Trevithick in St Columb Major] occupant Francis Munday:
    East Meadow, meadow, 1 ac.; Meadow under Towne, meadow, 3¼ ac.;
    Moore ground soe called, ½ ac.; East Close, pasture, 9¼ ac.; Parkinkrime, pasture, 14¼ ac.; Parkedraie, arable, 6¾ ac.; Drie Close, arable, 2½ ac.; North Moore, moor ground, ¾ ac.; Toppetts Lower Close, pasture, 5 ac.; Toppetts Higher Close, arable, 4 ac.; Bradbrooks, pasture, 5 ac.
In all 52¼ ac. Worth £37 18s.

Trevethucke, occupant Beniamin Strongman:
    'Meadow ground soe called', meadow, ¾ ac.; Joseph Close, pasture, 4 ac.; Drie Close, arable, 3¼ ac.; 'Moore Ground soe called', 4 ac.
In all 12 ac. Worth £6 10s.

Trevethucke, occupant 'one Brabin':
    'Meadow Ground soe called', 2 ac.; 'Meadow Ground soe called', 3 ac.; East Meade, 3½ ac.; Hill Close, arable, 14 ac.; Fure Close, 2½ ac.; Close above Towne, pasture, 3 ac.
In all 28 ac. Worth £13 17s.

Trevethucke, occupant Hugh Spry:
    South Hill, arable, 2½ ac.; North Hill, arable, 3 ac.
In all 5 ac. [Should be 5½]. Worth £1 17s.

Dennis [in St Columb Major], occupant Peter Jenkins: 2 small parcels of pasture called The Dennis, 31 ac. Worth £3 15s.

The Manors of Rialton and Reterth, with the 'Baylywicke of the Hundred of Pidershire' were granted by L. P. of 22 April 1599 to John Monday, for 31 years, beginning on the surrender of a lease dated 28 Oct. 1537, granted by Thomas Wansworth, late Prior of St Mary and St Peter [should be Petrock] of Bodmin to John Monday, William M. and Elizabeth Prideaux for 99 years. Rent £60. Imp. val. £919 7s 7¼d. Anthony Monday gent. is in possession as executor to his f. Thomas Monday, who was executor for his f. John Monday.

Md. 'Wee are informed that the foresaid premisses are granted to Francis Godolphin of Godolphin by indenture of the late Queene Henrietta Maria and Henry late Earle of Holland' on 22 March 1638, for 21 years, beginning at the expiry of Monday's lease, paying an additional rent of £60 besides the £60 now paid for the same. But no such lease has been produced 'although wee sent to him for it.'

[BOUNDS]

'This Mannor is not to be bounded but by distinct parcells which are . . . The villages of Gustavean, Gustavered, Trevenson and Tretheris are bounded on the south west for the most part with a little brooke; on the west side with a hedge that leadeth to the sea; on the north parte with the said sea and the lands of Sir John Arundle unto the High Way, and by the High Way unto the Barton gate called Parke Marten. On the north east it is bounded by a river; on the east side with the lands of Sir Samuel Cuswarth to Rialton Bridge; on the south side by lands of Sir John Arundle kt.

The Barton or Demeasnes lands is bounded on the north side with a river to the village of Trewassecke; on the east side with a little brooke and parte of the lands of Collen Bluetts to the village of Langwith; on the south with the lands of Collon Hambleys to the village of Trewallecke, and soe with the lands of the said Hambley to the tenement called Gustavean on the south west side; and on the west with the lands of Thomas Trefusis till it come to the brooke first named.

The third parte of the said Mannor, knowen by the name of Higher Porthe, two partes whereof doe belong to this mannor, is bounded on the north with the river and on the other partes with the rest of Porthe not being of this mannor.

The fouerth parte, knowen by the name of Trethilian lyinge in Crantocke, is bounded on the south side with the strand; on the west side with the lands of Thomas Lower; on the north side partely with the sea and the Highway, and on the east side with the lands of Humphrey Noy esq.

The last parte, knowen by the name of Treworrecke in the parish of Enoder [St Enoder] is bounded on the south side with the lands of Peter Courtney and the lands of Allexander Cottle; on the west side and north with the lands of Sir Samuell Cuswarth kt, and on the east side with the lands of the heires of Rewe.

The Mannor of Reterth lieth wholely within the Parish of Collumb Major, but wee cannott finde out the particular bounds thereof.

There are divers comons lyinge in the Parish of Collombe Major . . . and other parishes nigh adjoyning in which the tennants of this Mannor claime to have right of comon with others therabouts.'

CUSTOMS

A Court Baron is held every three weeks and a Court Leet twice yearly. The Lord is to provide overseers of weights and measures within the Mannor so 'that they may be good according to the custome of the Countrey and that none may be deceaved by them.' Free tenants pay a relief of 12s 6d for every acre Cornish.

AN ABSTRACT

Rent reserved by lease	£60
Improved value of demesne and leasehold lands	£919 7s 7¼d
Timber trees are worth	£80

'This is an exact survey . . . [Sd.]

35   MANOR OF RILLATON

DCO S/5; PRO E 317 (C)/37. The manor occupied the western part of the parish of Linkinhorne. It was one of the ancient manors of the Duchy.

'A Survey of the Mannor of Rillaton . . . retorned [1 Feb. 1649/50].

There is not any demeasne lands within the said Mannor, all the tenements there being freehold and held in free convenconary. Onely there are severall woodes within the said Manor belonginge to the Lord thereof, the herbage and weedeings of which woodes the tennants within whose tenements the said woodes doe grow have been accustomed to take at theire pleasure not spoyleing the said woods, soe that the Lord hath onely the fallinge of the said woodes, which are as followeth vizt Broade Woode alias Treowese Wood, Kilquite Wood, Darley Wood and Darley Parke Wood now in the tenure of the severall tennants followinge:

All that wood and woodground called Broadwood alias Treowes Wood' of 20½ ac., the herbage of which is granted to John Daw jn., Alice Martin wid., Elizabeth John wid. and John Kneebone. Worth, besides herbage £3 p.a. Wood now standing in Broadewoode of 20 years' growth is worth £83.

Darley Wood of 10 ac., herbage of which is granted to Thomas Bridge sn. and Thomas B. jn.; worth besides the herbage 30s p.a. Wood of 20 years' growth is worth £35.

Darley Park Wood of 2 ac., herbage of which is granted to George Foote; worth besides the herbage 6s p.a. Wood now standing thereon of 20 years' growth worth £5.

Kilquite Wood of 9 ac., worth £1 7s p.a. Trees of 20 years' growth thereon are worth £27.

'The tolle of the tinne mines' comes on average to £2 10s.

FREEHOLDERS

John Lampen of Paderda esq., lands previously held by Robert de Paderda of 4 ac.; suit to the Lord's mill 'and to carry the letters of the Lord, his servants and ministers throughout the whole Hundred of East Wivellshire when there shalbe neede and shold drive the distresses of the said Lord throughout the whole Hundred . . . which shalbe taken by the Bayliffe when and as often as he or they shalbe thereof forewarned.' He pays a relief. The lands lie in Wescott [Westcott], Linkinhorne, Mulle Combe [Millcombe], Pengelley [Pengelly], Brugeton, Haidon and Combe [Black Combe?]. Rent 4s 8d and 2 lb of cummin or 2d.

John Lampen also holds a moiety of the Manor of Rillaton Peverley, previously Hugh of Peverley, and 8 ac. in ½ farl. C. The heirs of John Vincent hold a quarter of the said manor and lands, and the heirs of Sampson Olver the other quarter. The lands are in Hen Wood [Henwood], Blackcoombe [Black Coombe], Broad Willake, Mulle, Mullecombe [Millcoombe], Lourdescombe [Liverscoombe], Benethwood [Beneathwood], Clampitt [Clampit], Uphill [*id.*], Combe, Tremolla [Tremollett] and Lawrane [Lewarne]. Relief according to custom. Rent 2s.

William Beere, mill leat or headweir within the above Manor 2d.

Jonathan Rashly esq., Manor of Rillaton Pengelly of 8 ac. C. and $\frac{1}{2}$ farl., by like service and relief. The manor lies in Henwoode, Blackcombe, Broadewillake, Wescott, Millcombe, Beneth Woode, Combe, East Tremolla, West Tremolla and Lawarne. Rent 2s.

id., Manor of Tremolla alias Rillaton Tremolla of $8\frac{1}{2}$ ac. C., lying in 'the villages and fields of' Pengelly, West Tremolla, East Tremolla, Combe and Notter (*id.*). Relief, as above. Rent 1 lb of pepper or 1s.

John Escott gent., lands in above Manor called Stoke or Stokadon [Stockaton in South Hill]. Rent 3d.

William Corriton esq. pays at Michaelmas a sum called Modlett money 'for a certeine tenement in his lands of old the lands of Roger Deferriers' 10s p.a.

William Edgecombe of Gressen in Lezant pays yearly to the Reeve out of a ten. in Gressen called Timbrell Ham the sum of 6s 8d 'in recompence to the said Reeve for the like some which the said Reeve payeth yeerely to the Lord for the office of Bedell of the said Mannor'.
Md. 'Wee have not accounted the last mentioned some of (6s 8d) as parte of the rent of assize for that the same is paid by the Reeve as a parte of the rent of the convenciouary tennants'.

CONVENTIONARY TENANTS OF INHERITANCE
John Beare, a moiety of a mess. in Rillaton and 31 ac. in $\frac{1}{2}$ ac. C., and a quarter of the other moiety; Joan Bridge wid., another quarter; John Kneebone, an eighth; Edward John, a sixteenth; John Curtis, the rest. Fine £2 12s. Rent 5s 2d.

id., a moiety of 1 landyoke[1] in Haydon and 16 ac. of waste in 1 farl.; Edward John, the other moiety. Fine 4s 4d. Rent 2s 6d.

William Charke, quarter of mess. and $36\frac{1}{2}$ ac. in $\frac{1}{2}$ ac. C.; John Oliver, a seventh of a quarter; William Staunton, third of a quarter, except a house and garden; Thomas Treloders, the said house and garden, being an eighth of the said third; William Chearke, another third of the said quarter; John Dill, a fifth of a quarter and a third of a quarter; John Oliver, a seventh of a quarter; Thomas Vine, a third of another moiety; John Dingle, third of a quarter; William Luskey, a thirty-second of a moiety; Walter Combe, a sixteenth of the said moiety. Fine £2 12s. Rent 2s 10d.

Henry Jackeman, moiety of 16 ac. of waste in 1 landyoke in Haydon; John Lampen, quarter of the other moiety; Nicholas Foote, another quarter. Fine 8s. Rent 2s 6d.

William Staunton, moiety of ten. and 32 ac. in $\frac{1}{2}$ ac. C. in Rillaton; Edward S., the other moiety. Fine 8s 8d. Rent 4s 1d.

id., moiety of 16 ac. of waste in 1 landyoke in Heydon alias Higham; John Beare, quarter of another moiety; John Roberts the other quarter. Fine 7s. Rent 2s 6d.

[1] A landyoke appears to have been a small clearing, possibly only temporary, made in the waste. In this manor they occur on the margin of Bodmin Moor.

id., moiety of the pinfold of the said Manor; Edward Staunton, the other moiety. Fine 1s. Rent 1s.

John Daw sn., moiety of a mess. and 32 ac. in ½ ac. C. in Beare [Berriow in North Hill?]; John D. jn., the other moiety. Fine £4 4s. Rent 5s 4d.
id., moiety of a landyoke and 8 ac. in Beare; John D. jn., the other moiety. Fine 2s. Rent 8d.

Thomas Budge jn., an eighth of a quarter of a mess. and 32 ac. in ½ ac. C. in Broadwoode; Henry Grills, fortieth of a quarter; Joan Clothworthy, eighth of a quarter; George Foote, rest of the said quarter; Thomas Budge, a house, being an eightieth of the said ten.; Henry Grills, a garden, being 'the twoe hundreth parte'; Edward Kneebone, a twelfth; Robert John, a fifth of a quarter; Johan Coltworthy, rest of the quarter; John Daw, another quarter. Fine £3. Rent 6s 8d.

John Dingle, moiety of a landyoke containing 18 ac. in 1 farl. in Oves; Thomas Budge, quarter of the said landyoke; George Foote, the other quarter. Fine 6s. Rent 1s 6d.

id., and the others in like parts, another landyoke there containing 24 ac. in 1 farl. (C) Fine 7s 4d. Rent 2s.

Thomas Budge sn., moiety of ten. in Darley [*id.* in Linkinhorne] and 24 ac. in 1 farl.; Thomas B. jn., the other moiety. Fine £1 9s. Rent 3s.

Thomas Budge sn., moiety of a landyoke, being 'in the whole eight acres of land waste' in Darley; Thomas B. jn., the other moiety. Fine 3s 4d. Rent 8d.

Edward Roberts, moiety of ten. and 16 ac. in 1 farl. in Henwoode; Henry Oliver, the other moiety. Fine 13s 10d. Rent 2s 6d.

John John alias Broadlake, moiety of a landyoke, being 5⅓ ac. at Windgate; Faith Oliver, the other moiety. Fine 8d. Rent 1s.

Edward Roberts, moiety of a mess. in Henwoode and 16 ac.; Thomas Daw, quarter and an eighth of the other moiety; John Warne, a sixteenth of a moiety and the residue. Fine 15s. Rent 2s 6d.

John Warne, moiety of a landyoke of 5½ and 1/3 ac. in Windyate; Marvell Harp, the other moiety. Fine 8d. Rent 1s.

Edward Roberts, a sixteenth of a moiety of a mess. and 32 ac. in ½ ac. C. in Henwoode; Faith Oliver, the rest; John Barrett, the other moiety. Fine 6s 4d. Rent 2s 4d.

John Barrett, third of a landyoke consisting of 5 ac. and 3 parts of an ac. in Windgate; Marvell Harp, the rest. Fine 1s 4d. Rent 1s.

The Reeve: 'the driveing of the Moore called Langston Downe'. No fine. Rent 3s 4d.
The Reeve 'taketh for the use of all the tennants . . . to be held as aforesaid all the comons within the said Mannor'. No fine. Rent 5s 3d.

Edward Davie, quarter of a ten. and 33 ac. in ½ ac. C. in Uphill; Alice Davie, quarter except a ninth; John Kneebone, the said ninth and also a quarter; Henry Jackeman, a third of a quarter; John Kneebone, a third of a quarter; Edward Harrie, a sixth of a quarter; John Beare, a seventh of a quarter; William Pomerine, a sixtenth; John Kneebone, the rest. Fine 11s 6d. Rent 2s 9d.

Edward Davie and the rest, as above: 'like severall partes of another messuage' in Uphill of 33 ac. Fine 11s 6d. Rent 2s 9d.

Edward Davie, moiety of a landyoke in Haydon containing 16 ac.; William Hooper gent., 2 parts of another moiety; John Lampen esq., 3 parts of the same. Fine 10s. Rent 2s 6d.

Edward Davie, moiety of a landyoke in Kilquitt Woode of 2 ac.; William Hopper, the other moiety. Fine 6d. Rent 2d.

Andrew Fenton, mess. in Benethwoode alias Brewoode and 33 ac. and 3 roods in ½ ac. C. Fine £1 18s. Rent 4s 11d.

id., 'two-fourths' of a ten. and 21 ac. in Beneth Woode; John Whall, 1 ac. of the other moiety; Robert John, the rest. Fine £1 13s 4d. Rent 5s.

William Hooper, 1½ ac. in Combe. Fine 3s 6d. Rent 9d.

John Beare, moiety of a mess. and 16 ac. in 1 farl. in Rilla Mill [*id.* in Linkinhorne]; Elizabeth Lawndrie, quarter of the other moiety; Richard Lawndrie, Sibill L. and Bridgett L. the other quarter. Fine 13s 6d. Rent 2s 6d.

John Lampen esq., 'the Lord's mill (with the multure of the tennants) called Rilla Mill'. Fine 10s. Rent £1 13s 4d.

Pierce Mannaton esq., moiety of the royalty of fishing in the River of Linner; Elizabeth Lawndrie, the other moiety. No fine. Rent 2d.

'The Reeve . . . taketh to the use of all the tennants of the Mannor the office of Bedle for which there is paid p.a.' 6s 8d.

John Daw jn., Elizabeth John wid. and Elizabeth Martin wid., a cottage with the pasture of Broadwoode alias Treowes Woode. Fine 6s. Rent 6s 8d.

William Davie, moiety of a landyoke containing 2 ac. of waste in Kilquitt Woode; John Beare, a quarter; Elizabeth Tozer, a quarter. No fine. Rent 2s.

'THE SAID MANNOR OF RILLATON IS THUS BOUNDED

By the Mannor of Callyland [?] in the parish of North Hill on the south east being the lands of Sir John Trelawny kt.; by the Mannor of Carnedon Liar [Caradon] the lands of Robert Trelawny gent.; on the south by the Mannor of Carnedon Prior; on the south west by the Mannor of Retradocke [?]; on the west by the lands of Henry Spoore esq., by the Mannor of Carnedon Prior (see No. 7) to the lands of John Lampen esq. and thence to the Mannor of Landreyne on the north; thence by the Mannor of Trefreis [Trefrize in Linkinhorne], and so by the Mannor of Clymsland Prior [see No. 8] to the foresaid Mannor of Carnedon Prior and by the said Mannor to the Mannor of Callyland where it began on the east.'

CUSTOMS

An Assessions Court is held every seven years, and new knowledge money is paid by all new tenants. This is double the rent and fine and is paid over three years. It amounts on average to £1 2s 6d. A court baron is held every three weeks and a court leet twice a year. At one of the courts the reeve, tithingman and beadle are chosen. The reeve is to collect rents and also such casualties and perquisites as arise, the value of which is on average £3 3s 3d. Free tenants pay a relief and customary tenants a heriot on every surrender. New tenants pay 8d as acknowledgement of fealty. Widows of customary tenants are to hold for life. The land of customary tenants is not forfeited if they die for treason or felony, but descends to the next heir, but goods and chattels are forfeited.

An Abstract of the present Rents and other Profits

Rents of assize and perquisites	£4 3s 4d
Rents of conventionary tenants	£5 19s 6d
Fines to be paid within six years of each Assessions	£4 11s 5d and 1/7 of 1d
New knowledge money	£1 2s 6d
Toll of tin miners	£2 10s
Woodground in hand p.a.	£6 3s
Total	£24 8s 9d and 1/7 of 1d.

Woods are worth £150.

'This is an exact survey . . . [Sd].'

36   BOROUGH OF ESSA *alias* SALTASH

DCO S/4; PRO E 317 (C)/38. The borough of Saltash was created within the manor of Trematon (no. 48). Both were ancient manors of the Duchy.

'A Survey of the Borrough of Salt Ash . . . retorned [28 May 1650].

High rents or rents of assize

High Street
The heires of Hutchin hold freely to them and their heires for ever three burgages and four half burgages for which they pay 2s 6d.'

	Burgages	Half Burgages	Rent
Sir Richard Buller	3	3	2s 3d
Sir Richard Edgecombe	1		6d
Sir William Wrey		1	3d
Henry Clowbery	5	1	2s 9d
Thomas Wivell esq.	2	3	1s 9d
Nicholas Symons	1		6d
John Symons		1	3d
John Darton	1		6d
Nicholas Shipheade gent.		1	3d
William Herringe		1	3d
James Crosman gent.		1	3d

	Burgages	Half Burgages	Rent
Richard Porter gent.	1		6d
John Trelawney		1	3d
John Randall merchant		1	3d
John Holster		1	3d
Heirs of Hodge and Bray	1		6d
Heirs of Paschoe	1		6d
William Wills gent.		1	3d
Elias Wills		1	3d
Richard Furlonge		1	3d
Ciprian Cooke		1	3d
Heirs of Kempe		1	3d
Heirs of Strong		1	3d
Heirs of Paschoe		1	3d
William Wills gent.		1	3d
Abraham Jennins, merchant	1		6d
Heirs of John Edgecombe	1		6d
Phillip Launder		1	3d
William Rogers		1	3d
Edmond Dowrish	1		6d
Mathew Lambert		1	3d
Walter Brasy		1	3d
John Trerisa		1	3d
Peter Bayliffe		1	3d
Richard Furlonge		1	3d
Sampson Bond	1		6d
John Trerisa	1		6d
William Wills		1	3d
Edmond Herringe		1	3d
John Trerisa	1		6d
Heirs of Flamancke	1		6d
Heirs of Stronge	1		6d
William Bond		1	3d
William Wills	1		6d
William Maynard gent.		1	3d
William Bickton		1	3d
William Michell	1		6d
Edmond Dowrish	2	1	1s 3d
William Bickton		1	3d
Elizabeth Dowrish		1	3d
Edmond Luscombe		1	3d
Heirs of Gifford Wills		1	3d
John Trerisa		1	3d
Heirs of John Edgecombe		1	3d
William Preston	1		6d
Heirs of Brendon		1	3d
John Randle		1	3d
Edmond Herringe	1		6d
Heirs of Breade		1	3d

	Burgages	Half Burgages	Rent
Heirs of Beare		1	3d
Richard Wills gent.		1	3d
Stephen Easties		1	3d
Heirs of Bevill	1		6d
Edmond Herringe		1	3d
The Streete by the Water Side			
Sir Richard Buller and [blank] Harden	2		1s
Henry Clowberry		1	3d
Richard Carew esq.		1	3d
William Maynard gent.		1	3d
William Wills gent.	1		6d
Roger Beile		1	3d
Ambrose Ough		1	3d
Richard Porter gent.		1	3d
Thomas Webb		1	3d
William Beile		1	3d
William Wills gent.		1	3d
Heirs of Hutchin		1	3d
William Grills		1	3d
Roger Stacy		1	3d
William Beile		1	3d
Heirs of Lowell		1	3d
The Lucas Streete			
John Lucas	1		6d
Heirs of Hutchin	1		6d
William Moulton	1		6d
Thomas Trott	1		6d
Sir Richard Buller	1		6d
Middlestreete			
William Wills gent.	2		1s
Heirs of Heechin	1		6d
Richard Thomas	2		1s
Heirs of Bevill	1		6d
Thomas Edgecombe	1		6d
William Wills gent.	1		6d
John Andrew	1		6d
James Thomas		1	3d
John Reade	1	1	9d
Richard Porter gent.		1	3d
Heirs of Lowell		1	3d
Henry Clowberry		1	3d
Sir William Wrey kt		1	3d
Heirs of Hethins	1		6d
Sir Richard Buller		1	3d
Heirs of Peterfield		1	3d
William Baylie		1	3d

	Burgages	Half Burgages	Rent
John Reade		1	3d
Richard Porter		1	3d
Heirs of Hetchings		1	3d
Edmond Dowrish		1	3d
Daniell Dodge		1	3d
John Gliddon	1		6d
Thomas Hardwen		1	3d
Thomas Wiwell	1		6d
Heirs of Hetchings	3		1s 6d
Backstreete			
Heirs of John Strong	1		6d
Heirs of Skinner		1	3d
James Finch gent.	2		1s
William Wills gent.	2		1s
Heirs of Strong	1		6d
Richard Wills	1		6d
Richard Porter		1	3d
John Marchant		1	3d
Henry Clowberry gent.	1		6d
Heirs of Paschoe	3		1s 6d
Heirs of Hechins	1		6d
John Lampen gent.	1		6d
William Wills		1	3d
Sir Arthur Georges	1	1	9d
Thomas Norman		1	3d
Heirs of Stronge	1		6d
William Cloke		1	3d
William Beile	1		3d
Richard Carew esq.	1		6d
William Beile, merchant		1	3d
William Wills gent.		1	3d

Total £1.

Henry Wills, Sampson Bond, William Biell jn. of Salt Ash, who is 'liveing beyond the seas as we have heard and are credbly informed', and the Mayor and Burgesses, by grant of King Charles when Prince of Wales and Duke of Cornwall of 30 May 1618: 'passadge of the water of Tamer and ferry boate of Essa alias Salt Ash with the rents of men and oares and other services and things to the said passadge or passadge boate belonging'. Term 90 (sic.) years, on lives of H.W., S.B., and W.B. Rent £20. It is worth £100.
Excepted: 'all escheats, lands . . . in the charge of the bayliffe of the Mannor of Trematon . . . and all passage, butlerage, traventree and all Admirall iurisdicon (other than such power of holding Admirall Cortes for determyning of sea causes within the water aforesaid and lymitts thereof as the Major and Burgesses of right have used and enioyed. And alsoe except all arrests for hues and cries there which ought to be impleaded or presented in the court of the Mannor of Trematon.

There is to be reprised to the purchaser of the premises out of the foresaid improved value for and towards the decaies of rents reparacons of the passadge boates and other casualties belonging to the said Borrough the come of (£20) and soe that the improved value is de claro p.a. £80.
Md. The present Major and Aldermen . . . produced before us a charter under the Great Seale of England graunted unto them by the late Queene Elizabeth whereby confirmation is made of divers charters and letters pattents from Reginald de Valetorta, Richard II, Edward IV and Henry VIII, and alsoe all the premises in the forecited lease with many lardge priviledges therein specified are confirmed and graunted to them by the said charter of Queen Elizabeth to hold in fee farm for ever at the old yearely rent' of £18.

Annotated by William Webb, Surveyor General: 'I understand the premisses conteyned in this survey are by order of the Comittee of Obstructions to be accompted as in fee farme, and the fee farme rent of (£18 p.a.) sold accordingly.' [Sd] William Webb.

'This is an exact survey . . .'